Get the eBook FREE!

(PDF, ePub, Kindle, and liveBook all included)

We believe that once you buy a book from us, you should be able to read it in any format we have available. To get electronic versions of this book at no additional cost to you, purchase and then register this book at the Manning website.

Go to https://www.manning.com/freebook and follow the instructions to complete your pBook registration.

That's it!
Thanks from Manning!

Kubernetes for Developers

Kubernetes for Developers

WILLIAM DENNISS

MANNING
SHELTER ISLAND

For online information and ordering of this and other Manning books, please visit
www.manning.com. The publisher offers discounts on this book when ordered in quantity.
For more information, please contact

Special Sales Department
Manning Publications Co.
20 Baldwin Road
PO Box 761
Shelter Island, NY 11964
Email: orders@manning.com

The authors and publisher have made every effort to ensure that the information in this book
was correct at press time. The authors and publisher do not assume and hereby disclaim any
liability to any party for any loss, damage, or disruption caused by errors or omissions, whether
such errors or omissions result from negligence, accident, or any other cause, or from any usage
of the information herein.

Manning Publications Co.
20 Baldwin Road
PO Box 761
Shelter Island, NY 11964

Development editor:	Elesha Hyde
Technical development editor:	Shawn Smith
Review editor:	Adriana Sabo
Production editor:	Deirdre Hiam
Copy editor:	Alisa Larson
Proofreader:	Mike Beady
Technical proofreader:	Mayur Patil
Typesetter:	Dennis Dalinnik
Cover designer:	Marija Tudor

ISBN: 9781617297175
Printed in the United States of America

For Peter.

brief contents

contents

preface

Over the Christmas holidays in 2016, I sat down to learn Kubernetes. I was soon to join the Google Kubernetes Engine (GKE) team and needed to learn how this platform worked—and quickly. I'd previously used several Platform as a Service (PaaS) environments to deploy stateless applications in a scalable way, and I was excited by the opportunity that Kubernetes presented: the flexibility to run anything you could package in a container paired with the versatility of various workload constructs from stateless to stateful applications and batch jobs. Like many, perhaps, I found there was a bit of a learning curve when starting out.

By early 2017, I'd gained some knowledge and was now a product manager on the GKE team, interacting frequently with developers. One such developer was my brother, who was migrating his startup from a PaaS to Kubernetes. I was able to share everything I'd learned so far and hopefully helped him skip some of the newbie mistakes I made. But I wished there was a simpler way to transfer this knowledge: content specifically written for the application developer who wants to deploy onto a production-grade system without needing to learn the whole system at the outset.

This book is essentially the book I wish I had for those moments. I don't assume any prior knowledge of Kubernetes or even containers. The book takes you through the development and deployment of a simple containerized application, starting by getting something up and running online and then gradually layering on additional Kubernetes concepts like stateful applications and background task queues to build up your knowledge.

My hope is to give you the confidence to deploy your own applications to Kubernetes while challenging the notion that "Kubernetes is hard." It's certainly a large and complex system, but as I hope to convince you, its wide scope gives you a lot of powerful functionality that will come in handy when you have complex workloads to deploy. But that can wait. You don't need to learn it all at once! In fact, deploying a stateless application is pretty straightforward, so start there and add on the rest as you need.

By the end of the book, you'll hopefully appreciate the flexibility of the platform, which I expect you will when you have requirements that wouldn't have easily been met on a more special-purpose platform like many PaaSs environments.

I was a bit nervous writing a technical book, especially since it would take multiple years, for fear that things would change so much that parts would become out of date and I would be forever rewriting to catch up. Fortunately, I can report that for every generally available (GA) concept that I wrote about, specifically Kubernetes APIs with a v1 version, the content remained current. This experience gives me hope both in the stability of Kubernetes as you use it in your own projects and the longevity of this book. As I was drafting the content, I covered a few non-GA APIs, and those did change substantially. Fortunately, by the time I was done writing, everything had made it to GA, and I was able to update the content to use those stable versions (based on this, I would also steer well away from beta APIs except to experiment).

When I joined the GKE team, Kubernetes was rapidly gaining in popularity but was not yet ubiquitous. I remember being excited by the prospect of working on what looked to be a pivotal piece of open source software but, at the same time, with some uncertainty as to how things would unfold (and, thus, a chance to influence in a positive way). Well, in that time, we've seen basically every cloud platform offer its own managed platform (fortunately, with high compatibility among them and a culture of maintaining software conformance) and Kubernetes's rise to be the primary way people orchestrate containers in production. I've enjoyed being a part of the Kubernetes community and working on such a pivotal computing platform. I hope this book helps you as you embark on your own journey with Kubernetes!

acknowledgments

First, I want to thank my development editor, Elesha Hyde, who taught me how to weave a story out of this technical content and greatly influenced the final product. To Shawn Smith, my technical development editor, I appreciate your detailed review of the early drafts and your suggestions, which helped to fine-tune the narrative. Thank you, Michael Stephens, for having the confidence in me to write this book when I pitched it to you four years ago, and thanks to everyone at Manning who helped make it what it is: Deirdre Hiam, my project editor; Alisa Larson, my copyeditor; and Mike Beady, my proofreader. Before starting the project, I was unaware just how much working with you all would contribute to the quality of the book, but it became apparent quickly.

To all the reviewers: Amar Manigandan, Andres Sacco, Ariel Gamiño, Atul S. Khot, Becky Huett, Bonnie Malec, Chase Sillevis, Chris Heneghan, Chris Viner, Conor Redmond, David Paccoud, Davide Fiorentino, Deepika, George Thomas, Giuliano Latini, Gregorio Piccoli, Guy Ndjeng, Hans Donner, Harinath Mallepally, Ioannis Polyzos, Javid Asgarov, Juan Jimenez, Julien Pohie, Kamesh Ganesan, Karthikeyarajan Rajendran, Kelum Prabath Senanayake, Kelvin Johnson, Kosmas Chatzimichalis, Krzysztof Kamyczek, Mark Dechamps, Michael Bright, Mike Wright, Mitchell Fox, Najeeb Arif, Pierre-Michel Ansel, Rahul Modpur, Rajaseelan Ganeswaran, Rambabu Posa, Richard Vaughan, Robert Kielty, Satadru Roy, Sebastian Czech, Sergiu Popa, Simeon Leyzerzon, Suhas Krishnayya, Basheeruddin Ahmed, Venkatesh Sundaramoorthy, Waldemar Modzelewski, and Zalán Somogyváry, your suggestions helped to make this a better book.

I greatly appreciate the technical staff at Manning who built the incredible tools that power the Manning Early Access Program (MEAP), which meant I could share the content while it was still a work in progress and get feedback directly from my early readers. Thank you as well to everyone who bought the book via MEAP when it was still half done.

Thank you to my team at work: Drew Bradstock and Yochay Kiriaty for believing in me and supporting me to work on this 120% project and for the team environment you have created that makes building things fun. Thanks to Tim Hockin, Chen Goldberg, Kelsey Hightower, Eric Brewer, Jeremy Olmsted-Thompson, Jerzy Foryciarz, and Brian Grant, who influenced me greatly, and Aparna Sinha, who bet on me early on.

Tom Edwards is the photographer and site reliability engineer who took my profile photo during one KubeCon; check out his work at tomedwardsphotography.com. Thanks, mate!

Lastly, thank you to my family for supporting me to work on this project. Aaron and Ashleigh, though you were too young to know what I was working on, those months when we walked every day to Imua so I could get some quiet space to work on the manuscript while you played nearby are moments I will treasure. To my wife, Fiona, thank you for supporting all my endeavors and being a reality check when I need one. Xianqiong, thank you for supporting our family—without your help, I would barely have time to make anything. To Julie, Graeme, and Laurel, thank you for fostering my interest in technology from a young age, and to my siblings, Jessica and Peter, thanks for always being there for each other and our various endeavors.

about this book

Got an application you want to host in a production-grade environment on the cloud with the power and flexibility to handle your requirements as they evolve and with the potential to scale massively? This book will give you what you need to take an application, whether it's Python, Java, Ruby, or whatever else, and confidently deploy it to the cloud in a professional-grade platform that can meet your needs now and in the future using containers and Kubernetes.

If you don't have an application of your own ready to deploy, one is provided for you to use as a sample. No prior knowledge of Docker or Kubernetes is required. By the end of this book, you should feel confident to deploy workloads to Kubernetes in production, from stateless applications to batch jobs and databases.

Who should read the book

There are many books on Kubernetes out there, written with different audiences in mind. This one is specifically written for developers, intended to cover the journey that goes something like, "I have a bunch of code sitting on my laptop. How do I publish it to the world and do so on a platform that can scale if my product becomes a hit?" When I was learning Kubernetes, I wanted an end-to-end demo of how to get my code into Kubernetes, updated, running smoothly without intervention, and ready to scale if needed. I hope this book provides that for you.

If you're new to containers, no worries, as this book has you covered with a chapter on containerizing applications so you can get them ready to deploy. If you're already familiar with Docker and containers and want to start deploying to Kubernetes right away, you can skip straight to chapter 3.

How this book is organized

The book is split into two parts. The first is designed to give you the basics of Kubernetes, starting with building containers and running them in Kubernetes. You'll learn how to set the right resources and configure them to make the most of Kubernetes's automated operations and, of course, how to update your application. If your goal is to deploy a stateless application to Kubernetes, this might be all you need:

- Chapter 1 is a high-level overview of Kubernetes and its benefits.
- Chapter 2 is a crash course in Docker for application developers. Feel free to skip it if you're already familiar.
- Chapter 3 gets you going with your first Kubernetes deployment. Deploy, expose to the internet, and update. You're now live with Kubernetes.
- Chapter 4 adds essential health checks for a more reliable deployment.
- Chapter 5 helps you right-size your workload so it gets the resources it needs without wastage.

The second part goes deeper into the production aspects of Kubernetes. You'll learn about scaling apps, configuring internal services, and deploying workload constructs like stateful applications and background processing queues. The book concludes by covering configuration as code, continuous deployment, and security considerations:

- Chapter 6 is about scaling up (and down): manual, automated, nodes, and Pods—it's all here.
- Chapter 7 discusses how to configure internal services and microservice architectures and introduces HTTP-based load balancing.
- Chapter 8 covers how you can indicate in your workloads the specific hardware requirements of your containers, as well as how to group or spread out Pods on nodes.
- Chapter 9 gets you set up with stateful workloads like databases.
- Chapter 10 is about all the activity that happens outside of the request/response chain, including task queues and batch jobs.
- Chapter 11 is an introduction to GitOps, covering how to use namespaces for different environments and treating configuration as code.
- Chapter 12 rounds out the book with several security topics worth considering as a developer.

About the code

The code in this book is open source under the Apache 2.0 license and can be downloaded in full at https://github.com/WilliamDenniss/kubernetes-for-developers.

Examples are organized into folders by chapter number. Kubernetes configuration can be found in subfolders prefixed with the section or subsection in which they appear, along with a descriptive suffix. For example, the configuration appearing in chapter 3, section 3.2, can be found in Chapter03/3.2_DeployingToKubernetes. The example containerized application is built on throughout the book and can be found in the relevant chapter folder. For example, it first appears in chapter 2, located at Chapter02/timeserver, and is updated in chapter 4 as Chapter04/timeserver2, and so on.

Each code listing is titled with the complete path to the file for easy reference. The example commands, which appear throughout, start from the base folder, so you can follow the sections out of order; just reset your command-line shell to the base directory when starting a new section, and you're good to go.

Mac, Linux, and Windows can all be used to run the examples in the book, and setup instructions are provided in chapters 2 and 3.

For Google Cloud users, the browser-based Cloud Shell (https://cloud.google.com/shell) can be used to run every example instruction in the book, including those that use Docker and minikube, without needing to install anything locally, with the exception of Docker Desktop's local Kubernetes environment (follow the instructions for minikube instead).

This book contains many examples of source code both in numbered listings and in line with normal text. In both cases, source code is formatted in a `fixed-width font like this` to separate it from ordinary text. Sometimes code is also **in bold** to highlight code that has changed from previous steps in the chapter, such as when a new feature adds to an existing line of code.

In many cases, the original source code has been reformatted; we've added line breaks and reworked indentation to accommodate the available page space in the book. In rare cases, even this was not enough, and listings include line-continuation markers (➡). Additionally, comments in the source code have often been removed from the listings when the code is described in the text. Code annotations accompany many of the listings, highlighting important concepts.

You can get executable snippets of code from the liveBook (online) version of this book at https://livebook.manning.com/book/kubernetes-for-developers. The complete code for the examples in the book is available for download from the Manning website at https://www.manning.com/books/kubernetes-for-developers, and from GitHub at https://github.com/WilliamDenniss/kubernetes-for-developers.

liveBook discussion forum

Purchase of *Kubernetes for Developers* includes free access to liveBook, Manning's online reading platform. Using liveBook's exclusive discussion features, you can attach comments to the book globally or to specific sections or paragraphs. It's a snap to make notes for yourself, ask and answer technical questions, and receive help from the author and other users. To access the forum, go to https://livebook.manning.com/book/kubernetes-for-developers/discussion. You can also learn more about Manning's forums and the rules of conduct at https://livebook.manning.com/discussion.

Manning's commitment to our readers is to provide a venue where a meaningful dialogue between individual readers and between readers and the author can take place. It is not a commitment to any specific amount of participation on the part of the author, whose contribution to the forum remains voluntary (and unpaid). We suggest you try asking the author some challenging questions lest his interest stray! The forum and the archives of previous discussions will be accessible from the publisher's website as long as the book is in print.

Additional online resources

- The official Kubernetes docs at https://kubernetes.io/docs/
- Container base images at https://hub.docker.com/
- StackOverflow at https://stackoverflow.com/questions/tagged/kubernetes

More content by the author on the topic of Kubernetes and GKE can be found at https://wdenniss.com/kubernetes.

The resource icons used in the figures throughout the book are from the Kubernetes Icons Set by the Kubernetes Authors, licensed under CC BY 4.0. They can be found at https://github.com/kubernetes/community/.

The Kubernetes logo is by the Kubernetes Authors and is licensed under CC BY 4.0. It can be downloaded along with the source code to Kubernetes itself at https://github.com/kubernetes/kubernetes/.

about the author

WILLIAM DENNISS is a Group Product Manager at Google where he works on Google Kubernetes Engine (GKE). He co-founded the Autopilot experience for GKE, building a fully managed Kubernetes platform that offers a complete Kubernetes experience without the overhead of managing the underlying compute nodes. A strong believer in open standards and open source software to drive the industry forward, his first project on the GKE team was to work with the Kubernetes community and the Cloud Native Computing Foundation to create the Certified Kubernetes Conformance Program to encourage broad compatibility among Kubernetes providers.

Joining Google in 2014, he first worked in the identity space, where his goal was to improve how users interact with identity systems on mobile devices. He wrote the best current practice OAuth for Native Apps, published as RFC 8252, and co-founded the open source library AppAuth for iOS, Android, and JavaScript to provide a common implementation of that best practice.

He enjoys learning through teaching and spends a good chunk of his spare time coding and iterating on various projects. If he has a device, he's likely coding something for it, whether it's a graphics calculator (in high school), a computer running Windows, Linux, or Mac (at various times), a PlayStation Portable (in the 2000s), or an iPhone (since the iPhone 3G). Eventually, projects required a server component, which first led him to deploy code on a Platform as a Service (PaaS) over a decade ago and sparked his interest to later work on Kubernetes when the opportunity arose, to help make life easier for developers with similar requirements.

His product management superpower is to be an avid user of the products he builds.

about the cover illustration

The image on the cover of *Kubernetes for Developers* is an illustration titled "A Seaman with a Man of War's Barge" by Dominic Serres, created in 1777. This artwork belongs to a collection of images depicting the Royal Navy's uniforms, from the sailor seen in this illustration through the mid-officer ranks to that of the admiral. The seaman in the illustration wears a short blue jacket with a row of cloth-covered buttons, scalloped mariner's cuffs with a three-button closure, and a plain white waistcoat. He also sports petticoat trousers that stretch from his waist to the top of the calf, plain white stockings, and shoes with white metal buckles.

At a time when it's hard to tell one computer book from another, Manning celebrates the inventiveness and initiative of the computer business with book covers based on the rich diversity of historical figures and costumes of the past, brought back to life with illustrations such as this one.

Part 1

Getting started with Kubernetes

Kubernetes is a popular platform for orchestrating containers. This first part of the book demystifies what Kubernetes is and why it's useful. It also covers basics such as how to containerize apps so they can be used in this environment and how to deploy your first containerized application into Kubernetes and make it available on the internet. You'll learn how to configure an application to take advantage of Kubernetes automation to keep everything running without downtime, including during application updates, and how to determine what resources to allocate to each container.

By the end, you'll have a working stateless containerized application running in Kubernetes and available online to the world if you want it to be. You'll know how to configure it so that Kubernetes can keep it online without you needing to monitor it closely, even if your application crashes or the cluster is upgraded.

You might have heard that Kubernetes is a little complex to use, which stems in part from the system's large number of capabilities. I hope to show you in this part that it's actually pretty easy to deploy a simple stateless application to Kubernetes and publish it live. There's no need to learn all the intricate capabilities of Kubernetes on day one, although it's nice to know they exist for when you need them. Deploying a stateless application is a great place to start.

Kubernetes for application deployment

This chapter covers

- The benefits of packaging applications in containers
- What makes Kubernetes an ideal platform to deploy containers with
- Deciding when to use Kubernetes

It's 5 pm on a Friday, and the product you've been working on for the last year just went viral. You need to scale everything—and fast. Is your application and the platform it runs on capable of scaling 100×, ready to capture your success, or are you stuck with brittle code and an inflexible platform, meaning all your work will be for naught?

You built an amazing stateless application on a popular application platform capable of scaling rapidly, and everything is working great. Until one day, your business requirements shift, and suddenly you need to run a bespoke stateful application for some critical business data or configure a nightly batch processing pipeline. Will these new workloads fit in seamlessly with your existing ones, or will you need to start over from scratch or patch together multiple disparate systems?

Kubernetes is fast becoming the industry standard for running workloads of all different shapes and sizes and at different scales by promising to solve these concerns and more. It enables you to launch containerized applications with the ability to scale rapidly while, at the same time, handling a variety of complex deployment patterns, from stateless applications to stateful databases, batch jobs with ephemeral storage, and so on. Invented at Google,[1] open-sourced, and used by countless organizations like Spotify,[2] CapitalOne,[3] and OpenAI,[4] Kubernetes is an open, vendor-agnostic, and well-proven platform that is to cloud deployments what Linux is to operating systems.

However, all this flexibility comes with a bit of a learning curve. Being a general-purpose platform capable of handling so many different deployment constructs, Kubernetes can be a daunting thing to learn. I'm here to tell you, though, that (a) it's not as hard as people make it out to be and (b) it's worth learning. If you start with the basics and gradually layer on new constructs (which is how this book is structured), it's a lot more approachable. You can get a stateless app deployed with a few lines of YAML and build your knowledge from there.

As a professional, when you are faced with a problem, like how best to deploy your applications, I believe the right answer isn't always to pick the simplest option available that can solve your immediate concern but rather to invest your time to learn a system that can meet your needs both now and in the future, one that allows you to develop your skills and grow professionally as your requirements evolve. Kubernetes fits this bill. You can get up and running in hours with some simple deployments while knowing a wealth of functionality exists, ready for you to learn and employ when, and if, you need it.

If you're already sold on the idea of Kubernetes, I suggest skipping to chapter 2 to start building a Docker image, and if you already know what a Docker container is and want to start deploying to Kubernetes, go right to chapter 3. The rest of this chapter covers why Kubernetes and containers are proving so popular for application deployment.

1.1   *Why containers?*

Kubernetes is a deployment platform for containers. All code deployed into Kubernetes, like your application, needs to be first packaged into a container. What are containers, and why bother with them at all?

Containers are the modern way to package and run applications. Unless you're running one application per host (which is pretty inefficient), you typically want some way to deploy multiple applications onto a machine or collection of machines. What are the choices?

---

[1] https://cloud.google.com/learn/what-is-kubernetes
[2] https://kubernetes.io/case-studies/spotify/
[3] https://kubernetes.io/case-studies/capital-one/
[4] https://kubernetes.io/case-studies/openai/

Before virtual machines (VMs), it was common to install each application into a different directory on a shared host, with each served on a separate port. This presents a few problems in that the various applications need to cooperate with each other to some extent when it comes to sharing dependencies and the resources of the machine, like CPU, memory, and available ports. It can also be hard to scale: if you have one application that suddenly is receiving more traffic, how do you scale just that application while leaving the others as they are?

More recently, with VMs, the solution was to package each application into a VM of its own. In this way, each application has its own operating environment so that dependencies can be isolated and resources divided up and allocated. Since each VM has the complexity of an individual host, though, you now need to maintain the operating system and all packages for each application, which has high overheads and is complex to maintain.

This brings us to containers. Containers are a way to package just your application and its required dependencies for hosting in an isolated environment, much like a VM but without needing to install and manage an operating system with the application.

Figure 1.1 illustrates the evolution of hosting services, from running multiple workloads on a single host, to running them on separate VMs, and, finally, containers. Containers provide many of the benefits of VMs but without the overheads of running another operating system kernel, making them the logical modern path forward.

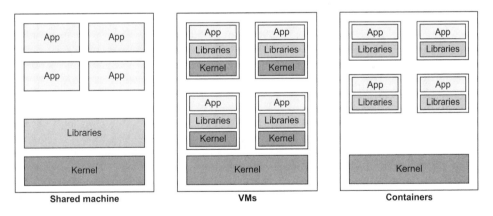

Figure 1.1 Evolution of shared hosting architectures

1.1.1 Container benefits

Some of the top reasons people choose containers are for the language flexibility (being able to run any language or environment on a container platform), lightweight isolation (protecting your workloads from interfering with each other without using VMs), developer efficiency (bringing production closer to development and allowing easy setup), and reproducibility (recording the steps used to create the environment in the container build file).

LANGUAGE FLEXIBILITY

Containers unbind you from language or library requirements from your deployment systems. You can bring any language and update any package. No longer are you locked into specific languages and versions or stuck with some outdated version of a critical dependency that shipped in the operating system years ago, as you might be on a traditional platform as a service (PaaS).

There are no shared libraries between two containers running on the same host, meaning the configuration of one will not interfere with the other. Need two different versions of Java or some random dependency? No problem. This isolation extends beyond just the libraries of the containers: each container can use a completely different base OS and package manager—for example, one using Ubuntu and APT, while another uses CentOS and RPM. This flexibility makes it simpler to potentially string together a system from multiple services (a pattern known as *microservices*), each maintained by separate teams, with their own dependencies or languages. Containers keep these different app dependencies isolated from each other, making it simple to run them all on the same host (figure 1.2).

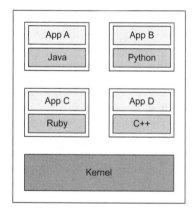

Figure 1.2   Four containers with different languages sharing a host

ISOLATION WITHOUT OVERHEAD

In the past, to achieve isolation between multiple apps running on the same host, you would use VMs. VMs are heavier, both in image size and CPU/memory resource overhead, as the kernel and much of the OS are duplicated in each VM. While containers are lighter than VMs, they still offer most of the same resource isolation benefits. You can limit your containers on Kubernetes to use only some of the resources of the host, and the system will restrict them from using more. This ultimately means you can pack more applications onto a single host, reducing your infrastructure costs (figure 1.3).

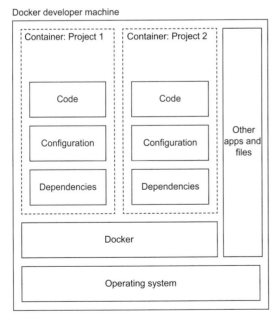

Figure 1.3 Four containers running on the same host, fully isolated but sharing the kernel

DEVELOPER EFFICIENCY

What makes containers great for production by isolating dependencies also makes them great for development, as you can develop a myriad of applications on a single machine without needing to configure the host with the dependencies of each (figure 1.4). In addition to developing Linux applications directly on Linux, with Docker you can use macOS or Windows workstations to develop a Linux container, without needing to create a version of the app that runs natively on those platforms, eliminating platform-specific configurations for development.

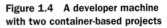

Figure 1.4 A developer machine with two container-based projects

No longer do you need to have pages of setup instructions for developers to get started either, as setup is now as easy as installing Docker, checking out the code, building, and running. Working on multiple projects within a team or for different teams is now simple as well, as each project is nicely isolated in its container without needing a particular host configuration.

With containers, your development and production app looks very similar and can be the exact same container—no more development-specific idiosyncrasies getting in the way, like MacOS having a different MySQL library or subtle differences in the way the code is packaged for production. Trying to diagnose a production problem? Download that exact container, run it against your development environment, and see what's up (figure 1.5).

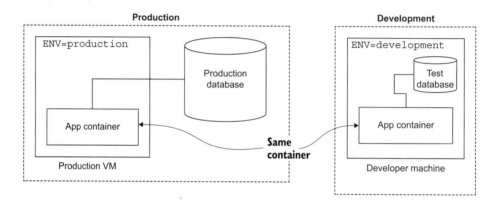

Figure 1.5   The same container being deployed in the production and development environments

REPRODUCIBILITY

Containers make it easier to reproduce your application environment as well. Imagine you have a VM on which your application is deployed, and you need to configure Transport Layer Security (TLS) for secure HTTPs connections. You SSH into the production host, and add the TLS certificates to a folder. It didn't work, so you add them to another folder. Soon they're in three folders, and it's working so you don't touch it. A year later, you need to update the TLS certificate. Can you remember how, and which of the three locations needs to be updated?

Containers solve this. Rather than SSHing and tweaking the state, you would add the TLS certificate as a build step in the container. If it didn't work, you'd tweak that build step until it does but, crucially, only keep the step (or steps) that actually do work. The files added in this step are also nicely isolated from the rest of the system, so essentially you're capturing the delta, or differences, over the base system—just those modifications you needed to make. This means that a year later when you need to update the certificate, you just replace the certificate file and rerun the container build, and it will put it in the right place.

The following listing provides a pseudocode example of a Dockerfile—that is, the code to configure the container expressed in plain English (in chapter 2, we'll use some real ones).

Listing 1.1 Chapter01/1.1.1_Pseudocode Dockerfile

```
Use the Ubuntu OS
Copy and configure TLS certificate
Copy the application
```

> **NOTE** Docker as a tool for creating containers isn't perfect for reproducibility. Commands like `apt-get` to install a dependency operate on a live system, so you won't actually get the same output for the same input, as those dependent systems (like the APT repository) may have changed between builds. Tools like Bazel, open-sourced by Google, are designed to solve this problem and more but come with their own complexities and are more recommended for sophisticated enterprise deployments. Despite this limitation, Docker's build system is still a heck of a lot more reproducible than trying to remember what you did a year ago when you SSHed into that Linux box to fix a problem, and it is good enough for most projects.

1.2 Why Kubernetes?

If containers sound like a great idea for packaging your application, you'll still need a way to actually run and manage those containers. Sure, you could just run a container or a handful of containers on each host in much the same way it is possible to run a bunch of different applications from folders or VM images, but operating like this tends to create special snowflakes of machines and limits your ability to scale due to the high-touch required to configure and manage hosts.

A better option is to have a shared pool (cluster) of machines (nodes) and use a so-called container orchestrator (like Kubernetes) to run your containers on this resource pool. In this way, machines are managed together as a group, where none need to be ascribed any special meaning. Should one fail, another will be there to pick up the slack. This pattern gets you out of the individual-machine business and allows you to scale your application faster than your team size.

Previously, systems that could flexibly orchestrate containers at scale were the domain of large companies. Kubernetes—in particular, managed Kubernetes offerings on public clouds—makes this operations model accessible to deployments of all sizes, from a single container application running on one machine to a set of microservices, each published by a different team running on a 15,000-machine behemoth.

Kubernetes also makes it easy to achieve *high availability* for your applications. As illustrated in figure 1.6, we can deploy the same service across multiple availability zones, where the loss of an entire zone would not result in downtime. With a manual deployment system, this can be complex, but we can achieve such deployment patterns

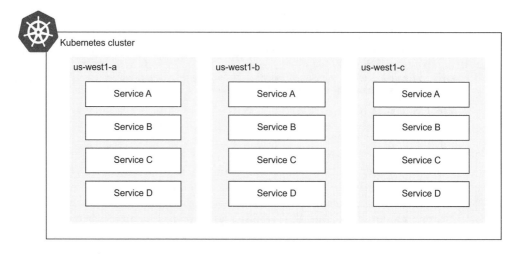

Figure 1.6   A Kubernetes cluster operating in three zones, managing four services

rapidly in Kubernetes by simply defining what we want to see (in this case, containers spread over multiple zones). Section 8.2.1 covers this.

The best part is that updating a service in Kubernetes requires a single line of config to be changed, and Kubernetes will handle the rollout of the update to each of the zones for you, per your requirements. Updates to the Kubernetes platform itself happen in a similar, automated fashion (provided you are using a managed platform, which handles this), where nodes are replaced gradually with updated versions, and your workload is migrated to avoid downtime. If your app isn't big enough to require a high-availability multizone deployment, fear not: Kubernetes can run at a small scale too, with the added benefit that you can scale up when you need.

Kubernetes has gained popularity as it automates much of the operational aspects of scheduling and running containers on a pool of resources and provides the level of abstraction to developers that seems to have hit the sweet spot. It isn't so low level that you are worried about individual machines, while also not being so high level as to constrain what workloads you can deploy.

1.2.1   *Composable building blocks*

In Kubernetes, containers are grouped into what are called *Pods*. A Pod is simply a set of containers that get scheduled together and treated as a single unit. Quite often, a Pod is just a single container, but it could be multiple containers in the case where your app consists of multiple connected parts. Conceptually, the Pod is your application and its dependencies. Services are used to provide connectivity to groups of Pods, both internally within the cluster and externally. Figure 1.7 illustrates the resources of a typical app deployed to a Kubernetes cluster.

Kubernetes has several higher-order workload constructs, described throughout this book, that encapsulate Pods. For a stateless application, you will create a *Deployment*

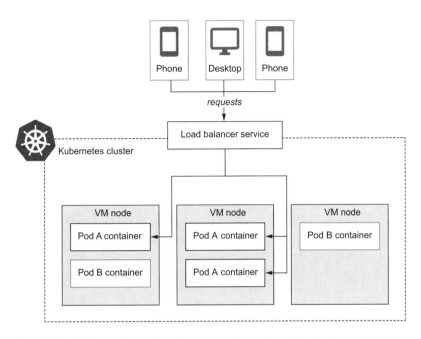

Figure 1.7 A Kubernetes cluster with several VMs running two different application containers, exposed with load balancing

object that wraps the Pod definition (specifying your container versions), where you specify how many replicas (instances) you want. In all these cases, Kubernetes will do the heavy lifting of finding space in your cluster to place the Pods according to your requirements.

The range of workload types you can describe in Kubernetes configuration is wide and varied and includes the following:

- Stateless applications
- Databases and other applications with persistent state
- Applications formerly configured in a VM
- A batch process you wish to run at a certain schedule
- A batch task you want to run once, like training a machine learning model

In all cases, the applications are containerized and grouped in Pods, and you describe to Kubernetes in configuration files how you want your workload to be run.

1.2.2 Features and benefits

In this section, we will discuss some of the top reasons why people choose Kubernetes to deploy their containers.

AUTOMATED OPERATIONS

Provided you configure your deployment correctly, Kubernetes will automate various operational aspects for you. Processes running on the node restart containers that crash, while liveness and readiness probes continue to monitor the container's health and ability to serve live traffic. Pod autoscalers can be configured on your deployments to automatically increase the number of replicas based on metrics like utilization.

Kubernetes itself doesn't repair compute node–level problems. However, you can choose a managed platform that will provide such automation. Take, for example, the Autopilot mode of Google Kubernetes Engine: it automatically provisions the compute capacity for your Pods, scaling up and down automatically as you change your replica count, and will repair and upgrade nodes as needed.

HIGH SCALABILITY

No matter the size of your application, you will want to think about how it will scale. Whether you are deploying a huge enterprise application or you are a bootstrapped startup, you will need a solution that can scale as you do. The time when you need to scale is not the time to start thinking about how you are going to scale!

It is hard enough to create a successful product; the last thing you want in your moment of success—when everyone is beating down your door trying to use your product—is for your application to go offline. At that moment, and perhaps even in the months and years to come, you're likely not going to be able to completely re-architect your application for scale.

Kubernetes can handle applications of any size. You can have a single-node cluster with a single CPU and a bunch of memory or a multi-thousand-node behemoth like the 10s of thousands of cores Niantic used to run Pokémon Go when it launched.[5] Of course, your application itself will need to have properties that enable it to scale, and so will any dependencies, particularly database ones, but at least you can rest assured that your compute platform will scale as you do.

WORKLOAD ABSTRACTION

Abstraction layers are great, until they aren't. It is a challenge to find tools that abstract away precisely those things you do not want to care about, without hiding details you do care about. But, in my experience, Kubernetes comes the closest to achieving exactly that.

Infrastructure as a service (IaaS) is a hardware-level abstraction. Rather than interacting with actual machines with spinning disks and network cards, you interact with an API that provides software that implements those same interfaces.

Kubernetes, by comparison, is a workload-level abstraction. Meaning that you describe your application in workload terms. For example, I have a server that needs to run in a distributed fashion; I have a database that requires certain disk volumes to be attached; I have a logging utility that needs to run on every node; or maybe I have a movie to render, one frame at a time, on the cheapest resources available. All these deployment constructs and more can be represented natively in Kubernetes.

Kubernetes provides a layer above compute instances (VMs), freeing you from the need to manage or care about individual machines. You specify what resources your

---

[5] https://cloud.google.com/blog/products/gcp/bringing-pokemon-go-to-life-on-google-cloud

container needs: CPU, memory, disk, GPU, etc. A managed Kubernetes platform will also typically provision the compute capacity to handle your workloads. You don't need to worry about individual machines, but you can still do things that you would expect at a machine level, like write to a persistent local disk, tasks that until recently were often not possible at this level of abstraction.

The abstraction layer also remains quite clean by not interfering with your application (figure 1.8). Unlike many traditional PaaS environments, Kubernetes does not modify how your app runs; for example, no code is injected or changed, and very few restrictions are placed on what your app can do. If the app can be run in a container, then it can likely be run on Kubernetes.

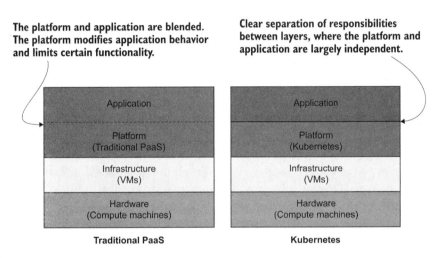

Figure 1.8 Illustration of the separation of concerns between the different compute layers

DECLARATIVE CONFIGURATION

Kubernetes uses a declarative resource model. You describe your workload in the configuration (primarily YAML files), and the system strives to enact your configuration and make it a reality. For example, if, in the Deployment, you specify that you want three replicas (copies) of your application connected by a load balancer to the outside world, Kubernetes will find space in your cluster to run those three replicas and attach a load balancer. Not only does Kubernetes place these replicas initially, but it will continue to monitor them and attempt to keep them running in the event of a crash or failure.

A declarative configuration is useful because it allows you to describe what your desired state is (e.g., run three copies of my application) and lets Kubernetes do the work of actually producing that state, as opposed to issuing imperative commands (e.g., create three copies of my application) and doing the monitoring and adjusting yourself (like querying how many copies of my application are currently running and adjusting accordingly).

COST EFFICIENCY

Kubernetes takes the lowest-level compute building blocks (VMs) and makes them easy to manage. Whereas in the past, you might have assigned one app per VM for maintenance reasons, Kubernetes allows you to efficiently host multiple instances of an app or apps on a single machine for high efficiency (so-called bin-packing). The combination of using commodity building blocks (raw compute nodes) with robust orchestration of the workloads often makes Kubernetes attractive from a price perspective.

Beyond bin-packing, resource pooling is another benefit of Kubernetes that improves efficiency. Your workloads can be configured in a way where they have a set amount of guaranteed resources and, when there's a usage spike, utilize the capacity that other containers have reserved but are not currently using.

EXTENSIBILITY

When you need to do something that Kubernetes can't, you can source or even write your own Kubernetes-style API to implement it. This isn't for everyone and definitely isn't needed to deploy most workloads like stateless or stateful web applications, but it can be extremely handy when you need to add particular business logic or some new construct that Kubernetes doesn't support. The custom resource definition object and operator patterns allow you to create your own Kubernetes-style APIs.

OPEN SOURCE

Kubernetes is open source and available on all major clouds as a managed offering. Despite the proliferation of many different platforms, distributions, and installers, most such offerings have been certified under the Cloud Native Computing Foundation's certification program,[6] which offers several guarantees around workload portability and compatibility. In fact, the only way for a product to include the name *Kubernetes* in it (as in Google Kubernetes Engine) is to have formally passed these tests.

You can also run Kubernetes yourself from scratch. And if you do run Kubernetes yourself, then the quality of the code will matter to you. Not all open source is created equal. While open source does typically remove you from propriety lock-in, you might end up having to maintain it yourself (you use it, you own it) unless there is a strong community. The exception is for large, well-maintained open source projects of the caliber of, say, Linux, where so many people depend on it and so many people use it that you can rest assured you won't need to take over maintenance. Fortunately, Kubernetes, as the leading open source container orchestrator, fits into this category.

> **TIP** While it is possible to host Kubernetes yourself, whether on a public cloud or on a cluster of Raspberry Pis, I don't recommend this approach for production use (i.e., outside of learning how to manage a cluster) in most cases. Spend the time doing what you do best—building great applications— and let someone else handle the minutiae of running Kubernetes for you.

---

[6] https://www.cncf.io/certification/software-conformance/

Beyond the project itself being open source, Kubernetes is surrounded by a vibrant community. There are open source tools for accomplishing pretty much anything, so you typically have the option to go with a managed service or deploy an open source tool yourself. This is a break from proprietary-only marketplaces in PaaS systems of the past, where your only option for any type of component was a paid one. Do you get value from a managed monitoring tool? Use a proprietary product. Want to just manage it yourself? Go install open source Prometheus. Kubernetes has a large and growing number of practitioners as well, so whatever the topic is, you should be able to find help on Stack Overflow or in books like this one.

CUSTOMIZED WORKFLOWS

Kubernetes is very unopinionated about how you set up development workflows. Want a "git push to deploy" style workflow? There are a bunch of ways to do that, some with only minimal setup. Typically, you'll start with a bunch of CI/CD building blocks, which you assemble into your desired workflow, from simple push-to-deploy to complex pipelines with admissions control, auto-injecting secrets, and security scanning. The downside is that it's not quite as ready to use out of the box as, say, a traditional PaaS, but this book will show you it's not *that* hard to get started.

Particularly for larger teams, the flexibility provided by Kubernetes in this area is often a huge advantage. Companies with a central core platforms team will create opinionated pipelines for their application developer teams to use. The pipeline can be used to ensure certain development practices around things like security, resource usage, and so on.

1.2.3 *Kubernetes vs. platforms as a service*

Another approach to application deployment is to use a PaaS. A PaaS makes it easy to deploy your application code at scale by taking care of a lot of the packaging and deployment aspects for you. As long as your application fits within the scope of what the PaaS offers in terms of languages, dependencies, how it handles state, etc., you can launch each application into the PaaS and not worry about the machines underneath.

However, what happens when you need to highly customize your dependencies, like using a specific version of Java? Can you host a stateful backend alongside your stateless frontends? And is it cost-effective when you have many applications, each needing many replicas? At a certain point, the limitations of a PaaS can be prohibitive, and once you move out of the PaaS world, you have to start over from scratch—a daunting prospect.

A traditional PaaS is often fast to learn but slows down as you mature, and there's a potential cliff if you exceed the capabilities of the system and need to start from scratch. Kubernetes has a slower learning curve at the beginning but expansive possibilities as you grow (figure 1.9).

If you're using a PaaS and everything is going great, there may not be a need to move to Kubernetes. However, a common problem I've seen is that teams hit a certain

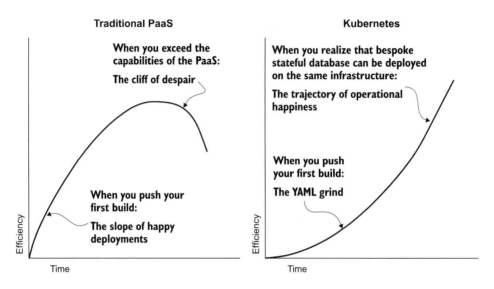

Figure 1.9   Developer efficiency using a traditional PaaS and Kubernetes

level of complexity where their requirements exceed what the PaaS is capable of. One of the scariest things about being in that position is that you can't simply "break the glass" and assume more control yourself. Often, you'll need to re-architect the entire system, losing even the bits you were happy with, to build the new parts that you need. In this book, I'll show you how Kubernetes can run PaaS-type workloads with marginal added complexity over a dedicated PaaS, as well as how to run various other workload constructs like stateful workloads, background processing, and batch jobs, which set you up for success in the future by enabling you to implement more complex product requirements.

A word on simplicity

I like to say, be wary of tools that make the simple easier but the complex harder. Sure, it's nice when something helps you get up and running sooner, but is it leaving you in a good state, with the right knowledge and tools to get the job done? Kubernetes is easy enough to get started on, while being powerful enough to serve your needs as you grow and expand. When choosing your platforms, prioritize making hard tasks possible over making simple tasks even easier.

Kubernetes will enable you to run a simple, 12-factor stateless application; migrate over a bespoke stateful custom application previously installed on a VM; or even run your own database. The abstraction layer doesn't limit what you can do, while still allowing you to get started using only the bits you need at first.

Some more modern PaaSs support containers, so you could run there and get the best of both worlds: the flexibility of containers with easy deployments. A downside is that even modern PaaSs come with many restrictions on the types of workloads you can run. Can it, for example, run a stateful application with a block-based volume attached, as you might need if you have a legacy application to migrate, or run a bespoke database where no managed offering exists? I suggest you carefully consider your current and future needs and choose a platform that will be able to grow and scale as you do.

1.2.4   *When (not) to use Kubernetes*

Like most tools, the goal of Kubernetes is to improve your efficiency—in this case, managing your application deployments. It's best to ignore the hype and really consider whether Kubernetes will help or hinder your ability to run your service. Managed Kubernetes platforms exist to keep your cluster components running smoothly, but be aware that there is some overhead to running a general-purpose platform like Kubernetes. Operational tasks include allocating CPU and memory resources to containers, updating deployments, configuring your network, and keeping everything up to date without disrupting your running services.

If you can predict the exact scope of your business requirements now and in the future and don't need the flexibility that Kubernetes provides, don't care about the vendor portability of the Kubernetes ecosystem, and can fit your application architecture neatly into the expectations of a more special-purpose platform, then go ahead and use it instead! Honestly, you'll probably have a simpler time of it.

I don't generally recommend using Kubernetes for deployments of software where fully-managed equivalents exist. For example, why run a SQL database in Kubernetes when your cloud provider can do that for you? There are some exceptions where it becomes desirable to self-manage, but, in general, I believe if the managed service exists, you should use it!

Kubernetes *is* really good at a few things, though, like running stateless applications at high density; mixing multiple workloads like a modern stateless application and legacy stateful monolith; migrating services from outdated systems to a unified platform; handling high-performance compute, like batch processing jobs for data analytics and machine learning; and, of course, running a bunch of microservices. In each of these cases, Kubernetes brings a lot to the table by enabling high efficiency, unifying your hosting platform, automating your systems, and running your batch jobs.

Kubernetes does introduce a new level of management overhead, which needs to be considered. There's a risk of simply replacing one problem with another if you take what you're doing (assuming it's working well) and throw it onto Kubernetes. Some cases where you may want to consider carefully would be replacing a stateless platform *if* it's already handling your requirements and moving standardized stateful workloads that have well-established deployment patterns like SQL databases. While you may see benefits in Kubernetes for such workloads, the advantages may not be as many, and so the tradeoff needs to be more carefully considered.

To help decide, I suggest weighing the benefits of moving to containers and unifying your compute platform around one deployment system suitable for varied workloads, with the added knowledge needed to administer Kubernetes. If what you're starting with is a bunch of services running on bespoke VMs in various stages of disrepair, it's likely not going to be a hard choice. Similarly, if you've outgrown your PaaS or have a highly proficient team wanting to deploy faster with modern tools, go for it. But that MySQL cluster that's running like a charm on a custom clustering setup with four 9s of reliability? Maybe that one's OK to leave for now.

Going to Kubernetes doesn't need to be an all-or-nothing decision. I'd suggest starting with those workloads that make the most sense and gradually migrating them as you and your team build up knowledge in operating Kubernetes.

Summary

- Containers are the modern way to run applications that achieve isolation between multiple applications running on the same host and do so with low overhead compared to VMs.
- Kubernetes is a deployment platform for containerized applications.
- Kubernetes has a bit of a learning curve, but it enables you to express a vast variety of deployment constructs and takes care of configuring infrastructure and keeping applications running.
- Hosted platforms (like Google Kubernetes Engine) take away the administrative burden of managing Kubernetes, allowing you to focus on your application deployments.
- Application developers can focus on describing their application configuration in Kubernetes terms, after which the system is responsible for running it in the way you described.
- A key benefit of Kubernetes is that it allows you to grow as your needs evolve; you likely won't need to change platforms due to new requirements like an application needing to have its own local state.
- When you need to scale up due to increased demand, Kubernetes can help you do so in an efficient way.

Containerizing apps

This chapter covers

- How to containerize apps
- Running your container locally
- Executing commands in the container context

Containerizing your application—that is, packaging your application and its dependencies into an executable container—is a required step before adopting Kubernetes. The good news is that containerizing your application has benefits beyond being able to deploy it into Kubernetes; it's a valuable step in its own right, as you're packaging the application's dependencies and can then run it anywhere without needing to install those dependencies on the host machine.

Regardless of how you deploy your app, containerizing it means that your developers can begin working on it locally using Docker, enabling them to get started on a new project with no setup beyond installing Docker. It provides easy context switching between the different applications developers are working on, as the environments are completely isolated (figure 2.1). These properties make it a valuable way to improve developer productivity even if you don't end up deploying your app into production with containers (although you'll probably want to do that, too).

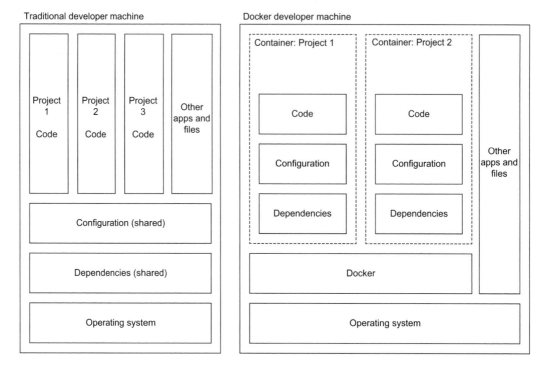

Figure 2.1   Comparison of multiple projects on a development machine with and without containerization

Having your application packaged into containers means that all your dependencies and configurations are captured by a container configuration file—the Dockerfile—rather than a mix of bash scripts, text-based instructions, human memory, and other nonstandard configuration systems. It makes it possible to deploy multiple applications on a single host machine without worrying that they will interfere with each other but with greater performance and less overhead than full virtualization.

2.1   *Building Docker containers*

Let's take an application and put it in a container.

2.1.1   *Developer setup*

Docker is distributed as a developer tool that is available for most platforms as Docker Desktop (https://www.docker.com/products/docker-desktop), which includes some convenient utilities such as a local Kubernetes environment (covered in chapter 3). For Linux (including Windows Subsystem for Linux [WSL]), you can also install the Docker Engine standalone.

MAC
On Mac, simply install Docker Desktop.

WINDOWS

On Windows, I highly recommend first configuring the WSL (https://learn.microsoft
.com/en-us/windows/wsl/install). WSL 2 is the one you want so that Docker can
use it as well. With WSL 2 installed, you can also install a distribution of Linux like
Ubuntu (http://mng.bz/pP40), which gives you a bash shell and is a convenient way
to run the samples presented in this section. Once WSL is configured, install Docker
Desktop.

LINUX

For Linux, there is another option in addition to Docker Desktop—the Docker Engine.
You can find instructions for various platforms, including Ubuntu, here: https://docs
.docker.com/engine/install/ubuntu/. Docker Engine is also an option when you use
Linux via WSL.

2.1.2   Running commands in Docker

To explore how Docker works before we build our own application container, we can
bring up a containerized Linux shell in Docker, like so:

```
$ docker run -it ubuntu bash
root@18e78382b32e:/#
```

This downloads the base `ubuntu` image, starts a container, and runs the bash command against it. The `-it` parameters make it an interactive bash terminal. Now we are
in the container, and anything we run will happen in the container.

   Since we're going to be building an application on Ubuntu, let's install the language package. I'm going to be using Python for many of the examples in this chapter, but the concept applies equally to any other language.

   Run the following two commands in the container shell:

```
apt-get update
apt-get install -y python3
```

Now we can try out Python interactively, for example:

```
# python3
>>> print("Hello Docker")
Hello Docker
>>> exit()
#
```

We can capture this most basic of commands into our own Python script:

```
# echo 'print("Hello Docker")' > hello.py
# python3 hello.py
Hello Docker
```

When you're done playing around in this container, exit using `exit`.

The beauty of this is that we installed Python and ran our Python command on the container, not on our local system. The Docker `run` command actually created a *container*, from our *image*. The image, `ubuntu`, is a prebuilt filesystem from which the container process runs in. When we exit our interactive session with the container, it will be stopped, but you can easily start it up again using `docker ps -a` to get the container ID, `docker start $CONTAINER_ID` to boot it, and `docker attach $CONTAINER_ID` to reconnect our shell:

```
$ docker ps -a
CONTAINER ID    IMAGE     COMMAND     CREATED         STATUS
c5e023cab033    ubuntu    "bash"      5 minutes ago   Exited (0) 1 second ago

$ CONTAINER_ID=c5e023cab033
$ docker start $CONTAINER_ID
$ docker attach $CONTAINER_ID
# echo "run more commands"
# exit
```

After running a lot of Docker containers, you'll end up with a pretty big list of stopped containers (and lots of hard drive space used). To clean up these images, which typically you don't need to keep, at any time, run:

```
docker system prune -a
```

> ### Container image vs. container instance
> In Docker terminology, the container *image* is the file artifact (whether downloaded from a registry as in this section or built locally), and the container instance (or just container) is an invocation of the container. In Kubernetes, configuration refers only to images, while container instances are created at run time and are ephemeral in nature (they are deleted when the Pod is stopped). When using Docker locally, the instance concept is important, not least because every invocation creates a container instance that persists, so eventually you'll need to clean them up to recover the disk space.

With these steps, we now have a Linux environment, which we can use for testing and running random commands, all without needing to install anything (beyond Docker) on our local machine. Want two Linux container environments with a different config? No worries—just run another container!

If you've ever set up a virtual machine (VM) before, you'll appreciate just how fast this is to set up! Containers are simple to create. As you'll see in the next section, they are also easy to build on and expand.

2.1.3   *Building our own images*

In the previous section, we started a Linux container, installed Python, and created a simple Python script, which we ran in the container. Let's say we want to make this repeatable. That is, we want to capture the configuration of the container (installing Python) and our application (the Python script) in our own container image. Such an image would be useful so we don't have to remember the steps we took and also so that others can build our amazing application!

While this example uses only a simple Python script, you can imagine that the application can be as large and complex as you want to make it. It doesn't just have to be Python either; these steps work for any interpreted language (see section 2.1.7 for how to deal with compiled applications). Just substitute the Python configuration for whatever language you are using.

The process of building our container image so we can make a repeatable application deployment uses a configuration file known as a Dockerfile. The Dockerfile is a set of procedural instructions used to build your container. Think of it like a bash script that configures a VM image with your app and its dependencies; only the output is a container image.

Running the examples

The example Docker applications and Kubernetes configuration listed in this book can be found in the source repository. Clone the repository and change into the root directory with the following:

```
git clone https://github.com/WilliamDenniss/kubernetes-for-developers.git
cd kubernetes-for-developers
```

The examples are arranged by chapter and section. For example, the code from chapter 2 is in a folder named Chapter02, and the examples from section 2.1.3 are in folder 2.1.3_Dockerfile. Each code listing includes the path to the sample file so you can locate it.

The shell commands given start from the root sample code folder (`kubernetes-for-developers`, if you cloned the repo per the previous command), so just change back to that directory after running any example or exploring the code, and you should be ready to pick up where you left off and follow the next example.

We'll start with the basic Python program we created in the previous section, as shown in the following listing.

Listing 2.1   Chapter02/2.1.3_Dockerfile/hello.py

```
print("Hello Docker")
```

To build a container image for this script, you'll need to create a Dockerfile, pick a base container image to use as the starting point, configure Python, and add the program. For now, we'll start with the generic base image `ubuntu`, which provides a containerized Linux environment. The following listing shows a basic Dockerfile to capture these steps.

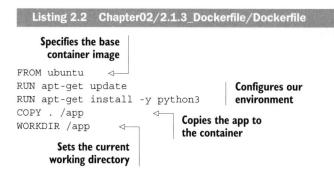

Listing 2.2   Chapter02/2.1.3_Dockerfile/Dockerfile

Build this container and name (tag) it `hello`, like so:

```
cd Chapter02/2.1.3_Dockerfile/
docker build . -t hello
```

Once built, we can run the `python3 hello.py` command on the container named `hello`, like so:

```
$ docker run hello python3 hello.py
Hello Docker
```

Notice how the commands in our Dockerfile are essentially the same as the ones we used in the previous section. Rather than starting the `ubuntu` container image directly, we use it as our base image of the Dockerfile. Then we run the same two `apt-get` commands as before to install Python, copy our Python script into the image, and specify the default working directory to indicate where commands will be run. Also, notice that the command to run the code is still `python3 hello.py`; it's just now prefixed to run in our new container image.

We've now encapsulated the environment we built and our script into a neat package that we can use and run ourselves and share with others. The wonderful thing about containers is that they encapsulate the configuration steps along with the program itself. The best part is that when the `ubuntu` base image is updated, we can rebuild our image by simply running that one `build` command again.

Compare this to installing Python on your developer machine and running everything locally. For one, if you'd done that, you would now have Python installed. You probably would be happy to have Python installed, but imagine a more complex application that brings with it dozens of tools and libraries. Do you really want all these on your system? Furthermore, what if you're developing a few different applications, all with their own dependencies or with the same dependency but requiring particular versions of that dependency, making it impossible to satisfy the dependencies of both applications simultaneously (a situation sometimes referred to as "dependency hell")?

Containers solve this by isolating applications along with their dependencies in their own container images. You can happily work on multiple projects, share Dockerfiles with your development team, and upload container images to your production environment without messing up your developer machine.

For a different language, like Ruby, the setup is fairly similar, as shown in the following two listings.

Listing 2.3   Chapter02-ruby/2.1.3_Dockerfile/hello.rb

```
puts "Hello Docker"
```

Listing 2.4   Chapter02-ruby/2.1.3_Dockerfile/Dockerfile

```
FROM ubuntu
RUN apt-get update
RUN apt-get install -y ruby
COPY . /app
WORKDIR /app
```

To run, the only difference is the command that is passed:

```
$ cd Chapter02-ruby/2.1.3_Dockerfile
$ docker build . -t hello_ruby
$ docker run hello_ruby ruby hello.rb
Hello Docker
```

2.1.4   Using base images

The previous section uses the Linux container `ubuntu` as a base to configure our Linux-based app. Base images, including `ubuntu` and other distributions such as `centos` and the `alpine`, are a good starting point for configuring any Linux-based app. However, for convenience, the container community has created several more-specific images designed for various languages and environments.

Instead of installing Python ourselves onto the `ubuntu` base image, we can just start with the `python` image and save some steps. The added bonus is that these base images are generally created by experts and thus are well-configured to run Python apps. The following listing shows the same container but starting with the `python` base image.

Listing 2.5   Chapter02/2.1.4_BaseImage/Dockerfile

```
FROM python:3
COPY . /app
WORKDIR /app
```

Simpler, right? Building and running it is the same as before:

```
$ cd Chapter02/2.1.4_BaseImage
$ docker build . -t hello2
$ docker run hello2 python3 hello.py
Hello Docker
```

> **What is a base image, really?**
> The base image used in this example, `python`, is itself built with a Dockerfile and configures an environment with everything needed to run Python programs. For container images from Docker Hub, their Dockerfile sources are linked so you can see how they are composed. Base images often start with another base image, and so on, until one that starts with a completely empty container known as `scratch`.

If you're using Ruby instead of Python, setup is pretty similar. Just use the `ruby` base image, as shown in the following two listings.

Listing 2.6   Chapter02-ruby/2.1.4_BaseImage/hello.rb

```
puts "Hello Docker"
```

Listing 2.7   Chapter02-ruby/2.1.4_BaseImage/Dockerfile

```
FROM ruby
COPY . /app
WORKDIR /app
```

To build and run:

```
$ cd Chapter02-ruby/2.1.4_BaseImage
$ docker build . -t hello_ruby2
$ docker run hello_ruby2 ruby hello.rb
Hello Docker
```

More than just operation system and language-specific base images exist. If you're using an environment like Apache, you can start with the `httpd` base image. Sometimes you'll have a situation where there are multiple base images that could serve as the base. The best rule of thumb is to pick the one that saves you the most configuration (and you can always crib from the Dockerfile of the one you didn't pick!).

Base images—or at least public examples that you can copy—exist for pretty much every common language, environment, and open source application. Before building your own from scratch, it is wise to search Docker Hub or Google for a base image to see if someone has an example for your environment that you can use as a starting point.

2.1.5   Adding a default command

Typically, the command executed in the container (`python3 hello.py` in the earlier Python example) is the same each time. Rather than repeating it each time, you can specify that in the Dockerfile as well.

Listing 2.8   Chapter02/2.1.5_DefaultCommand/Dockerfile

```
FROM python:3
COPY . /app
```

```
WORKDIR /app
CMD python3 hello.py
```

To build and run this container, execute the following from the command line:

```
$ cd Chapter02/2.1.5_DefaultCommand
$ docker build . -t hello3
$ docker run hello3
Hello Docker
```

Unlike the other lines in the Dockerfile we've used so far, CMD is unique as it doesn't actually change how the container is built. It merely saves the default command that will be executed if you call docker run without a command specified. This doesn't stop you from overriding it and executing a different command at run time. With the command now specified in the Dockerfile, to build and run the Ruby version of this program, it is also simply docker run $IMAGE_NAME:

```
$ cd Chapter02-ruby/2.1.5_DefaultCommand
$ docker build . -t hello_ruby3
$ docker run hello_ruby3
Hello Docker
```

2.1.6 Adding dependencies

Most nontrivial applications will have their own dependencies not included in the base image. To load those dependencies, you can run commands during the container build process to configure the image as you need. This was how we added Python to the Linux base image in the previous example, and this method can be used to install all the dependencies that your application needs. If your application establishes a database connection to a MariaDB database, you might build your container as in the following listing.

> **Listing 2.9 Chapter02/2.1.6_Dependencies/Dockerfile**

```
FROM python:3
RUN apt-get update                          Use apt-get to configure your Linux
RUN apt-get install -y mariadb-client       container with everything your app needs.
COPY . /app
WORKDIR /app
CMD python3 hello.py
```

The python base image is built from Debian, a distribution of Linux widely used for containers, which uses the apt-get package manager, so we can use apt-get to install pretty much any other dependency we need.

You don't just have to use apt-get either. Say you have a service that's creating PDF files, and you need to include a Unicode font. You can build an image that includes Google's Noto free font, like in the following listing.

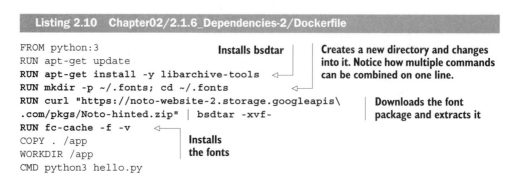

Listing 2.10   Chapter02/2.1.6_Dependencies-2/Dockerfile

```
FROM python:3
RUN apt-get update
RUN apt-get install -y libarchive-tools
RUN mkdir -p ~/.fonts; cd ~/.fonts
RUN curl "https://noto-website-2.storage.googleapis\
.com/pkgs/Noto-hinted.zip" | bsdtar -xvf-
RUN fc-cache -f -v
COPY . /app
WORKDIR /app
CMD python3 hello.py
```

Installs bsdtar

Creates a new directory and changes into it. Notice how multiple commands can be combined on one line.

Downloads the font package and extracts it

Installs the fonts

It is common for containers to have many dependencies, and you can configure any part of the operating system you need to in this way, such as installing fonts or TLS certificates.

2.1.7   *Compiling code in Docker*

What about programs that need compilation, like Java, .NET, Swift, and C++? Obviously, a COPY command will not suffice in the Dockerfile, unless you already have compiled binaries lying around.

Precompiling the application locally would be one option, but why not use Docker to compile your application as well! Let's re-implement our "Hello World" example in Java and compile it into our container, as shown in the following two listings.

Listing 2.11   Chapter02/2.1.7_CompiledCode/Hello.java

```
class Hello {
    public static void main(String[] args) {
        System.out.println("Hello Docker");
    }
}
```

Listing 2.12   Chapter02/2.1.7_CompiledCode/Dockerfile

```
FROM openjdk
COPY . /app
WORKDIR /app
RUN javac Hello.java
CMD java Hello
```

The compile command

This Dockerfile is similar to the previous ones: we start with the OpenJDK (openjdk) base image and copy the app. In this case, however, we'll use the RUN command to build the app, prefaced with a WORKDIR directive to specify where this action (and subsequent actions) should be performed.

To build and run this example, do the following:

```
$ cd Chapter02/2.1.7_CompiledCode
$ docker build . -t compiled_code
```

```
$ docker run compiled_code
Hello Docker
```

Another example that compiles a server-side Swift application is given in the Chapter02-swift/2.1.7_CompiledCode folder. It can be built and run in the same way.

2.1.8 *Compiling code with a multistage build*

Using RUN to compile code or perform other actions is a viable path; however, the drawback is that you end up configuring your container image with tools it needs to execute the RUN command. These tools end up in the final container image along with any source code.

For example, if you look at the image we created in the previous section and run ls,

```
$ docker run compiled_code ls
Dockerfile
Hello.class
Hello.java
```

you'll see that the source code remains. Also, the Java compiler (javac) is still present in the image, even though it will never be used again (we don't need the compiler when running our application).

This mixing of responsibilities of the container image—to both build and run—is less than ideal. Not only do all those extra binaries bloat the container image, but they also needlessly increase the attack surface area of the container (as any process running in the container now has a compiler to work with). You could clean up the container with a bunch of additional Docker commands (e.g., deleting the source code, uninstalling tools that are no longer needed), but it's not always practical, particularly if all these extra tools came from the base image.

A better way to solve this problem is to use a multistage container build (figure 2.2). With a multistage build, we first configure a temporary container with everything needed to *build* the program, and then we configure a final container with everything needed to *run* the program. This keeps the concerns separated and neatly isolated to their own containers.

Let's rework the example in the previous section to be built using a multistage Dockerfile.

Listing 2.13 Chapter02/2.1.8_MultiStage/Dockerfile

```
FROM openjdk:11 AS buildstage          ◁──┐  The build container is named buildstage and
COPY . /app                               │  has the responsibility to build the code.
WORKDIR /app
RUN javac Hello.java
                                          ┌─ The runtime container uses a slimmed-down
                                          │  base image, without the compile tools
FROM openjdk:11-jre-slim          ◁──────┘
COPY --from=buildstage /app/Hello.class /app/   ◁──┐  --from= is used to reference
WORKDIR /app                                       │  files from the build container.
CMD java Hello
```

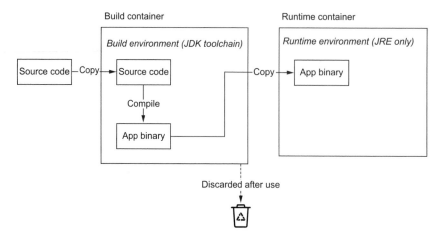

Figure 2.2   A multistage container build, where an intermediate container is used to build the binary

As you can see from this example, there are what looks like two Dockerfiles in one (each beginning with a FROM command). The first is configured and built purely to compile the app, using the full openjdk base image, which includes the Java compiler, and the second has only what is needed to run the app and is built from the jre base image, which only includes the Java Runtime Environment.

This Dockerfile produces, as its final artifact, a production container that only contains the compiled Java class and dependencies needed to run it. The intermediate artifact of the first container that built the app is effectively discarded after the build completes (technically, it's saved in your docker cache, but no part is included in the final artifact that you would use in production).

To run this example, do the following:

```
$ cd Chapter02/2.1.8_MultiStage
$ docker build . -t compiled_code2
$ docker run compiled_code2
Hello Docker
```

If we run the ls command on this new container, we can see that there is only the compiled code:

```
$ docker run compiled_code2 ls
Hello.class
```

Another example that compiles a server-side Swift application with the multistage build process is given in the Chapter02-swift/2.1.8_MultiStage folder. It can be built and run in the same way.

2.2 Containerizing a server application

The examples in the previous section were all simple programs that run once then exit. This is a use case for containers such as command-line programs and batch workloads or even to serve requests in a functions-as-a-service environment. One of the most common workloads to deploy in Kubernetes, however, is HTTP services—that is, an application that listens for and processes incoming requests (i.e., a web server).

A server application is no different from any other application from Docker's perspective. There are a few differences in how you start and connect to the container, owing to the fact that you likely want to keep the container running (so it can serve requests). You'll also likely want to forward ports from your local machine so you can connect to it.

2.2.1 Containerizing an application server

Until now, the example program has been a basic "Hello World" Python script. To demonstrate how to containerize HTTP servers, we'll need something that is an HTTP server! Listing 2.14 is an example of a bare-bones HTTP server in Python that returns the current date and time. Don't worry too much about the code itself. This book is language agnostic, and the Python used here is purely an example. You can apply these principles to any HTTP server.

> **Listing 2.14   Chapter02/timeserver/server.py**

```
from http.server import ThreadingHTTPServer, BaseHTTPRequestHandler
from datetime import datetime

class RequestHandler(BaseHTTPRequestHandler):
    def do_GET(self):
        self.send_response(200)
        self.send_header('Content-type', 'text/plain')
        self.end_headers()
        now = datetime.now()
        response_string = now.strftime("The time is %-I:%M %p, UTC.")
        self.wfile.write(bytes(response_string, "utf-8"))

def startServer():
    try:
        server = ThreadingHTTPServer(('', 80), RequestHandler)
        print("Listening on " + ":".join(map(str, server.server_address)))
        server.serve_forever()
    except KeyboardInterrupt:
        server.shutdown()

if __name__ == "__main__":
    startServer()
```

Containerizing this server application is very similar to the earlier command-line program as follows.

Listing 2.15   Chapter02/timeserver/Dockerfile

```
FROM python:3.12
ENV PYTHONUNBUFFERED 1
COPY . /app
WORKDIR /app
CMD python3 server.py
```

Containerizing your own application

If you're containerizing your own application, follow these generic steps:

1 Find an ideal base image that provides as much of your configuration as possible. For a Ruby on Rails app, start with `ruby` and not the more generic `ubuntu`. For Django, use `python`, and so on.
2 Configure any application-specific dependencies you need (via `RUN` statements, as we did previously).
3 Copy your application.

I find that Google search is really your friend for this. Unless you're doing something new and exotic, someone's probably figured out and shared an example Dockerfile of how to configure an application using your framework. If you're using a popular framework like Django, Ruby on Rails, WordPress, Node.JS, or SpringBoot I can say with certainty that there are a lot of resources for you to draw on. Every application is different—your dependencies won't exactly match everyone else's all the time—but you can get a huge head start this way.

Now that we have our HTTP server application, we can build it like usual:

```
$ cd Chapter02/timeserver
$ docker build . -t timeserver
```

Running it is a little different this time since we'll need to forward ports from the host machine to the container, so we can actually try this application in the browser. Let's forward port 8080 on our local machine to port 80 in the container that the application is listening on:

```
$ docker run -it -p 8080:80 timeserver
Listening on 0.0.0.0:80
```

Now you should be able to browse to http://localhost:8080 and view the application. Or, with `curl`, do the following:

```
$ curl http://localhost:8080
The time is 1:30 PM, UTC.
```

The `-it` parameter (actually two parameters but normally used together) allows us to terminate by sending SIGTERM (often Ctrl/Command+C). This makes the typical developer loop of build–run–fix–repeat easy (run, Ctrl+C, fix, repeat). Alternatively, you can run Docker in the background with `docker run -d -p 8080:80 timeserver`. Without using `-it`, you'll need to stop the process manually: `docker ps` to list the process and `docker stop $CONTAINER_ID` to stop it, or `docker stop $(docker ps -q)` to stop all running containers.

For a neat development loop, I like to use the following one-liner that will build and run the image in one go. When you need to rebuild, you can just press Ctrl+C (or equivalent), the Up arrow to show the last-used command, and Enter to do it all again. Just be sure to watch the console output for any errors during the build stage, as otherwise it will run the last built image:

```
docker build . -t timeserver; docker run -it -p 8080:80 timeserver
```

That's it! We now have a containerized application running in Docker. In section 2.3, I cover how to use Docker Compose to configure and run a local debug setup (useful if your application consists of a few different containers) and, in the next chapter, how to deploy this web application into Kubernetes.

2.2.2 Debugging

If you're having trouble getting your app to run after configuring a Dockerfile, it can be useful to shell into the container's environment to poke around and see what's going wrong. While the container is running using the previous instructions, you can shell into the running container from a new console window, like so:

```
$ docker ps
CONTAINER ID    IMAGE        COMMAND               CREATED        STATUS
6989d3097d6b    timeserver   "/bin/sh -c 'python3…"  2 minutes ago  Up 2 min

$ CONTAINER_ID=6989d3097d6b
$ docker exec -it $CONTAINER_ID sh
# ls
Dockerfile   server.py
# exit
$
```

You can run any command other than `sh`, too; for example, on a Ruby on Rails project, you might run `bundle exec rails console` here to bring up the rails console directly without an intermediate step.

I won't list out every Docker command, as the docs do a great job at that, but another one I find especially useful for debugging is `docker cp`. It allows you to copy files between your host and the container. Here's an example:

```
docker cp server.py $CONTAINER_ID:/app
```

Or to copy a file out of the container, do the following:

```
docker cp $CONTAINER_ID:/app/server.py .
```

If you do fix anything by running commands via `exec`, or copying files, be sure to capture the change in the Dockerfile. The Dockerfile is your primary specification, not the container instance. If you rely on manual changes to the container instance, it's no better than the old "shell into a VM and change things" model that we're moving away from.

2.3   *Using Docker Compose for local testing*

At this point, we have built a container image and are ready to start using Kubernetes. If you like, skip ahead to the next chapter and deploy this newly built container into Kubernetes right away to a cloud or local Kubernetes environment. This section covers how you can use Docker Compose for local container testing and development before deploying to Kubernetes.

In the previous section, we booted our server application using Docker and forwarded ports to our host for testing. Using this approach for testing during development has a couple of drawbacks. You have to set up the ports to forward each time, and if you're developing an application with a few containers, it can be complex to get everything up and running with the right ports forwarded, and so forth.

This is where Docker Compose comes in. Compose is a mini container orchestrator that can bring up and tear down multiple containers in a logical group and preserve the runtime settings in between runs, which is useful for local testing. To run the web server container from section 2.2.1 with Compose, we can configure a docker-compose.yaml file, such as in the following listing.

> #### Listing 2.16   Chapter02/2.3_Compose/docker-compose.yaml

```
services:
  web:
    build: ../timeserver          ⟵┘  The path to the directory
    command: python3 server.py    ⟵─┐ containing the docker
    ports:                            container to be built
      - "8080:80"
```

The path to the directory containing the docker container to be built

Command that will be run on the container. It can be skipped if your Dockerfile specifies CMD.

Ports to forward to the container from the local machine. In this case, port 8080 on the local machine will be forwarded to the container's port 80.

To build and run the container, do the following:

```
cd Chapter02/2.3_Compose
docker compose build
docker compose up
```

When developing, I tend to run both these steps as one so I can create a tight rebuild loop:

```
docker compose build; docker compose up
```

With this simple configuration, there's no need to remember the specific Docker command to boot and test the application—everything is stored neatly in the compose file. With this example, that mostly consists of some ports to forward, but this benefit will become apparent as you add more configuration and dependencies.

2.3.1 Mapping folders locally

Earlier, we used `docker cp` to copy files into and out of container instances. One really useful feature of Compose is that you can actually map local folders right into the container. In other words, instead of the container having a copy of your application, it will actually just link to the application folder on your hard drive. During development, this can be really handy, as it allows you to work on the files in the container right from your desktop without needing to copy things back and forth or rebuild the container.

Recall from the Dockerfile in listing 2.15 that our server app is copied into the `/app` directory within the container. What we want to do now is mount our local directory into the container at that same directory using volume binding, as follows.

Listing 2.17   Chapter02/2.3.1_VolumeMount/docker-compose.yaml

```
services:
  frontend:
    build: .
    command: python3 server.py
    volumes:
      - type: bind          Binds the local container build
        source: .           directory into the container's /app
        target: /app        directory (matching the Dockerfile)
    environment:
      PYTHONDONTWRITEBYTECODE: 1      Sets a new environment variable
    ports:                            so that Python can be made to
      - "8080:80"                     reload our source
```

With this volume binding, the files from our local machine are used instead of the ones copied when we built our container. When we update those files locally, the changes can be immediately read in the container without a rebuild. For interpreted languages like Python, Ruby, and PHP, as well as markup languages like HTML and CSS, this means you can potentially have a setup where you just hit Save in your editor and reload the page in the browser for a really tight development loop.

> **NOTE** For compiled code, this may not be of much help. You could build the binary locally, replacing it in the container, but if you prefer to build everything through Docker (or there is an architectural difference between your local environment and the container), then this won't help. For compiled code, I recommend using other developer tools like Skaffold[1] to give you a tight development loop.

[1] https://skaffold.dev/

There's a trick to get this to work with the sample application, however. Our Python code, by default, isn't reloaded from the disk when there are changes. So, while we can modify the source code, it won't have any effect once the container is running. This will be true for many other build systems as well.

Let's update the Python timeserver app to support reloading the code while it's running and configure a local mount in Compose. The steps here will vary by language and framework. For Python, we can use the *reloading* library to have our GET function reloaded from disk each time there is a new request.

Listing 2.18   Chapter02/2.3.1_VolumeMount/server.py

```python
from reloading import reloading
from http.server import ThreadingHTTPServer, BaseHTTPRequestHandler
from datetime import datetime

class RequestHandler(BaseHTTPRequestHandler):
    @reloading
    def do_GET(self):
        self.send_response(200)
        self.send_header('Content-type', 'text/plain')
        self.end_headers()
        now = datetime.now()
        response_string = now.strftime("The time is %-I:%M %p, UTC.")
        self.wfile.write(bytes(response_string,"utf-8"))

def startServer():
    try:
        server = ThreadingHTTPServer(('',80), RequestHandler)
        print("Listening on " + ":".join(map(str, server.server_address)))
        server.serve_forever()
    except KeyboardInterrupt:
        server.shutdown()

if __name__ == "__main__":
    startServer()
```

By adding the @reloading tag to our method, it will be reloaded from disk every time it runs so we can change our do_GET function while it's running.

Since we're using a new library, we'll need to add that dependency in the Dockerfile as well.

Listing 2.19   Chapter02/2.3.1_VolumeMount/Dockerfile

```dockerfile
FROM python:3
RUN pip install reloading
ENV PYTHONUNBUFFERED 1
COPY . /app
WORKDIR /app
CMD python3 server.py
```

With our app configured to reload files from the disk, we can now run it with Compose as before:

```
$ cd Chapter02/2.3.1_VolumeMount
$ docker compose build; docker compose up
Creating network "231_volumemount_default" with the default driver
Creating 231_volumemount_frontend_1 ... done
Attaching to 231_volumemount_frontend_1
```

As before, browse to the app at http://localhost:8080/. This time, open up the 2.3.1_VolumeMount/server.py code (listing 2.18) and make a change to the response. For example, we can change the response to 24-hour time by replacing line 12 with:

```
response_string = now.strftime("The time is %H:%M, UTC.")
```

Save the file in your editor and reload the page. You should see the new text in the response:

```
$ curl http://localhost:8080
The time is 17:23, UTC.
```

In this example, we had to make some code changes to make it work, but if you're using a standard development framework, that will likely not be necessary, as you'll be able to configure it to perform reloads automatically.

Being able to map local folders into the container to create a development loop that is as fast as clicking Save in your code editor, then reloading a page on the browser has to be one of my favorite features of Docker Compose and containers in general. You have all the benefits of containers, where you don't need to mess around installing the developer tools locally, with the same efficiency as if you were running it locally without any build step.

The binding works both ways, too. If you make any changes in the container within the bound volume, it will be reflected on your local disk. This can be useful when you want to run commands in the container and save their output. In fact, with this approach, you can completely avoid having the developer tools installed on your local machine at all. For example, a Rails developer will, from time to time, run `gem update rails` in their project directory to keep the framework up to date. With a volume binding, you can run that in the container and get the changed package list on your hard drive ready to commit to version control.

2.3.2 Adding service dependencies

In the case where your app is completely standalone, congratulations, you are done. The rest of the time, though, you'll likely have other services that you need to bring up alongside your application. These might be other separate servers that you build or standard components that might be run by your cloud provider, like a database. In both cases, you can add these dependencies in Compose to create a local development environment.

Compose or Kubernetes for local development?

Why use or consider Compose rather than Kubernetes itself to bring up dependent services for development? Kubernetes certainly can be used for local development, and if you want to replicate your production environment, it's the best option (chapter 3 includes a section on local development). What makes Compose popular for this task, however, is its simplicity.

Compose is easy to set up for local use if you just need a handful of dependent services, which for many simple applications is the case. Production, where you're not just running a few single instance services on one machine, is a different (more complex) story, which is where Kubernetes excels.

This duality means it's not uncommon to see Compose for local dev and Kubernetes in production. It does mean that your runtime configuration is essentially duplicated, but this configuration has two separate purposes—development and production—so it likely won't look identical even if it was all in Kubernetes. I suggest simply using whichever approach makes life as a developer easier.

Multiple services can easily be added to the Compose. These can reference standard images (in the case of a dependency like MySQL) or other projects on your computer. A common project structure is to have one root folder for all services, with each checked out in a subfolder and a Docker Compose file that can reference them all.

Listing 2.20 provides an example of a Compose file with two containerized services: our app that's built locally and a database instance using the public MySQL container. The demo app here doesn't actually use MySQL, but, hopefully, you can see how easy it is to add the dependencies that your app needs. You can add all the services you need here, including multiple locally built containers and multiple external images.

> **Listing 2.20   Chapter02/2.3.2_MultipleServices/docker-compose.yaml**

```
services:
  frontend:
    build: ../timeserver
    command: python3 server.py          Our app that is
    environment:                        built locally; you
      PYTHONDONTWRITEBYTECODE: 1        can have multiple
    ports:                              locally built apps.
      - "8080:80"

  db:
    image: mysql:5.7
    volumes:
      - db_data:/var/lib/mysql
    restart: always                     A service running
    environment:                        a public image;
      MYSQL_ROOT_PASSWORD: super secret password   you can have
      MYSQL_DATABASE: my_database                   multiple such
      MYSQL_USER: dev_user                          services as well.
      MYSQL_PASSWORD: another secret password
```

```
volumes:
    db_data:
```
| Volume definition for the
development database so that
it will persist between restarts

This is one of the key reasons to use Compose, rather than just Docker, for local testing—the ability to bring up a complete testing environment and tear it down all with a single command.

> **TIP** When configuring your application for local development and for production, all configuration changes should be made by environment variables. Even a single environment variable that indicates `prod` or `dev` to select which configuration file to use can suffice. Configuration should not be baked into the container in such a way that you need to modify it between environments. This allows you to reuse the same container in all environments and also means that you are testing the production artifact.

2.3.3 *Faking external dependencies*

If, to date, you've been testing against remote dependencies (like a cloud storage API), now might be a good time to see whether you can replace those remote dependencies with fakes. Fakes are lightweight implementations of the same API of the external dependency, which speed up development and testing by providing a local service.

In the past, you might have been constrained to finding a fake written in the same language as your application (for practical reasons, like not wanting to support multiple different environments for one project). One of the benefits of containers is that just like how you probably don't care what language a cloud service you consume is written in, you no longer need to care about what language your fake is written in either, as you don't need to maintain the environment—it runs in its own container.

This also brings the opportunity for high-quality fakes that are really just lighterweight implementations of the same API you'll use in production. Just as in listing 2.20 where we used real MySQL in a container (rather than a fake), you can use a real object storage provider to test against, even if you ultimately use a cloud provider service like Google Cloud Storage or Amazon S3.

Taking the object storage example, say your application does cloud storage using S3-compatible APIs (e.g., with S3 itself or one of the many object stores that support the API, like Google Cloud Storage). To set up a local fake for fast iteration, you could get a container like Adobe's S3Mock[2], but with containers, it's equally easy to use a fully fledged S3-compatible local storage solution like MinIO[3]. MinIO is not really a fake—you can deploy it into production in cases where you want to manage your

---

[2] https://github.com/adobe/S3Mock
[3] https://min.io/

own block storage service—but you can still use it as a high-quality fake and get benefits like a convenient UI.

The ubiquity of the S3 API for object storage

Like SQL standardized database query languages, S3's API is surprisingly popular for
object storage providers. For example, Google Cloud, Azure, and (of course) AWS all
implement the S3 API, along with most other clouds and several bare metal storage
options as well. The benefit of this ubiquity is you can easily switch between providers
and have several fakes to choose from to develop locally.

Earlier, I discussed how containers make it easy to mix and match services, all running
in their own environments. Here, we see how this ability can make development better as well. Rather than implementing a fake yourself or finding a rudimentary fake
for your environment, you can either use the same service locally as in production
(such as with MySQL) or find a production-grade replacement for another cloud service that you use (like with MinIO subbing in for cloud object storage). Let's add
MinIO as another service to our Docker Compose file.

Listing 2.21   Chapter02/2.3.3_Fakes/docker-compose.yaml

```
services:

  storage:
    image: minio/minio
    command: minio server /data
    volumes:
      - storage_data:/data              The new
    restart: always                     storage
    environment:                        fake
      MINIO_ACCESS_KEY: fakeaccesskey
      MINIO_SECRET_KEY: fakesecretkey
    ports:
      - "9000:9000"

  frontend:
    build: ../timeserver
    command: python3 server.py
    environment:
      PYTHONDONTWRITEBYTECODE: 1
      S3_ENDPOINT:              http://storage:9000
      S3_USE_PATH_STYLE:        1                       The application
      S3_ACCESS_KEY_ID:         fakeaccesskey           configured to use
      S3_SECRET_ACCESS_KEY:     fakesecretkey           the new fake
    ports:
      - "8080:80"

volumes:
  db_data:
  storage_data:
```

Typically with services used as fakes, as we are using MinIO here, you can specify the access keys it will accept and then simply specify those same secrets to the application using environment variables.

Summary

- Containerization captures your app's build, environment, and configuration into a standardized format that can then be run with VM-like isolation but without the VM overhead.
- Containerization is key step toward adopting Kubernetes, as this is the executable environment that Kubernetes supports.
- Not just for production, containers help developers work on multiple projects at once, without the environments conflicting and without needing complex setup instructions.
- The process of building a container image uses a configuration file known as a Dockerfile, which contains a set of procedural instructions used to build your container.
- To build a Dockerfile, start with the base image that is the most complete for your needs, then configure with your application and its dependencies.
- Multistage builds are useful for complied applications.
- With a multistage container build, we first configure a temporary container with everything needed to *build* the program, and then we configure another container with everything needed to *run* the program. This keeps the concerns separated and neatly isolated to their own containers.
- Docker Compose is a lightweight container orchestrator that can give you a quick container-based development environment for multiple services.
- Mapping folders locally with Compose enables the editing of noncompiled applications in real time, creating a tight development loop.
- During testing, containers allow for high-quality fakes of external dependencies that are really just lighter-weight implementations of the same API you'll use in production, such as MySQL in a container or a real object storage provider.

Deploying to Kubernetes

This chapter covers

- Kubernetes concepts related to specifying and hosting application deployments
- Deploying a containerized application to Kubernetes on a cloud platform
- Updating deployments with new versions of the application container
- Running a version of Kubernetes locally for testing and development

In the previous chapter, we covered how to containerize your application. If you stopped there, you would have a portable, reproducible environment for your app, not to mention a convenient developer setup. However, you may have trouble scaling that app when you go to production.

For ultra-simple deployments where you don't mind running one container per virtual machine (VM), you might be able to deploy containers to VMs directly and then scale your VMs as needed. You'd get a few of the advantages of containers, such as convenient packaging. However, if, like most, you have a number of different services to deploy, you'll probably need something more flexible.

This is where a container orchestrator like Kubernetes comes in. Container orchestration is just a fancy way of saying tooling that handles the scheduling and monitoring of a bunch of different containers on a bunch of different machines. It allows you to work primarily in terms of your application deployment—the container and its deployment attributes, such as how many replicas (instances) of the container there should be; and requirements such as high availability (spreading across failure domains), service networking, and so on—rather than needing to be overly concerned with the configuration of the underlying compute.

Being able to conveniently manage multiple services on a shared pool of compute resources gives you efficiency when running multiple applications or adopting patterns like microservices, where the various parts of your application are deployed and managed separately. You can mix different types of deployments, too, from a stateless application to a stateful database, batch jobs, and more—all without needing to worry too much about exactly which machine each container ends up actually running on.

3.1 Kubernetes architecture

Kubernetes is an abstraction layer that sits at the workload level on top of the raw compute primitives like VMs (or bare metal machines) and load balancers. VMs are referred to as *nodes* and are arranged into a *cluster*. Containers (one or multiple) are grouped into a scheduling unit known as a *Pod*. Networking is configured via a *Service*. Other higher-order building blocks like *Deployment* exist to make Pods even easier to manage. Let's explore some of the basic building blocks of this architecture before deploying our first workload.

3.1.1 The Kubernetes cluster

The Kubernetes cluster is a collection of nodes, which are the compute instances on which the containers are run. Most commonly, these are virtual machines, but they can also be bare metal (nonvirtualized) machines. Each of these nodes runs a special Kubernetes process called the *kubelet*, which is responsible for communicating with the control plane (the Kubernetes orchestration process) and managing the lifecycle of the containers, which run on nodes via the container run time. Other than the operating system, the kubelet, and the container runtime environment, the remaining processes, including your own workloads and some system components responsible for logging and monitoring, are run in containers, as shown in figure 3.1.

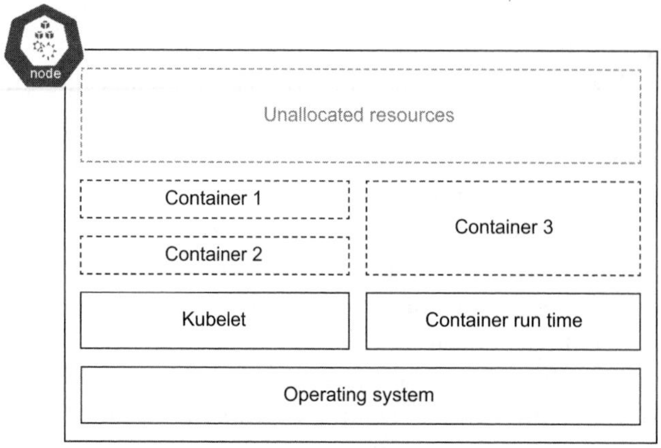

Unallocated resources

Container 1

Container 2

Container 3

Kubelet

Container run time

Operating system

Figure 3.1   Processes running on a VM, which Kubernetes calls a *node*

In the cluster, one or multiple (when operating in high availability mode) nodes have a special role, as shown in figure 3.2: running the Kubernetes orchestrator program itself. The special nodes that form the control plane are responsible for

- Running the API, which you use to interact with the cluster using tools such as the Kubernetes command-line interface (CLI) tool
- Storing the state of the cluster
- Coordinating with all the nodes in the cluster to schedule (start, stop, restart) containers on them

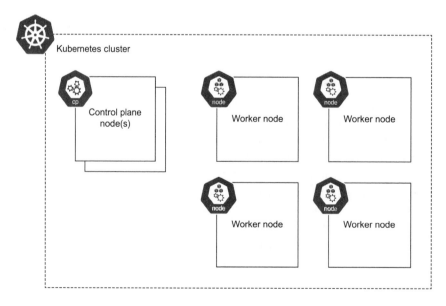

Kubernetes cluster

Control plane node(s)

Worker node

Worker node

Worker node

Worker node

Figure 3.2   Self-managed Kubernetes cluster with the control plane and worker nodes

In most cloud environments, the control plane is offered as a managed service. In such environments, the control plane nodes are typically not visible to the user, and the fact that the control plane may run on a node is an implementation detail. In these environments, you'll typically think of the cluster as the managed control plane with worker nodes, as shown in figure 3.3.

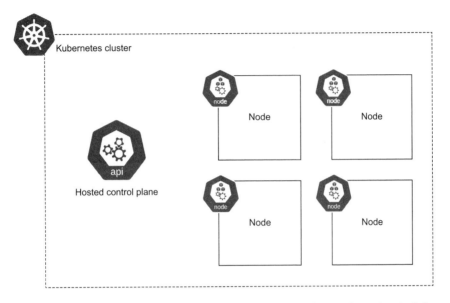

Figure 3.3   Cloud-based Kubernetes cluster with nodes connecting to a hosted control plane

Worker nodes (herein referred to simply as *nodes*) are responsible for managing the lifecycle of containers that run, including tasks such as starting and stopping containers. The control plane will instruct the node to run a certain container, but the actual execution of the container is then the responsibility of the node. The nodes also take some actions by themselves without needing to check in with the control plane, like restarting a container that has crashed or reclaiming memory when the node is running low.

Collectively, the control plane and nodes form the *Kubernetes cluster* and provide the Kubernetes platform on which you can schedule your workloads. The cluster itself is provisioned and managed by whatever platform provider you use to run Kubernetes, which is responsible for creating the cluster resources like nodes. This book, aimed at developers, focuses primarily on *using* the Kubernetes cluster to run your workloads rather than the platform provider tasks (which are more in the cloud provider domain) of offering this service to developers.

3.1.2   Kubernetes objects

Once the cluster is created, you interact with Kubernetes primarily by creating, inspecting, and modifying Kubernetes objects through the Kubernetes API. Each of these objects represents a particular deployment construct in the system. For example, there is an object that represents a group of containers (Pod), one that represents a group of Pods (Deployment), one for network Services, and so on. Even the node is represented as an object which you can query to view the aspects of the current status, like how much resources are being used. To deploy a typical stateless web application into the cluster, you'll use three objects: the Pod, a Deployment (which encapsulates the Pod), and a Service.

POD

The Pod is simply a collection of containers. Often, a Pod will be just a single container, but it could be multiple containers in the case where tightly coupled containers need to be deployed together (figure 3.4).

The Pod is used as the primary scheduling unit in Kubernetes. Encompassing your application and its containers, it's the unit of compute that Kubernetes schedules onto nodes according to the resources you require. For example, if your workload requires two CPU cores to run, you specify that in the Pod definition, and Kubernetes will find a machine with two available CPU resources.

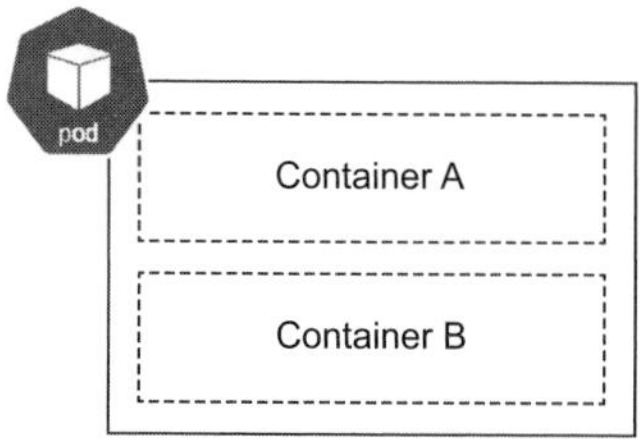

Figure 3.4   The Kubernetes Pod, which can have one or many containers

---

How many containers to a Pod?

Except for simple cases where a tightly coupled dependency exists between multiple containers, most containers are deployed individually with one container per Pod. Common situations where you might have multiple containers include so-called sidecars, where a second container is used for authorization, logging, or some other function, and other situations where multiple containers are tightly coupled, such that they benefit from being deployed together.

If you were to inspect the processes running on the node, you would not see the Pod itself, just a bunch of processes from the containers (figure 3.5). The Pod is just a logical grouping of containers. It's Kubernetes that binds these containers together, ensuring that they share a common lifecycle: they are created together; if one fails, they are restarted together; and they are terminated together.

DEPLOYMENT

While you can instruct Kubernetes to run Pods directly, you will rarely do so. Applications crash and machines fail, so Pods need to be restarted or rescheduled. Instead of

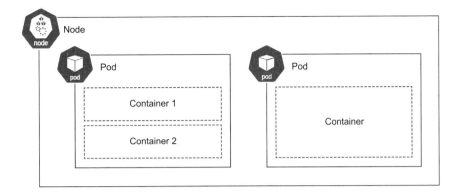

Figure 3.5 Multiple Pods running on a node

directly scheduling Pods, it's better to wrap them into a higher-order object that manages the Pod lifecycle.

For applications like web servers that need to run continuously, that object is a *Deployment.* Other options include a *Job* for running batch processes to completion, covered in chapter 10. In the Deployment, you specify how many replicas of the Pod you wish to be running and other information, like how updates should be rolled out.

Like all objects in Kubernetes, a Deployment (figure 3.6) is a specification for the desired state of the system, which Kubernetes seeks to actuate. You can specify things like the number of replicas of your Pod and, as we'll cover in later chapters, detailed requirements for how the Pods are spread across the cluster. Kubernetes continuously reconciles the observed state to the desired state while attempting to deliver what you requested. For example, if a Pod was to become unavailable sometime after it was deployed, like what would happen if the node it was running on failed, Kubernetes will observe that there are fewer Pods running than desired and schedule new instances of the Pod to once again meet your requirements. These automated operations for scaling and repairing are the primary reason for using a Deployment to manage the lifecycle of a service, rather than running Pods directly.

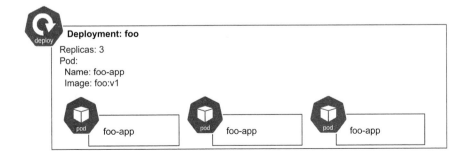

Figure 3.6 A Deployment with three replicas of Pod `foo-app`

SERVICE

Services are how you expose an application running on a set of Pods as a network service. A Service provides a single addressing mechanism and spreads the load across the Pods (figure 3.7). Services get their own internal IP address and DNS record, which can be referenced by other Pods running within the cluster, and can also be assigned an external IP address.

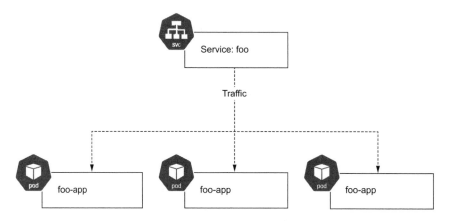

Figure 3.7   A Kubernetes Service

3.2   *Deploying an application*

Let's get started by deploying an application and making it available on the internet. Later, we'll update it with a new version. In other words, we will perform a basic application development–release–update cycle with Kubernetes. To do this, we'll use the Kubernetes objects discussed in the prior section: a *Pod*, which will be managed by a *Deployment*, and exposed with a *Service*.

3.2.1   *Creating a cluster*

Before deploying the application, you'll need a Kubernetes cluster to use. I recommend creating one on a public cloud, as it's less hassle to get set up, and people can check out your creations immediately as you can share a public IP for any services you deploy. Many cloud providers have free trials to help reduce costs while learning.

Developing with a local Kubernetes cluster is another option, but there are some inherent differences between the environment of a local Kubernetes cluster and a cloud-based cluster, particularly around things like load balancing. I prefer to learn the environment that I can use in production on day one, hence my suggestion to pick a cloud provider and start with that.

> ### Prefer a local cluster?
>
> If you'd prefer to use a local distribution of Kubernetes, I've got you covered. Follow the steps in section 3.4 to get your `kubectl` command connected to a local cluster instead and then come back to section 3.2.3 on deploying to Kubernetes and continue.
>
> Just note that when you go to deploy your own locally built container image, there are some considerations that are outlined in section 3.4 to ensure Kubernetes can find your image, and the way you access any Services you create will be different (also outlined in that section) due to the lack of public load balancers.

At the end of the day, all you need to run just about every sample in this book is a Kubernetes cluster hosted somewhere and the Kubernetes command-line tool `kubectl` (pronounced: "cube cuttle") authenticated to use that cluster, which any getting-started guide should get you. The next two steps use Google Cloud, but I'll also include some instructions along the way on how to substitute the platform of your choice.

GOOGLE KUBERNETES ENGINE

Google Kubernetes Engine (GKE) was the first Kubernetes product to market and is a popular choice for trying out Kubernetes due to its maturity and ease of use. I work on the GKE team, and I know this platform best, so it's the one I'll be using for the few places in this book with platform-specific requirements.

I've written this book to be applicable anywhere you find Kubernetes, and I expect that it will be useful for learning Kubernetes whether you're using GKE, OpenShift, Azure Kubernetes Service (AKS), Elastic Kubernetes Service (EKS), or any one of the other Kubernetes platforms and distributions out there. There are a few places where the platform plays a role (like now, when creating a cluster), and in those instances, I'll demonstrate the action with instructions for GKE, but I'll also be providing pointers on how to find the equivalents on other platforms.

> ### Creating a Kubernetes cluster on any cloud
>
> All you need to run the examples in this chapter after this setup section is the `kubectl` tool authenticated to the Kubernetes cluster of your choice. Creating and authenticating `kubectl` is the goal, and as you will see for GKE, this can be done with two commands. You can substitute those commands for the equivalent cluster creation and authentication for the platform of your choice.
>
> To run the following examples on any provider, follow the cluster creation guide for the provider of your choice and then continue to section 3.2.2. Uploading containers is also another provider-specific action, but I've got you covered with some general tips there on how to get that done on any platform.

To start with GKE, you'll need a Google Account (if you have an @gmail.com email address, then you have a Google Account). Head over to https://console.cloud.google .com/, select your account, and review the terms. Activate your free trial if you have not done so already or add billing info so you can run these samples (again, if you wish to run the samples locally, you can instead follow the steps in section 3.4 to get a local-only cluster).

With your account set up, head over to GKE in the console (direct link: https:// console.cloud.google.com/kubernetes) and create a cluster. I recommend Autopilot mode, which takes care of the provisioning and management of nodes for you. With Autopilot, you can set a name, pick a region (as I've done in figure 3.8), and leave the networking and advanced settings as the default.

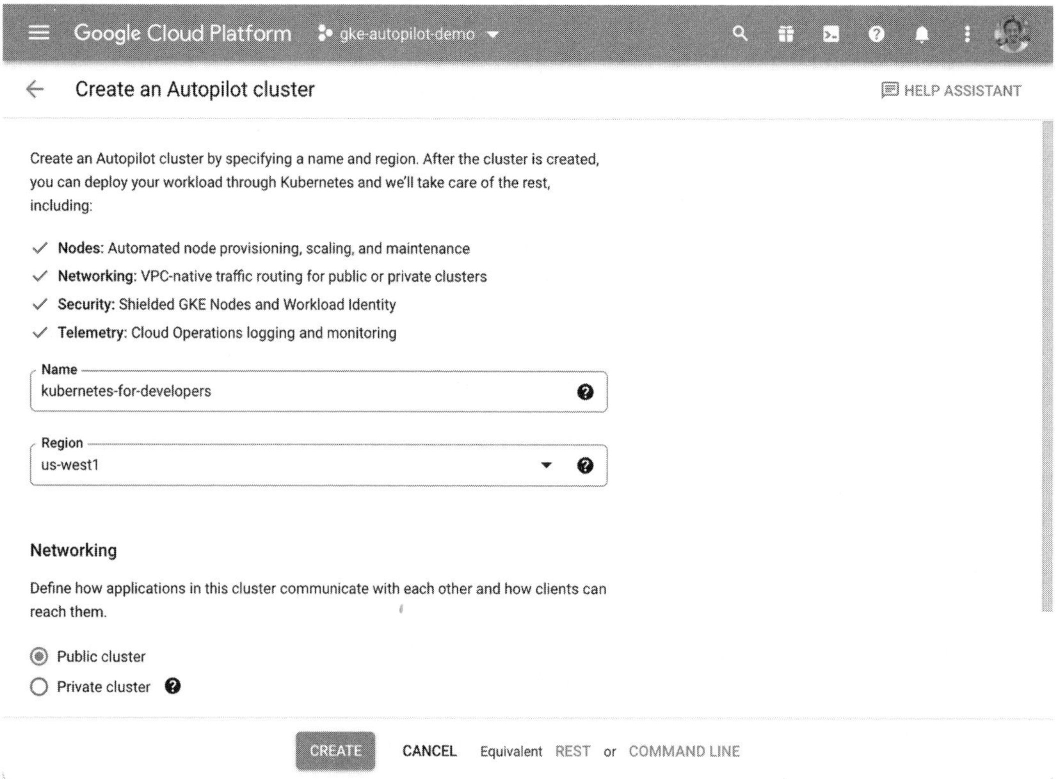

Figure 3.8   GKE Autopilot's cluster creation UI

Next, set up the command-line tools. You'll need the cloud provider CLI (in this case, `gcloud` for Google Cloud) to perform cluster operations like creating and authenticating, and `kubectl` for interacting with the Kubernetes API. Download the `gcloud` CLI at https://cloud.google.com/sdk/install and follow the installation instructions.

Once installed, run the `gcloud init` command to log in. If you have more than one Google Account, be sure to select the same account that you created the cluster in earlier:

```
gcloud init
```

The Kubernetes CLI, `kubectl`, can be installed standalone (following the instructions at https://kubernetes.io/docs/tasks/tools/) or via `gcloud`. It doesn't matter how you install it, but since this example uses `gcloud`, we can conveniently use it to install `kubectl`, like so:

```
gcloud components install kubectl
```

Once the cluster is ready and `gcloud` is configured, click Connect in the UI and copy the gcloud command provided (as seen in figure 3.9) into your shell to authenticate `kubectl`. Or, run the following command with your own cluster details:

```
CLUSTER_NAME=my-cluster
REGION=us-west1
gcloud container clusters get-credentials $CLUSTER_NAME --region $REGION
```

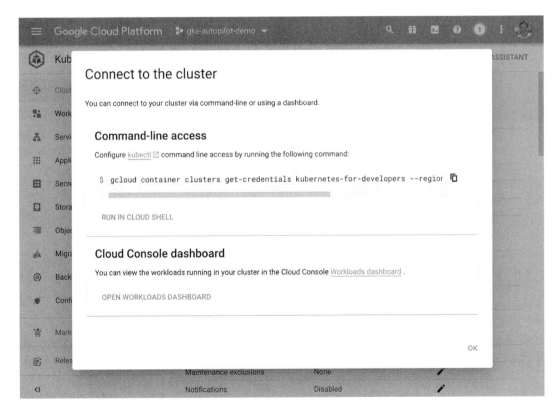

Figure 3.9   GKE's cluster connection UI

That command is the glue between the Google Cloud world and the Kubernetes one and authenticates the `kubectl` CLI with the right credentials to access your GKE cluster.

> **Creating clusters in the CLI**
> Rather than using the UI, you can do both the creation and connection steps from the command line, like so:
>
> ```
> CLUSTER_NAME=my-cluster
> REGION=us-west1
> gcloud container clusters create-auto $CLUSTER_NAME --region $REGION
> gcloud container clusters get-credentials $CLUSTER_NAME --region $REGION
> ```

With your cluster created and `kubectl` authenticated, you're ready to get going with your first application! To make sure everything is working, run `kubectl get pods`. It should state that there are no resources (since we've yet to deploy any Pods):

```
$ kubectl get pods
No resources found in default namespace.
```

If you get an error, it is likely that your cluster wasn't created or authenticated correctly. Try repeating the previous steps or lookup the error message.

3.2.2   *Uploading your container*

Until now, the containers we've created have been stored and run locally on your machine. Before you can deploy the container into Kubernetes running in the cloud, you'll need to upload your container image to a container registry. This is simply a place that stores the container image data and provides a way for Kubernetes to fetch the image. Most registries support options for public images, which anyone can use (like for open source projects and samples for a book), or private images, which require authentication (which you will use for your own proprietary applications).

If you prefer, you can skip this step and use the publicly available images referenced in the following examples. However, I'd recommend that you build and upload your own container to use, so you can deploy your own applications when the time comes.

Docker Hub is a popular choice as a container registry, particularly when it comes to public container images. This includes the base images (like the ones we used in the previous chapter), open source software like MariaDB, or perhaps your own software and demos you wish to share with the world. You can also access private container images from Docker Hub (and other registries) from any Kubernetes platform, with a bit of extra configuration to set up the credentials.

The default choice for most users who wish to keep their images *private* is to use the container registry of your cloud provider, as this generally gives you efficiencies in terms of image pull time, reduced network data costs, and simpler authentication. For

Google Cloud, that's Artifact Registry; on Amazon Web Services (AWS), it's Amazon Elastic Container Registry; on Azure, it's Azure Container Registry; and so on.

Once you have chosen your preferred location, follow these steps to get your containers uploaded.

ACCOUNT SETUP

To get started, first create an account at your preferred provider if you don't have one already and then create a repository where you'll be uploading the images. For Docker Hub, head over to https://hub.docker.com/, sign in, and then navigate to Create Repository.

For Artifact Registry, go to https://console.cloud.google.com/artifacts and create a new repository of type Docker in your desired location. Make a note of the path that is generated, which will look something like `us-docker.pkg.dev/my-project/my-repository`.

AUTHENTICATE

Next, you want to authenticate the `docker` command-line tool so it can upload images to your freshly created repository. Follow the instructions for your container registry to authenticate the docker command-line tool.

To do this in Docker Hub, you would run

```
docker login
```

For Artifact Registry, recall the path of the repository you created earlier. Take the host portion of that path (e.g., `us-docker.pkg.dev`) and run the following command to install a credential helper to the Docker tool so you can upload images there. You can run this multiple times, once for each separate host you use:

```
HOST_NAME=us-docker.pkg.dev
gcloud auth configure-docker $HOST_NAME
```

> **TIP** Authenticating Docker with the cloud provider of your choice is typically an easy operation. Just look for the cloud-specific command to configure the Docker CLI with the right credentials. The search query "authenticate docker with [your cloud provider] container registry" should do the trick!

TAG

When you build images, they are assigned a random hash-based name, like `82ca16cefe84`. Generally, it is a good idea to add your own tag that is somewhat meaningful so you can easily refer to your own images. In the previous chapter, we used these tags so we could run our images locally using nice names like `docker run timeserver` instead of `docker run 82ca16cefe84`.

When you upload containers into container registries, the tag takes on an additional meaning. You are required to tag the image with a name that follows a specific path convention dictated by the container registry for it to know which account and path to store the image in (and so that your local docker client knows which registry to upload it to). Tagging your image with a simple name like `timeserver` won't work when you're uploading to these repositories.

Docker Hub uses the convention

```
docker.io/$USERNAME/$REPOSITORY_NAME:$VERSION_TAG
```

where `$USERNAME` is your docker username, `$REPOSITORY_NAME` is the name of the repository you created in Docker Hub, and `$VERSION_TAG` is an arbitrary string (typically including a number). Putting it together, in my own case, where my username is "wdenniss", and my repository is "timeserver", the string I get is `docker.io/wdenniss/timeserver:1`.

The version tag

The version tag is an unstructured string used to refer to the version of the image. The convention is to use the version number (potentially constructed as major.minor .patch) and optionally with a suffix: for example, `2.2.1`, `2.1.5`, `2.1.5-beta`. A special version tag `latest` can be used to refer to the most recent image when running containers, but don't use `latest` when tagging the images for upload, as it's applied automatically by the container repository.

Each repository has its own format. For Google Cloud's Artifact Registry, the format consists of the following construction:

```
$LOCATION-docker.pkg.dev/$PROJECT_ID/$REPOSITORY_NAME/
➥ $IMAGE_NAME:$VERSION_TAG
```

After you create the Artifact Registry repository in the UI console, you should see the first portion of this string displayed (e.g., `us-docker.pkg.dev/wdenniss/ts`), which you can copy (or you can build the string using the previous formula). To this prefix, append any image name and tag that you like, such as `timeserver:1`. Put it together, and you'll get something, which, for me, looks like the following:

```
us-docker.pkg.dev/wdenniss/ts/timeserver:1
```

Container registry tag conventions

Every private container registry has its own magic string concatenation that you need to create the right tag, and they're all different. For example, Azure[a] documents `$REGISTRY_NAME.azurecr.io/$REPOSITORY_NAME:$VERSION_TAG` and AWS[b] documents `$AWS_ACCOUNT_ID.dkr.ecr.$REGION.amazonaws.com/$REPOSITORY_NAME:$VERSION_TAG`. One thing I'm sure about: make sure you follow the guidelines of whatever container registry you're using; otherwise, Kubernetes won't know where to push the image. The search term I use is "[cloud provider] registry container tag name."

---

[a] http://mng.bz/o1YD
[b] http://mng.bz/nWOd

Once you've worked out the right image tag to use (which we'll refer to as `$IMAGE_TAG` in the remaining examples), you can tag any existing Docker image for uploading. To upload one of the images we built in the earlier chapter to a container registry, you can reference the image from its previous tag and add a container registry tag (images can have multiple tags). If you built the example in section 2.2.1 using `docker build .` `-t timeserver`, this image will have the tag `timeserver`, which means we can retag it for the container registry, like so:

```
IMAGE_TAG=us-docker.pkg.dev/wdenniss/ts/timeserver:1
docker tag timeserver $IMAGE_TAG
```

> **NOTE** If you get the error "No such image," then keep reading as we are about to build it from scratch again anyway.

You can view the resulting list of images, like so:

```
$ docker images
REPOSITORY                                      TAG     IMAGE ID      CREATED
timeserver                                      latest  c07e34564aa0  2 minutes ago
us-docker.pkg.dev/wdenniss/ts/timeserver        1       c07e34564aa0  2 minutes ago
python                                          3.10    cf0643aafe49  1 days ago
```

You can also look up existing images and tag them based on image ID (`docker tag $IMAGE_ID $IMAGE_TAG`), but I suggest tagging when you build to avoid confusion. In fact, I generally find it quicker to simply rebuild the image than try to find the right image ID after the fact.

To build and tag the sample container, replace `$IMAGE_TAG` with your own repository image name, and from the root sample directory run

```
IMAGE_TAG=us-docker.pkg.dev/wdenniss/ts/timeserver:1
cd Chapter02/timeserver
docker build . -t $IMAGE_TAG
```

PUSH

Once our repository is set up, Docker is authenticated, and your image is tagged, you can push the image to the repository with

```
docker push $IMAGE_TAG
```

The previous authentication step installed a helper into the Docker configuration that enables Docker to speak with your cloud's container registry, whatever that may be. If you get a Permission Denied error, either you didn't authenticate Docker correctly, or your image tag string construction is wrong. Verify that you authenticated Docker to the appropriate repository and set the correct image tag. Refer to the up-to-date documentation for your chosen container registry for guidance.

If it goes well, you should see output like the following. Pay particular attention to the last line, which is where any authentication errors will be displayed:

```
$ docker push $IMAGE_TAG
The push refers to repository [us-docker.pkg.dev/wdenniss/ts/timeserver]
9ab1337ca015: Pushed
3eaafa0b4285: Layer already exists
a6a5635d5171: Layer already exists
8c25977a7f15: Layer already exists
1cad4dc57058: Layer already exists
4ff8844d474a: Layer already exists
b77487480ddb: Layer already exists
cd247c0fb37b: Layer already exists
cfdd5c3bd77e: Layer already exists
870a241bfebd: Layer already exists
1: digest: sha256:edb99776ae47b...97f7a9f1864afe7 size: 2425
```

Once the image has been uploaded, you're now ready to deploy your code into Kubernetes!

3.2.3   *Deploying to Kubernetes*

With a cluster created and `kubectl` authenticated, we can deploy our first application. To do this, we'll create an aptly named Deployment object. Kubernetes uses declarative configuration, where you declare the state you want (like "I want 3 copies of my container running in the cluster") in a configuration file. Then, submit that config to the cluster, and Kubernetes will strive to meet the requirements you specified.

For the configuration file, most developers use YAML as it's easier to edit manually. JSON is another option (primarily used with automated access), and some config can be created imperatively (discussed in section 3.3). Listing 3.1 is a minimal Deployment specification for the timeserver application from chapter 2. It references a public container image built from the included sample app, which I have uploaded to Docker Hub. If you have your own image, such as one pushed to a container repository in the previous section, edit this file and replace my image with yours.

Listing 3.1   Chapter03/3.2_DeployingToKubernetes/deploy.yaml

```
apiVersion: apps/v1
kind: Deployment
metadata:
  name: timeserver
spec:
  replicas: 3          ◁── How many Pod
  selector:                 replicas (instances)
    matchLabels:            to deploy
      pod: timeserver-pod
  template:
    metadata:
      labels:
        pod: timeserver-pod
    spec:
      containers:
      - name: timeserver-container
        image: docker.io/wdenniss/timeserver:1   ◁── Which container
                                                      image to deploy
                                                      and run
```

This manifest will create three replicas of our container. Later, we'll see how to configure a load balancer to split incoming requests over these three running instances. In this example of a minimalist Deployment config, the three most important lines are the name, which is needed to inspect, modify, and delete the Deployment; the replica count; and the container name. The rest is basically glue to make it all work (don't worry, I'll explain how the glue works as well).

The container image path is like a URL that references where to find the container. If you uploaded your container following the previous section, you already have this image path from that step. My container image with the docker.io prefix is available on Docker Hub, a popular place to host public images, including base images. One thing to note is that if you ever see an image path without a domain, like `ubuntu`, or `wdenniss/timeserver`, it's simply shorthand for an image hosted on Docker Hub.

So, that's the Deployment. Let's create it in the cluster. From the root sample directory, run

```
cd Chapter03/3.2_DeployingToKubernetes/
kubectl create -f deploy.yaml
```

This instructs Kubernetes to create the object defined by the configuration file. If you need to make changes once it's deployed (like changing the image version), you can make your changes locally and update the Deployment in the cluster with

```
kubectl apply -f deploy.yaml
```

To observe the state of the Deployment, run

```
$ kubectl get deploy
NAME        READY   UP-TO-DATE   AVAILABLE   AGE
timeserver  3/3     3            3           36s
```

As mentioned earlier, the Deployment is a declarative statement of your desired requirements, for example, "3 replicas of this Pod." When you create the Deployment and the system returns a success response, it simply means that Kubernetes accepted your Deployment for scheduling—not that it had completed scheduling in the manner you desired. Querying the Deployment with `kubectl get` will show you the current status, such as how many of the Pods are ready to serve traffic (the number in the READY column) and later, when you update the Deployment, how many of the pods are running the latest version during a roll out of a new version (the number in the UP-TO-DATE column). To see more detail about the Pods that form your Deployment, you can also query the Pods themselves:

```
$ kubectl get pods
NAME                          READY   STATUS    RESTARTS   AGE
timeserver-6df7df9cbb-7g4tx   1/1     Running   0          68s
timeserver-6df7df9cbb-kjg4d   1/1     Running   0          68s
timeserver-6df7df9cbb-lfq6w   1/1     Running   0          68s
```

NOTE If Pods show pending here, it may mean that your cluster doesn't have enough resources. In the case of a dynamically provisioned environment, simply waiting a minute or so is generally enough to see them scheduled. If they stay pending, review the advice that follows in the section "Troubleshooting: Stuck in Pending."

The kubectl get pods command returns the state of *all* pods in the active namespace, so once you have a lot of Deployments, this might get a bit jumbled. Instead, you can use a more verbose form where you pass the Pod's label (discussed in section 3.2.4) as a selector. Here's a complete example using the label of our example Deployment:

```
$ kubectl get pods --selector=pod=timeserver-pod
NAME                            READY   STATUS    RESTARTS   AGE
timeserver-6df7df9cbb-7g4tx     1/1     Running   0          2m13s
timeserver-6df7df9cbb-kjg4d     1/1     Running   0          2m13s
timeserver-6df7df9cbb-1fq6w     1/1     Running   0          2m13s
```

Once the Pod is running, we can interact with it! To connect to our fresh Deployment and visit the server that we deployed before creating a public IP, we can simply forward a port from our local machine to the containers, like so:

```
$ kubectl port-forward deploy/timeserver 8080:80
Forwarding from 127.0.0.1:8080 -> 80
Forwarding from [::1]:8080 -> 80
```

This allows you to interact with the Deployment from localhost by browsing to http:// localhost:8080. As you try out the containerized application, you can watch the log output in a new command-line shell, like so:

```
$ kubectl logs -f deploy/timeserver
Found 3 pods, using pod/timeserver-8bbb895dc-kgl81
Listening on 0.0.0.0:80
127.0.0.1 - - [09:59:08] "GET / HTTP/1.1" 200 -
```

The logs command, using the -f (follow) parameter, will stream the logs from one of the Pods in the Deployment. It's a good idea to log a statement to stdout in your own apps on startup, as was done here with "Listening on 0.0.0.0:80", so that you can be assured the container really did start as expected.

Most actions you take in Kubernetes are not instant. Creating a Pod takes time to provision new compute capacity (depending on what Kubernetes platform you are using), download the container from the container registry, and boot your container. If everything goes well, you should have running containers in a couple of minutes.

When things have succeeded, the Pods from your Deployment will report a status (when queried with kubectl get pods) of Running. You may see other statuses like Pending while it is waiting for capacity and ContainerCreating once the container has been scheduled to your nodes and is booting. Confusing matters is that sometimes a Pod can get stuck in `Pending`—it's a bit of an ambiguous state—and there can be other errors. What follows is a list of common error situations.

TROUBLESHOOTING: IMAGE PULL ERROR (ERRIMAGEPULL/ERRIMAGEPULLBACKOFF)

This error indicates that Kubernetes was unable to download the container image. This typically means that the image name was misspelled in your configuration, the image doesn't exist in the image repository, or your cluster doesn't have the required credentials to access the repository.

Check the spelling of your image and verify that the image is in your repository. For a quick fix just to get the Deployment running, try a public container image like the one I've provided. Any fixes you make to your Deployment configuration can be applied using `kubectl apply -f deploy.yaml`.

TROUBLESHOOTING: STUCK IN PENDING

If you see a Pod stuck in the `Pending` state for more than a minute or so, it typically means that the Kubernetes scheduler is unable to find space on your cluster to deploy the Pod to. Often, this problem can be resolved by adding additional resources to your cluster, like an additional or larger compute node.

You can see the details of the pending Pod by "describing" it as follows:

```
$ kubectl get pods
NAME                              READY   STATUS     RESTARTS   AGE
timeserver-6df7df9cbb-7g4tx       1/1     Pending    0          1m16s

$ POD_NAME=timeserver-6df7df9cbb-7g4tx
$ kubectl describe pod $POD_NAME
```

The `Events` section contains a list of any errors that Kubernetes has encountered. If you attempted to schedule a Deployment and no resources were available, you'll see a warning like `FailedScheduling`. Here's the event text I see for a Pod that I attempted to schedule but where there were not enough resources:

```
Warning  FailedScheduling  26s (x2 over 26s)   default-scheduler
⟶ 0/2 nodes are available: 2 Insufficient cpu.
```

As long as at least one of your Pods is in the `Running` state, you don't need to worry for now, as your Service should still run as long as one Pod exists to answer requests. However, if they are all pending, you'll need to take action—likely by adding more compute resources.

TROUBLESHOOTING: CRASHING CONTAINER (CRASHLOOPBACKOFF)

Another common error is a crashing container. There can be various reasons for a crashing container, including that the container failed to start (e.g., due to a configuration error) or that the container crashes soon after starting.

For the purposes of Kubernetes deployments, a *crash* is any container process that terminates—even one that terminates with a successful exit code. Deployments are designed for long-running processes, not once-off tasks (Kubernetes does have a way to represent a Pod that should be scheduled to run as a once-off task, and that is the Job object, covered in chapter 10).

The occasional crash of a container in a Deployment-managed Pod like the ones we are deploying here is handled gracefully by restarting it. In fact, when you run `kubectl get pods`, you can see how many times a container has been restarted. You can have a container that crashes every hour, and as far as Kubernetes is concerned, that's totally fine; it will keep restarting it, and it will go on its merry way.

A container that crashes either instantly at boot or quickly after, however, is put into an exponential backoff loop, where rather than continuing to restart it continuously (consuming the resources of the system), Kubernetes introduces a delay between restart attempts that increases exponentially (i.e., 10 seconds, then 20 seconds, 40 seconds, and so on).

When a container crashes the first time, it will have a status like `RunContainer-Error` (for a container that errored at start), or `Completed` for one that exited. Once the crash has been repeated a couple of times, the status will move to `CrashLoopBack-Off`. The chances are, any container in the `CrashLoopBackOff` state has a problem that needs your attention. One possibility is that the container may exit when an external dependency (like a database) is not being met, in which case you should ensure that the external service is running and can be connected to.

To debug crashed containers, I always start with `kubectl describe pod $POD_NAME` like the earlier problems to view the events for clues there. The container's logs are another good place to check. You can retrieve these with `kubectl logs $POD_NAME`. When dealing with crashing containers, you may wish to view the logs from the *prior* instantiation of the container (before it was restarted after crashing) to see any error printed when it crashed, as this often will indicate the cause. To do that, add `--previous` (or just `-p`) to your log request:

```
kubectl logs -p $POD_NAME
```

3.2.4 *The PodSpec*

It's worth taking a moment to understand how the Deployment object is composed since it actually encapsulates a Pod object, which has its own specification. You will see this pattern repeated with other higher-order workload types in Kubernetes like Job. It's also relevant because the way that we expose the Deployment in a Service is actually by referencing the Pods, not the Deployment.

When you create a Deployment of three replicas, in actuality, you are instructing the Kubernetes Deployment controller to create and manage three Pods. The Deployment controller manages the lifecycle of these pods, including replacing them with newer versions when you update the Deployment with a new container and rescheduling Pods that get evicted due to planned or unplanned maintenance events. Figure 3.10 has a visual breakdown of this object composition.

The Pod object template is referred to in the Kubernetes API documentation as the PodSpec. You can actually yank it out and run it by itself. To do so, you'll need to

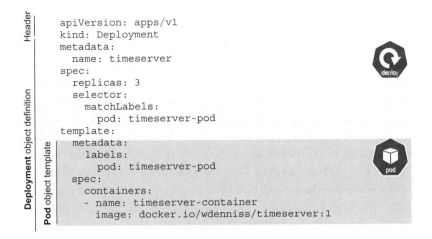

Figure 3.10   Pod object embedded in the Deployment object

provide a header specifying that this object is of kind Pod rather than a Deployment; then, you can copy the entire YAML under `template` into the root of the config, as shown in the following listing.

Listing 3.2   Chapter03/3.2.4_ThePodSpec/pod.yaml

```
apiVersion: v1
kind: Pod
metadata:
  name: timeserver
  labels:
    pod: timeserver-pod
spec:
  containers:
  - name: timeserver-container
    image: docker.io/wdenniss/timeserver:1
```

You can go ahead and create this Pod directly. Such pods are unmanaged by any Kubernetes controller. They will be rebooted if they crash, but if they are evicted due to causes such as an upgrade event or node failure, they won't be rescheduled. That's why typically you won't schedule the Pod directly but rather use a higher-order object like a Deployment or, as we'll see in the later chapters, StatefulSet, Job, and others.

> **NOTE** One of the key takeaways of this object composition in Kubernetes is that every time you see a PodSpec in an object like a Deployment, know that it carries all the capabilities of a Pod. That means you can look at the documentation for Pod and use any of the values within the Pod template of the managed object.

The PodSpec includes key information about your application, including the container or containers that comprise it. Each of these containers has its own name (so you can reference the individual containers in a multicontainer Pod), as well as the most important field: the container image path. There are a lot of optional fields as well, including some important ones to specify health checks and resource requirements, which are covered in the coming chapters.

There are also some seemingly repetitive labels in the Deployment and its embedded PodSpec. The Deployment's spec has a `selector` → `matchLabels` section, and the PodSpec has a `metadata` → `labels` section, both containing the same key–value pair `pod: timeserver-pod`. So, what's going on here?

Well, since the Pod object actually exists somewhat separately after creation (it is created as a separate object that is managed by the Deployment controller), we need a way to reference it. Kubernetes solves this by requiring that the Pod has a label (which is an arbitrary key–value pair), and that we reference (select) that same label from the Deployment. This is essentially the glue that binds the two objects together. It's easier to visualize in a diagram, as shown in figure 3.11.

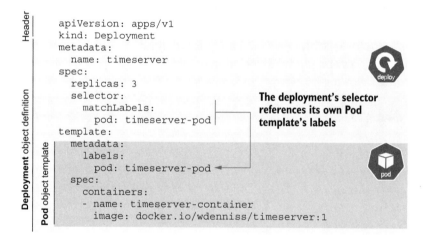

Figure 3.11   Relationship of the Deployment's selector and the Pod template's labels

This process may seem unnecessary, after all: can't Kubernetes do this object linking for us since the PodSpec is embedded in the Deployment? The reason you need to specify these labels manually is that they play an important role when referencing Pods directly in other objects. For example, in the next section, in which we configure a network Service, it references the Pods of the Deployment directly, not the Deployment itself. The same is true for other concepts covered later in the book, such as a Pod Disruption Budget (PDB). By specifying the label for your Pods, you will know what label to reference in these other objects. The Pod is the fundamental execution and scheduling unit in Kubernetes, and the Deployment is just one of many ways to create, manage, and interact with Pods.

As for the key–value label itself, it's completely arbitrary. You can use `foo: bar` for all Kubernetes cares. I used `pod: timeserver-pod`, as I find it reads well when selecting Pods in other objects. A lot of documentation uses something like `app: timeserver`. I have avoided repeating the name of the Deployment (`timeserver`) as the value of this label to avoid the misconception that the name of the Deployment has anything to do with the Pod label (since it doesn't).

So, that's how the Deployment object is constructed with an embedded PodSpec. I hope it's useful to understand this object composition and how the Pod is referenced. In the next section, we'll expose this Deployment to the world, which will reference the Pod by its labels.

3.2.5 Publishing your Service

With your container successfully deployed, no doubt you'll want to interact with it! Each Pod is given its own cluster-local (internal) IP address, which can be used for communication between Pods within the cluster. It's possible to expose Pods directly on the internet as well as on the node's IP (with the field `hostPort`), but unless you're writing a real-time game server, that's rarely what you'll do. Typically, and especially when Deployment is used, you will aggregate your Pods into a Service, which provides a single access point with an internal (and optionally external) IP, and load balance requests across your pods. Even if you had a Deployment of a single Pod, you'll still want to create a Service to provide a stable address.

In addition to load balancing, Services keep track of which Pods are running and capable of receiving traffic. For example, while you may have specified three replicas in your Deployment, that doesn't mean that three replicas will be available at all times. There might only be two if a node is being upgraded, or there could be more than three while you're rolling out a new version of your Deployment. The Service will only route traffic to running Pods (in the next chapter, we'll cover some key information you need to provide to make that works smoothly).

Services are used internally within the cluster to enable communication between multiple applications (a so-called microservice architecture) and offer convenient features, such as service discovery, for this purpose. This topic is covered in detail in chapter 7. For now, let's focus on using a Service and expose your new application to the internet by specifying a `LoadBalancer`-type Service to get it in the hands of end-users. As with the Deployment, we'll start with a YAML configuration.

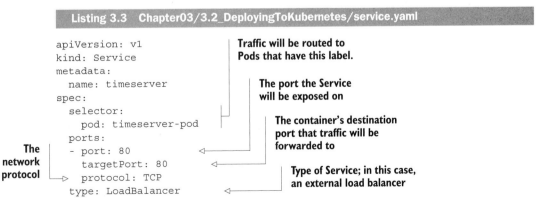

Listing 3.3   Chapter03/3.2_DeployingToKubernetes/service.yaml

```
apiVersion: v1
kind: Service
metadata:
  name: timeserver
spec:
  selector:
    pod: timeserver-pod
  ports:
  - port: 80
    targetPort: 80
    protocol: TCP
  type: LoadBalancer
```

Traffic will be routed to
Pods that have this label.

The port the Service
will be exposed on

The container's destination
port that traffic will be
forwarded to

Type of Service; in this case,
an external load balancer

The
network
protocol

The port list allows you to configure which port to expose for users of the Service (`port`) and which port of the Pod that this traffic will be sent to (`targetPort`). This allows you to, say, expose a service on port 80 (the default HTTP port) and connect it to an application in a container running on port 8080.

Each Pod and Service in Kubernetes has its own internal cluster IP, so you don't need to worry about port conflicts between Pods. Thus, you can run your application on whatever port you like (such as port 80 for an HTTP service) and use the same number for `port` and `targetPort` for simplicity, as with the previous example. If you do this, you can omit `targetPort` completely, as the default is to use the `port` value.

All Services (other than headless Services, covered in Chapter 9) are given an internal, cluster-local IP address that Pods in the cluster can use. If you specify `type: LoadBalancer` as in the previous example, an external IP address will be provisioned in addition.

Notice also that this Service has a section named `selector`, like our Deployment had. The Service doesn't reference the Deployment and actually has no knowledge of the Deployment. Instead, it references the set of Pods that have the given label (which, in this case, will be the Pods created by our Deployment). Once again, it's easier to visualize, as in figure 3.12.

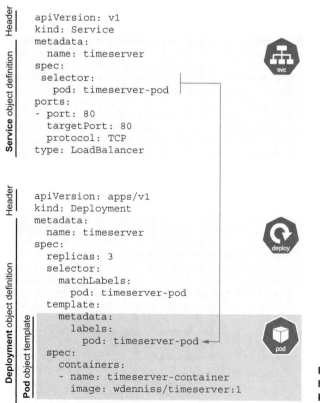

Figure 3.12   Relationship between the Service and the Pods it targets (selects)

Unlike in the Deployment object, the `selector` section has no `matchLabels` subsection. They are, however, equivalent. Deployment is just using a newer, more expressive syntax in Kubernetes. The selectors in the Deployment and in the Service are achieving the same result: specifying the set of Pods that the object is referencing.

Create the Service object on your cluster with

```
cd Chapter03/3.2_DeployingToKubernetes
kubectl create -f service.yaml
```

Notice how the creation command (`kubectl create`) is the same for the Deployment as the Service. All Kubernetes objects can be created, read, updated, and deleted (so-called CRUD operations) with four `kubectl` commands: `kubectl create`, `kubectl get`, `kubectl apply`, and `kubectl delete`.

To see the status of your Service, you can call `kubectl get` on the object type, like so:

```
$ kubectl get service
NAME          TYPE           CLUSTER-IP     EXTERNAL-IP    PORT(S)        AGE
kubernetes    ClusterIP      10.22.128.1    <none>         443/TCP        1h
timeserver    LoadBalancer   10.22.129.13   203.0.113.16   80:30701/TCP   26m
```

Notice that your Service is listed there (in this example, `timeserver`), as well as another Service named `kubernetes`. You can ignore the `kubernetes` Service if one is shown, as that's the Kubernetes API service itself running in your cluster. You can also specify just the Service you're interested in with `kubectl get service $SERVICE_NAME`.

If the `External IP` in the output indicates `Pending`, it just means the external IP is waiting for the load balancer to come online. It's common for this to take a minute or two, so no need to rush to debug why it's pending unless it's been that way for a while. Rather than repeating the previous `get` command repeatedly, you can stream any changes to the status by adding the `--watch/-w` flag (i.e., `kubectl get service -w`). Run that command, and within a couple of minutes, you should see output indicating that your Service now has an external IP.

> **NOTE** To have an external IP provisioned, you must be running Kubernetes on a cloud provider, as the provider is provisioning an externally routable network load balancer behind the scenes. If you're developing locally, see section 3.4.3 on how to connect using tools like `kubectl port-forward`.

Once the IP comes online, try accessing the Service by visiting the URL. Based on the preceding example output, this would mean visiting `http://203.0.113.16` (but replace it with your own external IP from `kubectl get service`!). The `curl` tool is great for testing HTTP requests from the command line (`curl http://203.0.113.16`); viewing it in a browser works just as well, too:

```
$ curl http://203.0.113.16
The time is 7:01 PM, UTC.
```

TROUBLESHOOTING: UNABLE TO CONNECT

Two common reasons for an `Unable to Connect` error are (1) the selector is incorrect and (2) your ports are wrong. Triple-check that the selector matches the labels in your Deployment's Pod template. Verify that the target port is, indeed, the port your container is listening on (a boot-time debug message in the container printing the port can be a good way to help verify this) and that you're connecting to the right port from your browser.

See whether you can connect to one of your Pods directly on the `targetPort` using `kubectl`'s port-forwarding capability. If you can't connect to the Pod directly, then the problem is likely with the Pod. If it does work, the problem could be an incorrect Service definition. You can set up a port forward to one of the Pods in the Deployment with

```
kubectl port-forward deploy/$DEPLOYMENT_NAME $FROM_PORT:$TO_PORT
```

where `$FROM_PORT` is the port you'll use locally, and `$TO_PORT` is the `targetPort` that you defined in your Service. Using our example earlier, this would be

```
kubectl port-forward deploy/timeserver 8080:80
```

Then browse to http://localhost:8080. This will select one of the Pods in the Deployment automatically (bypassing the Service). You can also specify a specific Pod to connect to directly with

```
kubectl port-forward pod/$POD_NAME $FROM_PORT:$TO_PORT
```

TROUBLESHOOTING: EXTERNAL IP STUCK IN PENDING

It can take a little while to get an external IP, so give it a few minutes. Verify that your cloud provider will provision external IPs for Services of type `LoadBalanacer`. Check the provider's documentation for any additional information about setting up load balancers in Kubernetes.

If you're running locally or just want to try out the Service without waiting for the external IP, you can forward a port on your machine to the Service, like so:

```
kubectl port-forward service/$SERVICE_NAME $FROM_PORT:$TO_PORT
```

3.2.6   *Interacting with the Deployment*

During development, it's convenient to be able to interact with the container to run commands or copy files back and forth. Fortunately, Kubernetes makes this about as easy as Docker does.

RUNNING ONE-OFF COMMANDS

Just as we can run one-off commands on the Docker image using the `docker exec` command (covered in chapter 2), we can also run one-off commands on our Pods with `kubectl exec`. A common command used to diagnose problems in the container is `sh`, which will give you an interactive shell on the container (provided that `sh` is available in the container). From there, you can perform whatever other debugging steps you need to do inside the container.

Technically, exec is run against a Pod, but we can specify the Deployment instead of a specific Pod, and kubectl will select one Pod at random to run the command on:

```
$ kubectl exec -it deploy/timeserver -- sh
# echo "Testing exec"
Testing exec
```

You can run any command on the container in this way, for example:

```
$ kubectl exec -it deploy/timeserver -- echo "Testing exec"
Testing exec
```

COPYING FILES TO/FROM THE CONTAINER

Again, similar to Docker, kubectl has a cp command allowing you to copy files between your system and the container. This command requires that the tar binary be present in your container image. This can be useful when you want to download your application logs or other diagnostic information. The default path is the container's working directory, so if you have a file in the container named "example.txt" you could copy it to your machine like so:

```
kubectl cp $POD_NAME:example.txt example.txt
```

You can also copy files in the other direction:

```
kubectl cp example.txt $POD_NAME:.
```

3.2.7 Updating your application

Now that your application has been deployed and published to the world, no doubt you'll want to be able to update it. Make a code change to the sample app and then build and push the container image to the container repository with a new version tag. For example, if you previously used us-docker.pkg.dev/wdenniss/ts/timeserver:1, your new image could be us-docker.pkg.dev/wdenniss/ts/timeserver:2. You can make this tag anything you like, but it's a good convention to use version numbers.

Once the container image has been pushed to the repository (as we did in section 3.2.2), update the deploy.yaml file from listing 3.1 with the new image name—for example (emphasis added):

Listing 3.4 Chapter03/3.2.7_Updating/deploy.yaml

```
apiVersion: apps/v1
kind: Deployment
metadata:
  name: timeserver
spec:
  replicas: 3
```

```
selector:
  matchLabels:
    pod: timeserver-pod
template:
  metadata:
    labels:
      pod: timeserver-pod
  spec:
    containers:
    - name: timeserver-container
      image: docker.io/wdenniss/timeserver:2
```

New image version

Save the file and apply the change to your cluster with

```
$ kubectl apply -f deploy.yaml
deployment.apps/timeserver configured
```

When you apply this change, an interesting thing happens. Remember how Kubernetes constantly seeks to actuate your requirements, driving the state it observes in the system to the state you require? Well, since you just declared that the Deployment is now using the image with the version tag 2 and all the Pods are currently tagged 1, Kubernetes will seek to update the live state so that all Pods are the current version.

We can see this in action by running `kubectl get deploy`. Here's some example output:

```
$ kubectl get deploy
NAME          READY    UP-TO-DATE    AVAILABLE    AGE
timeserver    3/3      1             3            10m
```

The READY column shows how many Pods are serving traffic and how many we requested. In this case, all three are ready. The UP-TO-DATE column, however, indicates that only one of these Pods is the current version. This is because, rather than replacing all the Pods at once, causing some downtime to the application, by default, Pods are updated with a so-called rolling update strategy—that is, one or several at a time.

Rolling updates and other rollout strategies are covered in detail in the next chapter, as well as important health checks that need to be configured to avoid glitches during the rollout. For now, it's enough to know that Kubernetes will actuate your changes and will replace the old v1 Pods with the new v2 Pods.

Once the UP-TO-DATE count is equal to the READY count, the rollout is complete. You can also observe the individual Pods being created and replaced with `kubectl get pods`, which will show a list of all Pods in the Deployment, both new and old.

MONITORING THE ROLLOUT

Since the output of the `kubectl get` commands displays the moment-in-time information, but the Deployment is continuously changing, most operators will monitor the Deployment in an automated way, avoiding the need to constantly rerun the same command. Kubernetes includes one such option, the `--watch/-w` flag, which can be added to most `kubectl` commands, such as `kubectl get pods -w` and `kubectl get deploy -w`. When `watch` is specified, any changes to the status will be streamed to the console output.

The disadvantage of the `watch` flag is that it kind of jumbles the output. If you have many Pods changing, you'll see line after line printed, and it's easy to lose sight of the current state of the system. My preference is to use the Linux `watch` command instead. Unlike the `watch` flag, the `watch` command refreshes the entire output, optionally showing you what changed between the current and the last update. This command is available in most Linux distros, macOS, and the Windows Subsystem for Linux (WSL) and can be found wherever you get your packages.

When `watch` is installed, you can simply prepend it to any `kubectl` command, such as

```
watch kubectl get deploy
```

My favorite `watch` flag is `-d`, which will highlight any changes:

```
watch -d kubectl get deploy
```

With a terminal window (or tmux session window) opened for watching each command, you can put together a real-time status dashboard with just `watch` and `kubectl`.

WATCHING THE DEPLOYMENT

The previously discussed `kubectl get deploy` and `kubectl get pods` commands return all Deployments and Pods, respectively, in the current namespace. As you make more Deployments, you may want to specify just the resources you're interested in:

```
kubectl get deploy $DEPLOYMENT_NAME
```

The name of the object can be found in the `name` field in the metadata section at the top of the file. Viewing all pods from a single Deployment is a little more tricky; however, you can use the label selector to get the status of a set of Pods with

```
kubectl get pods --selector=pod=timeserver-pod
```

where `pod=timeserver-pod` is the label selector specified in the Deployment.

3.2.8 Cleaning up

There are a number of ways to clean up the objects we've created. You can delete by object type and name:

```
$ kubectl delete deploy timeserver
deployment.apps "timeserver" deleted
$ kubectl delete service timeserver
service "timeserver" deleted
$ kubectl delete pod timeserver
pod "timeserver" deleted
```

NOTE You don't need to delete Pods that are managed by another object like Deployment, only those you created manually. Deleting the Deployment will automatically delete all the Pods it manages.

Or, you can delete objects by referencing individual configuration files or a directory of configuration files:

```
$ cd Chapter03
$ kubectl delete -f 3.2_DeployingToKubernetes
deployment.apps "timeserver" deleted
service "timeserver" deleted
$ kubectl delete -f 3.2.4_ThePodSpec/pod.yaml
pod "timeserver" deleted
```

If, after deleting, you change your mind, you can simply create them again (e.g., `kubectl create -f 3.2_DeployingToKubernetes`). That's the beauty of capturing your configuration in files: you don't need to remember any tweaks you made to the live state because everything is updated first in the configuration.

The cluster itself often carries a charge, so once you're done for the day, you can consider deleting it as well. This can be done using the UI console for most cloud providers. If you're using GKE with the command line, you can run `gcloud container clusters delete $CLUSTER_NAME --region $REGION`. Even without any Pods or Services running in the cluster, nodes themselves typically carry charges (unless you're using a platform like GKE Autopilot) but deleting the cluster should clean them up as well. If you're keeping the cluster and are using a platform that bills for nodes, pay attention to your node resources in addition to your Kubernetes objects, so you only have what you need.

TIP The rest of the book will assume you know how to delete resources you don't want to keep around. As you try out the examples in this book (and elsewhere), keep these steps in mind and be sure to delete any objects you created and no longer need to free up resources and reduce your bill!

3.3   *Imperative commands*

Kubernetes offers two approaches for interacting with the system: declaratively, where you specify (declare) in configuration files the state that you want and apply those configurations to the cluster, and imperatively, where you instruct the API one command (imperative) at a time to perform your wishes. The configuration-driven declarative model is the approach that is strongly preferred by most practitioners (including myself) and is what you'll most often encounter in a workplace.

In fact, it's possible to create a Deployment with our container and expose it to the internet using purely imperative commands. For completeness, here's how you would do that (provided the previous example was deleted following the cleanup steps in section 3.2.8):

1 Create the Deployment:

```
$ kubectl create deployment timeserver \
    --image=docker.io/wdenniss/timeserver:1
deployment.apps/timeserver created
```

2 Create a Service of type `LoadBalancer` on Port 80 to expose this Service:

```
$ kubectl expose deployment timeserver --type=LoadBalancer --port 80
service/timeserver exposed
```

3 Observe the result:

```
$ kubectl get deploy,svc
NAME                          READY   UP-TO-DATE   AVAILABLE   AGE
deployment.apps/timeserver    1/1     1            1           4m49s

NAME                    TYPE           CLUSTER-IP      EXTERNAL-IP   AGE
service/kubernetes      ClusterIP      10.22.128.1     <none>        5m2
service/timeserver      LoadBalancer   10.22.130.202   <pending>     31s
```

4 Update the container in the Deployment with a new version:

```
$ kubectl set image deployment timeserver timeserver=wdenniss/timeserver:2
deployment.apps/timeserver image updated
```

This option may look simpler at first brush when compared to controlling Kubernetes using configuration files that are, frankly, a little verbose at times. However, there are good reasons to prefer the configuration-based approach. The first is reproducibility. Let's say you need to reproduce the configuration on another environment, like production and staging, which is a pretty common use case. With the declarative approach, you can just apply the same exact config in the new environment (with any needed tweaks). If you went the imperative route, you would need to remember the commands, perhaps storing them in a bash script.

It's also harder to make changes. With configuration files, if you need to change a setting, you can just update the configuration and reapply it, after which Kubernetes will dutifully carry out your wishes. With a command-based approach, each change is itself a different command: `kubectl set image` to change the image, `kubectl scale` to change the number of replicas, and so on. You also run the risk that the command could fail, which may occur due to a network timeout, whereas with configuration, the changes will be picked up the next time you apply them. Chapter 11 covers taking configuration files and treating them just as you do the source code for your application, a so-called GitOps or configuration as code methodology where imperative commands would not be an option at all.

If you encounter a system previously built with imperative commands, fear not, as configuration can be exported from the cluster with `kubectl get -o yaml $RESOURCE_TYPE $RESOURCE_NAME`. When exporting a configuration like this from the live cluster, though, there are some extraneous fields you'll need to remove (covered in section 11.1.2). Fortunately, it's never too late to switch, as whether you use declarative or imperative commands, Kubernetes is still storing the object in the same way.

3.4   *Local Kubernetes environments*

This chapter so far has used a cloud-based Kubernetes provider as the deployment environment. You can, of course, run Kubernetes locally as well. I chose to lead with a public cloud provider instead of a local development cluster to demonstrate deploying on Kubernetes, as I assume, for most, the goal is to publish your service and make it accessible beyond your own machine. Indeed, if you're following the examples in this chapter in order, then congratulations: you can now deploy your apps to the world using Kubernetes! In future chapters, you'll learn how to operationalize them, scale them up, and more.

Local Kubernetes development clusters, however, definitely have their place. They are useful during development when you want to rapidly deploy and iterate on code while running in a Kubernetes cluster, particularly when your application consists of several different services. They're a great place to try out and learn Kubernetes constructs without paying for a cloud service and are a convenient option for testing your deployment configuration locally.

There are a lot of differences in using Kubernetes locally on a machine in a non-production-grade environment with a fixed set of resources compared to a production-grade cloud service with dynamic provisioning. In the cloud, you can scale up massively using multiple machines spread over a geographical region, while your local machine has a fixed set of resources. In the cloud, you can get a production-grade routable public IP for your Service—not so much on your local machine. Due to these differences and many more, I believe learning directly in your target product environment is more efficient. Hence, the focus in this book on production-grade clusters. That being said, as long as you understand the differences, a local development cluster can be a useful tool indeed.

> ### Do you need a Kubernetes cluster for application development?
> There's no requirement to use Kubernetes during application development just because you use it for production deployment. A fairly common app development pattern I've observed is using Docker Compose (covered in section 2.3) for local development and testing, with the resulting application deployed to Kubernetes for production.
>
> Docker Compose works pretty well for the development of apps with only a handful of interservice dependencies. The downside is you need to define the application config twice (once for development with Compose and once for production in Kubernetes), but this overhead is minor for apps with only a few service dependencies. The upside is that Docker has some useful tools for development, in particular, being able to mount local folders into the container, which means for interpreted languages like Python and Ruby, you can change code without a container rebuild. It's also simple to configure since you can skip all the production-related config like replica count and resource requirements.

(continued)

It's hard to understate the usefulness of Compose being able to mount your local app folder as a read/write volume, edit code without a container rebuild, get output from commands you run in the container like log files, and perform database upgrades right in your development folder. Kubernetes does have some tools to level the playing field here, like Skaffold, which gets you a tight development loop with Kubernetes (local or cloud) as the target, but Docker has a sterling reputation among developers for a reason.

As I always say, use the best tool for the job. Decide whether a local Kubernetes cluster or a Docker Compose setup works best for application development and use what works for you. Even if you choose to use Compose for application development, you may still utilize a local Kubernetes cluster for deployment testing.

There are a bunch of options for running a local Kubernetes cluster. The two most popular are Docker Desktop and Minikube. In fact, if you have Docker Desktop installed, then you already have a local single-node Kubernetes cluster! Minikube, created by the Kubernetes project, is also trivial to set up and offers a few more advanced options like multiple nodes, which are useful when you want to test more advanced Kubernetes constructs like Pod spread policies and affinity (chapter 8).

3.4.1 *Docker Desktop's Kubernetes cluster*

Docker Desktop comes with its own single-node Kubernetes development environment. If you have Docker Desktop installed, then you already have a local Kubernetes environment. Follow the instructions at https://docs.docker.com/desktop/kubernetes/ to get going in two simple steps:

1 Enable Kubernetes in Docker Desktop settings and ensure it's running.
2 Using `kubectl`, switch contexts to the Docker Desktop cluster.

NOTE Be aware that Docker's local Kubernetes option is packaged with the "Docker Desktop" product. If you are using Docker via the Docker Engine install on Linux, it does not have this functionality.

Once Docker Desktop is running with Kubernetes enabled, you can view the context and switch to it:

```
kubectl config get-contexts
kubectl config use-context docker-desktop
```

In fact, you can use these commands to switch to any cluster that you previously connected to, including a cloud platform like the one used previously in this chapter. Any time you wish to switch clusters, simply run

```
kubectl config get-contexts
kubectl config use-context $CONTEXT
```

I find those two commands a bit tedious to type when switching between clusters a lot, so I highly recommend the `kubectx` tool (https://github.com/ahmetb/kubectx), which makes it a lot quicker. To switch contexts with `kubectx`, use

```
kubectx
kubectx $CONTEXT
```

If you have any problems with Docker Desktop, then the Restart Kubernetes Cluster and Clean/Purge Data options found in the debug menu are your friends.

3.4.2   *Minikube*

Minikube is another great choice for testing locally and allows you to test more Kubernetes functionality by providing a multinode environment. It's maintained by the open source Kubernetes community. Follow the instructions at https://minikube.sigs .k8s.io/docs/start/ to install Minikube for your system.

Once installed, to boot a virtual multinode cluster (which I recommend, as it more closely resembles a production Kubernetes environment), run `minikube start` and pass the number of nodes you desire:

```
minikube start --nodes 3
```

The `start` command will automatically configure `kubectl` to use the Minikube context, meaning any `kubectl` commands will operate on the Minikube cluster. To change the context back to a different cluster, like your production cluster, use the `kubectl config` or `kubectx` commands described in the previous section.

Once Minikube is running, you can go ahead and use it like a regular Kubernetes cluster, following the instructions in this chapter. Before you start using it, to verify that things are running as expected, run `kubectl get nodes` to check that you can connect to the cluster:

```
$ kubectl get nodes
NAME           STATUS    ROLES            AGE      VERSION
minikube       Ready     control-plane    4m54s    v1.24.3
minikube-m02   Ready     <none>           4m32s    v1.24.3
minikube-m03   Ready     <none>           3m58s    v1.24.3
```

If you're done using Minikube and want to get your machine's CPU and memory resources back, run `minikube stop`. To delete all the data and make room for a new Minikube cluster next time with different settings (like a different node count), use `minikube delete`.

3.4.3   *Using your local Kubernetes cluster*

With `kubectl` set up to point to your preferred local Kubernetes cluster, you can deploy your application locally using the same `kubectl` commands shown earlier in this chapter. Two important differences, however, will be in how you expose and access Services and how you reference container images built locally. To deploy the sample application from this chapter, from the sample root directory, run

```
$ cd Chapter03/3.2_DeployingToKubernetes
$ kubectl create -f .
deployment.apps/timeserver created
service/timeserver created
```

> ### The benefit of declarative configuration
>
> Throughout this book, examples are given using declarative configuration rather than imperative commands. In other words, to create a Deployment, we first create the configuration of the Deployment and then apply it, as opposed to using `kubectl` to create the Deployment directly.
>
> One of the many benefits of this approach is that you can test out your configuration locally and then deploy it confidently to production later without needing to remember a bunch of one-off commands. Notice how we can deploy the same configuration files against the local cluster as we did against the production cluster. Neat!

ACCESSING THE SERVICE

Unlike when developing on a cloud Kubernetes provider, when creating a `Load-Balancer`-type Service locally, you won't get an external IP. For Docker Desktop, Minikube, and, in fact, any Kubernetes cluster, you can also use `kubectl` to forward ports from your local machine to the Service inside the cluster. This is useful for testing against a local Kubernetes cluster and debugging your cloud cluster. To expose the Service locally, use

```
kubectl port-forward service/$SERVICE_NAME $FROM_PORT:$TO_PORT
```

where `FROM_PORT` is the port you'll access the Service on locally, and `TO_PORT` is the IP of the Service. For our demo, choosing `8080` as a high-level port, the command can look like the following:

```
kubectl port-forward service/timeserver 8080:80
```

You can then browse to http://localhost:8080 to connect to the Service. There are a range of useful flags[1] for `port-forward`, including `--address 0.0.0.0`, to bind to all network interfaces so you can access the forwarded Service from other devices on the network (if your firewall allows it). Port forwarding is also useful to debug services running on a cloud Kubernetes platform.

Minikube offers an additional way[2] to route traffic to your Service. It can be accessed with

```
minikube service $SERVICE_NAME
```

---

[1] https://kubernetes.io/docs/reference/generated/kubectl/kubectl-commands#port-forward
[2] https://kubernetes.io/docs/setup/learning-environment/minikube/#services

For the sample in the earlier section, that would be

```
minikube service timeserver
```

Accessing Kubernetes Services locally from Docker

Are you running a Service in Kubernetes that you want to access directly from a Docker container running outside of Kubernetes for some reason? For example, you're doing some rapid iterating in Docker and want to access an established Service in Kubernetes.

The solution is easy. Forward the Service so that the port is open on your local machine as previously described. You can then reference it in containers running directly in Docker using `host.docker.internal` on whatever port you forwarded. `host.docker.internal` is how containers can talk to services on the local machine, and since you forwarded the port to your local machine, the connection can go through.

For example, say you deploy Redis in Kubernetes (see chapter 9) and forward the ports with `kubectl port-forward service/timeserver 6379:6379`. You then want to connect to it from a local container in Docker running Python using the redis-py library. You can do that with `redis.Redis(host='host.docker.internal', port= '6379')`. Happy coding!

DEPLOYING LOCAL IMAGES

By default, a local Kubernetes cluster will attempt to pull container images from the internet—behaving just like a production Kubernetes cluster. For public images like `ubuntu` or my sample image `docker.io/wdenniss/timeserver`, everything will just work. But extra steps are required to supply your own images built locally to the local cluster. Of course, you could upload them to a public container registry as you would for production, whereby your local cluster will pull them like in production.

Uploading every image you build during development, however, is a bit of a hassle. It slows down your development as you wait for the push and pull. Also, unless you're using public images, you'll need to provision credentials so your local cluster can access them (a step that is typically done for you when you're pulling private images from the container registry of your Kubernetes provider).

To get your local cluster to use a local image, you need to make two changes to your Kubernetes Deployment configuration. First, add the `imagePullPolicy` parameter and set it to `Never` and, second, refer to your image using its local image name without any repository prefix.

The path for locally built images is simply their repository and version tag, with no repository URL prefix. If you've built an image with `docker build . -t timeserver` as we did in chapter 2, you would reference this in your Pod spec as `image: timeserver:latest` in your config file (using `latest` as the version tag will give us the most recently built image). Run `docker images` to view a list of available local images. The following is an example of a Deployment referencing this locally built image:

Listing 3.5   Chapter03/3.4.3_LocalDevelopment/deploy.yaml

```
apiVersion: apps/v1
kind: Deployment
metadata:
  name: timeserver
spec:
  replicas: 3
  selector:
    matchLabels:
      pod: timeserver-pod
  template:
    metadata:
      labels:
        pod: timeserver-pod
    spec:
      containers:
      - name: timeserver-container
        image: timeserver:latest
        imagePullPolicy: Never
```

**Reference to a locally
available image**

**Image pull policy prevents
Kubernetes from attempting to
fetch this local image remotely.**

TIP Only apply the `imagePullPolicy: Never` configuration to images you plan to provide locally. You don't want to set this on remote images, as they won't be pulled and will error with a `ErrImageNeverPull` status. If you see that error, it means the image isn't available locally, yet the Deployment was configured to use a local image.

There is one more step if you're using Minikube. While Docker Desktop has access to all the images you built locally with Docker, Minikube does not (it has its own independent container run time and doesn't share images with your local install of Docker). To push local images you want to use into Minikube, simply run the command

```
minikube image load $REPOSITORY:$TAG
```

such as

```
minikube image load timeserver:latest
```

Then, apply your changes with `kubectl` as before:

```
kubectl apply -f deploy.yaml
```

Summary

- A Kubernetes cluster consists of a control plane and nodes on which your containers are run.
- You interact with the cluster via the Kubernetes API, typically with the command-line tool `kubectl`.

- To deploy your own application to Kubernetes, first, upload the container image to a container repository.
- Workloads are specified using objects such as a Deployment, which encapsulates a Pod, which defines your containers.
- Services are used to create network endpoints and expose containers to the internet.
- Pods are referenced by other objects, such as Deployments and Services, using labels.
- Kubernetes uses declarative configuration, typically YAML-formatted configuration files.
- You specify your requirements through the configuration, and the Kubernetes controller seeks to actuate and fulfill them continuously.
- Updating the application is as simple as modifying the configuration with the new container version and applying the change to the cluster.
- Kubernetes will compare changes across configuration versions and actuate any specified changes.

Automated operations

This chapter covers

- Creating long-lasting, reliable application deployments
- Having Kubernetes keep your applications running without your intervention
- Updating applications without downtime

Kubernetes can automate many operations, like restarting your container if it crashes and migrating your application in the case of hardware failure. Thus, Kubernetes helps to make your deployments more reliable without you needing to monitor them 24/7. These automated operations are one of the key value propositions of Kubernetes, and understanding them is an essential step to taking full advantage of everything Kubernetes has to offer.

Kubernetes can also help you update your application without outages and glitches by booting the new version and monitoring its status to ensure it's ready to serve traffic before removing the old version.

To help Kubernetes help keep your application running without downtime during normal operations and upgrades, you need to provide certain information about the state of your application with a process known as health checks. In the next section, we'll go through adding the various health checks to your application and, in a later section, how these can be used with Kubernetes' built-in rollout strategies to update your application without glitches or downtime.

4.1 Automated uptime with health checks

There are some conditions that Kubernetes can detect and repair on its own. If your application crashes, Kubernetes will restart it automatically. Likewise, if the node running your container fails or is removed, Kubernetes will notice that your Deployment is missing replicas and boot new replicas on available space in the cluster.

But what about other types of application failure, like a hung process, a web service that stops accepting connections, or an application that depends on an external service when that service becomes inaccessible? Kubernetes can gracefully detect and attempt to recover from all these conditions, but it needs you to provide signals on the health of your application and whether it is ready to receive traffic. The process used to provide these signals are named *health checks*, which Kubernetes refers to as *liveness and readiness probes*.

Since Kubernetes can't know what it means for each and every service that runs on the platform to be down or up, ready or unready to receive traffic, apps must themselves implement this test. Simply put, the probe queries the container for its status, and the container checks its own internal state and returns a success code if everything is good. If the request times out (e.g., if the application is under too much load) or the container itself determines that there's a problem (such as with a critical dependency), the probe is considered a fail.

4.1.1 Liveness and readiness probes

In Kubernetes, the health of a container is determined by two separate probes: *liveness*, which determines whether the container is running, and *readiness*, which indicates when the container is able to receive traffic. Both probes use the same techniques to perform the checks, but how Kubernetes uses the result of the probe is different (see table 4.1).

Table 4.1 Differences between liveness and readiness

	Liveness	Readiness
Semantic meaning	Is the container running?	Is the container ready to receive traffic?
Implication of probe failures exceeding threshold	Pod is terminated and replaced.	Pod is removed from receiving traffic until the probe passes.
Time to recover from a failed probe	Slow: Pod is rescheduled on failure and needs time to boot.	Fast: Pod is already running and can immediately receive traffic once the probe passes.
Default state at container boot	Passing (live).	Failing (unready).

There are a few reasons for having the two probe types. One is the state at boot. Note how the liveness probe starts in the passing, or live, state (the container is assumed to be live until the Pod proves otherwise), whereas the readiness probe starts in the unready state (the container is assumed to not be able to serve traffic until it proves it can).

Without a readiness check, Kubernetes has no way of knowing when the container is ready to receive traffic, so it has to assume it's ready the moment the container starts up, and it will be added to the Service's load-balancing rotation immediately. Most containers take tens of seconds or even minutes to start up—so sending traffic right away would result in some traffic loss during startup. The readiness check solves this by only reporting "Ready" when the internal tests are passing.

Likewise, with a liveness check, the conditions that require a container restart may differ from those that indicate the container is not ready to receive traffic. The best example is a container waiting for an external dependency, like a database connection. Until the container has the database connection, it should not be serving traffic (therefore it's unready), but internally, the container is good to go. You don't want to replace this container too hastily so that it has enough time to establish the database connection it depends on.

Other reasons for having two types of probes are the sensitivity and recovery times. Readiness checks are typically tuned to quickly remove the Pod from the load balancer (as this is a fast and cheap operation to initiate) and add it back when the check is passing again, whereas liveness checks are often tuned to be a little less hasty as the time needed to re-create a container is longer.

4.1.2 Adding a readiness probe

For a web service, a rudimentary health check could simply test "Is the service serving traffic?" Before building a dedicated health check endpoint for your service, you could just find any endpoint on the service that returns an HTTP 200 status code and use it as the health check.

If the root path returns HTTP 200 on all responses, you can just use that path. Since the root path behaves that way in our example container, the following readiness probe will work just fine.

Listing 4.1 Chapter04/4.1.2_Readiness/deploy.yaml

```
apiVersion: apps/v1
kind: Deployment
metadata:
  name: timeserver
spec:
  replicas: 3
  selector:
    matchLabels:
      pod: timeserver-pod
```

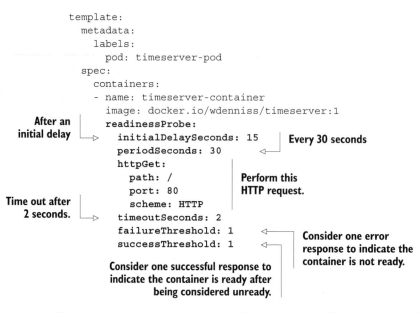

```
template:
  metadata:
    labels:
        pod: timeserver-pod
  spec:
    containers:
    - name: timeserver-container
      image: docker.io/wdenniss/timeserver:1
      readinessProbe:
        initialDelaySeconds: 15
        periodSeconds: 30
        httpGet:
          path: /
          port: 80
          scheme: HTTP
        timeoutSeconds: 2
        failureThreshold: 1
        successThreshold: 1
```

After an initial delay

Every 30 seconds

Perform this HTTP request.

Time out after 2 seconds.

Consider one error response to indicate the container is not ready.

Consider one successful response to indicate the container is ready after being considered unready.

From the root directory, update the `timeserver` Deployment with

```
cd Chapter04/4.1.2_Readiness
kubectl apply -f deploy.yaml
```

Now, any time the container fails to respond to the readiness check, that Pod will be temporarily removed from the Service. Say you have three replicas of a Pod, and one of them fails to respond. Any traffic to the Service will be routed to the remaining two healthy Pods. Once the Pod returns success (an HTTP 200 response in this case), it will be added back into service.

This readiness check is particularly important during updates, as you don't want Pods to be receiving traffic while they are booting (as these requests will fail). With correctly implemented readiness checks, you can get zero downtime updates, as traffic is only routed to Pods that are ready and not ones in the process of being created.

Observing the difference

If you want to see the difference between having a readiness check and not with your own experimentation, try the following test. In one shell window, create a Deployment without a readiness check (let's use the one from chapter 3):

```
cd Chapter03/3.2_DeployingToKubernetes
kubectl create -f .
```

Wait for the Service to be assigned an external IP:

```
kubectl get svc -w
```

(continued)

Now, set your IP and set up a watch on the service endpoint in a separate console window:

```
EXTERNAL_IP=203.0.113.16
watch -n 0.25 -d curl "http://$EXTERNAL_IP"
```

Back in the first window, trigger a rollout:

```
kubectl rollout restart deploy timeserver
```

As the Pods restart, you should see some intermittent connection problems in the curl window.

Now update the Deployment with a readiness check (like the one in this section) and apply

```
cd ../../
cd Chapter04/4.1.2_Readiness
kubectl apply -f deploy.yaml
```

This time, since the Deployment has a readiness check, you shouldn't see any connection problems on the `curl` window.

4.1.3 Adding a liveness probe

Liveness probes have the same specification as readiness probes but are specified with the key `livenessProbe`. How the probes are *used*, on the other hand, is quite different. The result of the readiness probe governs whether the Pod receives traffic, whereas a failing liveness probe will cause the Pod to be restarted (once the failure threshold is met).

The readiness check we added to our Deployment in the previous section was rudimentary in that it just used the root path of the service rather than a dedicated endpoint. We can continue that practice for now and use the same endpoint from the readiness probe for the liveness probe in the following example, with minor changes to increase the failure tolerance. Since the container gets restarted when the liveness probe fails the threshold and can take some time to come back, we don't want the liveness probe set up on a hair trigger. Let's add a liveness probe to our Deployment that will restart it if it fails for 180 seconds (six failures at a 30-second interval).

Listing 4.2   Chapter04/4.1.3_Liveness/deploy.yaml

```
apiVersion: apps/v1
kind: Deployment
metadata:
  name: timeserver
spec:
  replicas: 3
  selector:
    matchLabels:
      pod: timeserver-pod
```

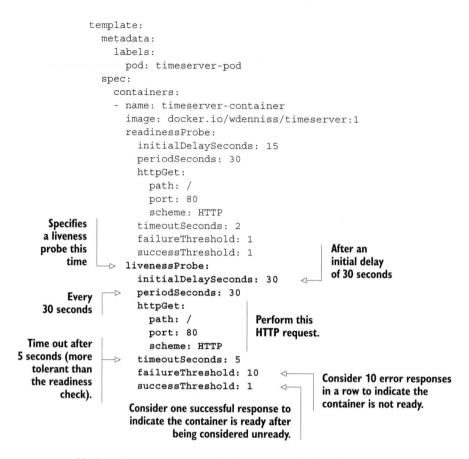

```
template:
  metadata:
    labels:
      pod: timeserver-pod
  spec:
    containers:
    - name: timeserver-container
      image: docker.io/wdenniss/timeserver:1
      readinessProbe:
        initialDelaySeconds: 15
        periodSeconds: 30
        httpGet:
          path: /
          port: 80
          scheme: HTTP
        timeoutSeconds: 2
        failureThreshold: 1
        successThreshold: 1
      livenessProbe:
        initialDelaySeconds: 30
        periodSeconds: 30
        httpGet:
          path: /
          port: 80
          scheme: HTTP
        timeoutSeconds: 5
        failureThreshold: 10
        successThreshold: 1
```

Specifies a liveness probe this time

After an initial delay of 30 seconds

Every 30 seconds

Perform this HTTP request.

Time out after 5 seconds (more tolerant than the readiness check).

Consider 10 error responses in a row to indicate the container is not ready.

Consider one successful response to indicate the container is ready after being considered unready.

Update the timeserver Deployment with these latest changes:

```
cd Chapter04/4.1.3_Liveness
kubectl apply -f deploy.yaml
```

Now, your Deployment has a readiness and liveness probe. Even these rudimentary probes improve the reliability of your deployment drastically. If you stop here, it's probably enough for a basic application. The next section details some further design considerations to bulletproof your probes for production use.

4.1.4 *Designing good health checks*

While using an existing endpoint as we did in the previous two sections, as the health check path is better than nothing, it's generally better to add dedicated health check endpoints to your application. These health checks should implement the specific semantics of readiness and liveness and be as lightweight as possible. Without understanding the semantic differences between liveness and readiness, you could see instability due to excessive restarts and cascading failures. In addition, if you're reusing some other endpoint, chances are it's heavier-weight than needed. Why pay the cost of rendering an entire HTML page when a simple HTTP header response would suffice?

When creating the HTTP endpoints to implement these checks, it's important to take into account any external dependencies being tested. Generally, you don't want external dependencies to be checked in the liveness probe; rather, it should test only whether the container itself is running (assuming your container will retry the connections to its external connections). There's not really any value in restarting a container that's running just fine or only because it can't connect to another service that is having trouble. This could cause unnecessary restarts that create churn and lead to cascading failures, particularly if you have a complex dependency graph. However, there is an exception to this principle of not testing dependencies in liveness probes, which I cover later in the section.

Since the liveness probe is only testing whether the server is responding, the result can and should be extremely simple, generally just an HTTP 200 status response, even one with no response body text. If the request can get through to the server code, then it must be live, which is enough information.

For readiness probes on the other hand, it's generally desirable that they test their external dependencies like a database connection (see figure 4.1). Say you have three replicas of a Pod, and only two can connect to your database. It makes sense to only have those two fully functional Pods in the load-balancer rotation. One way to test the connection is to look up a single row from the database in your readiness check.

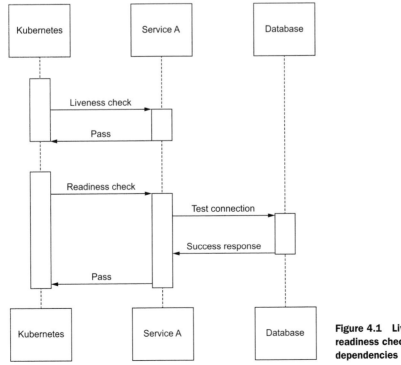

Figure 4.1 Liveness and readiness checks and external dependencies

For example, the pseudocode for a database connection check could look something like

```
result = sql.execute("SELECT id FROM users LIMIT 1;")
if result:
  http_response(200, "Ready")
else:
  http_response(503, "Not Ready")
```

Performing a simple SQL query should be enough to ensure that the database is both connected and responsive. Rather than using a SELECT query, you could perform any other database operation, but I personally like the legitimacy of a SELECT statement. If it works, I'm confident the other queries will work, too.

The Python timeserver example app doesn't have a database dependency. However, let's refactor the code to include specific paths, which we will name /healthz and /readyz, as it is best practice to have dedicated endpoints for these probes.

Listing 4.3   Chapter04/timeserver2/server.py

```
from http.server import ThreadingHTTPServer, BaseHTTPRequestHandler
from datetime import datetime

class RequestHandler(BaseHTTPRequestHandler):
    def do_GET(self):
        match self.path:
            case '/':
                now = datetime.now()
                response_string = now.strftime("The time is %-I:%M %p, UTC.")
                self.respond_with(200, response_string)
            case '/healthz':
                self.respond_with(200, "Healthy")              ┐
            case '/readyz':                                     │
                dependencies_connected = True                  │
                # TODO: actually verify any dependencies        │ The new health
                if (dependencies_connected):                   │ check paths
                    self.respond_with(200, "Ready")            │
                else:                                          │
                    self.respond_with(503, "Not Ready")        ┘
            case _:
                self.respond_with(404, "Not Found")

    def respond_with(self, status_code: int, content: str) -> None:
        self.send_response(status_code)
        self.send_header('Content-type', 'text/plain')
        self.end_headers()
        self.wfile.write(bytes(content, "utf-8"))

def startServer():
    try:
        server = ThreadingHTTPServer(('', 80), RequestHandler)
        print("Listening on " + ":".join(map(str, server.server_address)))
        server.serve_forever()
```

```
    except KeyboardInterrupt:
        server.shutdown()

if __name__ == "__main__":
    startServer()
```

After updating our Deployment configuration for these new endpoints, we get the code in the following listing.

Listing 4.4   Chapter04/4.1.4_GoodHealthChecks/deploy.yaml

```
apiVersion: apps/v1
kind: Deployment
metadata:
  name: timeserver
spec:
  replicas: 3
  selector:
    matchLabels:
      pod: timeserver-pod
  template:
    metadata:
      labels:
        pod: timeserver-pod
    spec:
      containers:
      - name: timeserver-container
        image: docker.io/wdenniss/timeserver:2
        readinessProbe:
          initialDelaySeconds: 15
          periodSeconds: 30
          httpGet:
            path: /readyz
            port: 80
            scheme: HTTP
          timeoutSeconds: 2
          failureThreshold: 1
          successThreshold: 1
        livenessProbe:
          initialDelaySeconds: 30
          periodSeconds: 30
          httpGet:
            path: /healthz
            port: 80
            scheme: HTTP
          timeoutSeconds: 5
          failureThreshold: 3
          successThreshold: 1
```

Updated endpoints → **path: /readyz**

→ **path: /healthz**

failureThreshold: 3 ← Now that the liveness probe is lightweight, we can reduce the failure threshold.

Apply this new config in the usual way. Your own application may have more complex readiness and liveness logic. The `healthz` endpoint here probably works for many HTTP applications (simply testing that the HTTP server is responding to requests is sufficient).

However, every application with dependencies like databases should define its own readiness test to determine whether your application is truly ready to serve user requests.

4.1.5 *Rescheduling unready containers*

The previous section detailed the standard way to set up liveness and readiness checks in Kubernetes where you only verify service dependencies in the readiness check. There is one problematic condition that can arise from not testing dependencies in the liveness check. By separating the concerns into readiness ("Is the container ready to receive traffic?") and liveness ("Is the container running?"), there could be a condition where the container is running, but due to a bug in the container's retry logic, the external connections are never resolved. In other words, your container could stay unready forever, something that a restart might resolve.

Recall that we don't generally test readiness in the liveness check, as this could cause the Pod to be re-created too quickly and not provide any time for the external dependencies to resolve. Still, it might make sense to have this Pod be re-created if it stays unready for too long. Sometimes it's best just to turn it off and on again!

Unfortunately, Kubernetes doesn't have a way to express this logic directly, but it's easy enough to add it to our own liveness check so that it will fail if the Pod doesn't become ready in a certain amount of time. You can simply record the time of each readiness success response and then fail your liveness check if too much time passes (e.g., 5 minutes). The following listing provides a simple implementation of this logic into the `timeserver` container.

Listing 4.5 Chapter04/timeserver3/server.py

```python
from http.server import ThreadingHTTPServer, BaseHTTPRequestHandler
from datetime import datetime, timedelta

last_ready_time = datetime.now()          ◁──────  The "last ready" time is initialized
                                                    at the current time to allow for
                                                    5 minutes after startup.
class RequestHandler(BaseHTTPRequestHandler):

    def do_GET(self):
        global last_ready_time

        match self.path:
            case '/':
                now = datetime.now()
                response_string = now.strftime("The time is %-I:%M %p, UTC.")
                self.respond_with(200, response_string)
            case '/healthz':
                if (datetime.now() > last_ready_time + timedelta(minutes=5)):
                    self.respond_with(503, "Not Healthy")
                else:
                    self.respond_with(200, "Healthy")
            case '/readyz':
                dependencies_connected = True
                # TODO: actually verify any dependencies
```

If 5 minutes have passed since the last successful readiness result (or since boot), fail the liveness check.

```
                  if (dependencies_connected):
                      last_ready_time = datetime.now()    ◁────┐  Each time the
                      self.respond_with(200, "Ready")           │  readiness passes,
                  else:                                          │  the time is updated.
                      self.respond_with(503, "Not Ready")
              case _:
                  self.respond_with(404, "Not Found")

      def respond_with(self, status_code: int, content: str) -> None:
          self.send_response(status_code)
          self.send_header('Content-type', 'text/plain')
          self.end_headers()
          self.wfile.write(bytes(content, "utf-8"))

  def startServer():
      try:
          server = ThreadingHTTPServer(('', 80), RequestHandler)
          print("Listening on " + ":".join(map(str, server.server_address)))
          server.serve_forever()
      except KeyboardInterrupt:
          server.shutdown()

  if __name__ == "__main__":
      startServer()
```

Having the liveness check fail eventually if the container doesn't become ready within a given timeframe gives it a chance to restart. Now, we have the best of both worlds: we don't test the external dependencies in the liveness check, but we do in the readiness one. That means our container won't receive traffic when its dependencies are not connected, but it's not rebooted either, giving it some time to self-heal. But if, after 5 minutes, the container is still not ready, it will fail the liveness check and be restarted.

An alternative approach to achieve this (restarting the container after a prolonged period of unreadiness) is to use the readiness endpoint for both the liveness and readiness probes but with different tolerances. That is, for example, the readiness check fails after 30 seconds, but liveness fails only after 5 minutes. This approach still gives the container some time to resolve any interdependent services before eventually rebooting in the event of continued downtime, which may indicate a problem with the container itself. This technique is not technically idiomatic Kubernetes, as you're still testing dependencies in the liveness check, but it gets the job done.

In conclusion, these two probes are incredibly important to giving Kubernetes the information it needs to automate the reliability of your application. Understanding the difference between them and implementing appropriate checks that take into account the specific details of your application are crucial.

4.1.6 *Probe types*

Until now, the examples have assumed an HTTP service, and the probes therefore were implemented as HTTP requests. Kubernetes can be used to host many different types of services, as well as batch jobs with no service endpoints at all. Fortunately, there are a number of ways to expose health checks.

HTTP

HTTP is recommended for any container that provides an HTTP service. The service exposes an endpoint, such as `/healthz`. An HTTP 200 response indicates success; any other response (or timeout) indicates a failure.

TCP

TCP is recommended for TCP-based services other than HTTP (e.g., a SMTP service). The probe succeeds if the connection can be opened:

```
readinessProbe:
  initialDelaySeconds: 15
  periodSeconds: 30
  tcpSocket:               TCP probe
    port: 25               specification
  successThreshold: 1
  failureThreshold: 1
```

BASH SCRIPT

A bash script is recommended for any container not providing an HTTP or a TCP service, such as batch jobs that don't run service endpoints. Kubernetes will execute the script you specify, allowing you to perform whatever tests you need. A nonzero exit code indicates failure. Section 10.4 has a complete example of a liveness probe for a background task.

4.2 *Updating live applications*

Once you've implemented readiness checks, you can now roll out changes to your application without downtime. Kubernetes uses the readiness check during updates to know when the new Pod is ready to receive traffic and to govern the rate of the rollout according to the parameters you set. You can choose from several different rollout strategies, each with its own characteristics.

4.2.1 *Rolling update strategy*

The default zero-downtime update strategy offered by Kubernetes is a rolling update. In a rolling update, Pods with the new version are created in groups (the size of which is tunable). Kubernetes waits for the new group of Pods to become available and then terminates the same number of Pods running the old version, repeating this until all Pods are running the new version (figure 4.2).

The goal of such a strategy is twofold:

- Providing continuous uptime during the rollout
- Using as few extra resources as possible during the update

Importantly, with this strategy, the two versions of your application (old and new) need to be able to coexist as they will both be running for a time. That is, your backend or any other dependencies must be able to handle these two different versions, and users may get alternating versions when they make different requests. Imagine reloading the page and seeing the new version and then reloading it and seeing the old version

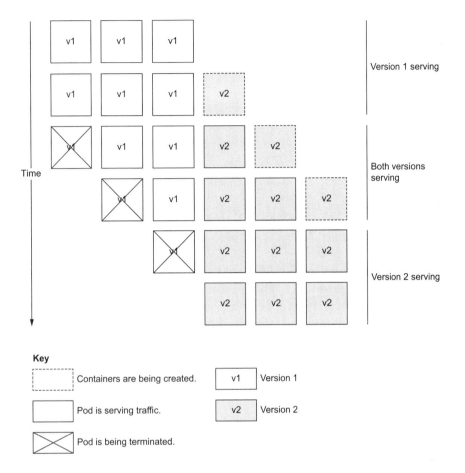

Key

☐ (dashed)   Containers are being created.

☐   Pod is serving traffic.

☒   Pod is being terminated.

| v1 | Version 1 |
| v2 | Version 2 |

Figure 4.2   Pod status during a rolling update. With this strategy, requests can be served by either the old or the new version of the app until the rollout is complete.

again. Depending on how many replicas you have, a rolling update can take a while to complete (and, therefore, any rollback can also take a while).

Let's configure our Deployment to use the rolling update strategy in the following listing.

Listing 4.6   Chapter04/4.2.1_RollingUpdate/deploy.yaml

```
apiVersion: apps/v1
kind: Deployment
metadata:
  name: timeserver
spec:
  replicas: 3
  selector:
    matchLabels:
      pod: timeserver-pod
```

Rolling update strategy

```
strategy:
  type: RollingUpdate
  rollingUpdate:
    maxSurge: 2
    maxUnavailable: 1          Optional
                               configuration
template:
  metadata:
    labels:
      pod: timeserver-pod
  spec:
    containers:
    - name: timeserver-container
      image: docker.io/wdenniss/timeserver:3
```

The options `maxSurge` and `maxUnavailable` can be used to govern how quickly the rollout happens.

MAXSURGE

`maxSurge` governs how many additional Pods you're willing to create during the rollout. For example, if you set a replica count of `5`, and a `maxSurge` of `2`, then it may be possible to have seven Pods (of different versions) scheduled.

The tradeoff is that the higher this number is, the faster the rollout will complete, but the more resources it will (temporarily) use. If you're highly optimizing your costs, you could set `maxSurge` to `0`. Alternatively, for a large deployment, you could temporarily increase the resources available in your cluster during the rollout by adding nodes and removing them when the rollout is complete.

MAXUNAVAILABLE

`maxUnavailable` sets the maximum number of Pods that can be unavailable during updates (percentage values are also accepted and are rounded down to the nearest integer). If you've tuned your replica count to handle your expected traffic, you may not want to set this value much higher than `0`, as your service quality could degrade during updates. The tradeoff here is that the higher the value, the more Pods can be replaced at once and the faster the rollout completes, while temporarily reducing the number of ready Pods that are able to process traffic.

A rollout could coincide with another event that lowers availability, like a node failure. Thus, for production workloads, I recommend setting `maxUnavailable` to `0`. The caveat is that if you set it to `0` and your cluster has no schedulable resources, the rollout will get stuck, and you will see Pods in the `Pending` state until resources become available. When `maxUnavailable` is `0`, `maxSurge` cannot also be `0` because, to preserve the full availability, the system needs to temporarily increase the replica count to allow time for the new Pods to become ready.

RECOMMENDATION

A rolling update is a good go-to strategy for most services. For production services, `maxUnavailable` is best set to `0`. `maxSurge` should be at least `1`, or higher if you have enough spare capacity and want faster rollouts.

DEPLOYING CHANGES WITH A ROLLING UPDATE

Once your Deployment is configured to use a rolling update, deploying your changes is as simple as updating the Deployment manifest (e.g., with a new container version) and applying the changes with `kubectl apply`. Most changes made to the Deployment, including readiness and liveness checks, are also versioned and will be rolled out just like a new container image version. If you ever need, you can also force a rollout without changing anything in the Deployment object with `kubectl rollout restart deploy $DEPLOYMENT_NAME`.

4.2.2 Re-create strategy

Another approach—some might say, the old-fashion approach—is to cut the application over directly, deleting all Pods of the old version and scheduling replacements of the new version. Unlike the other strategies discussed here, this approach is *not* a zero-downtime one. It will almost certainly result in some unavailability (figure 4.3). With the right readiness checks in place, this downtime could be as short as the time to boot the

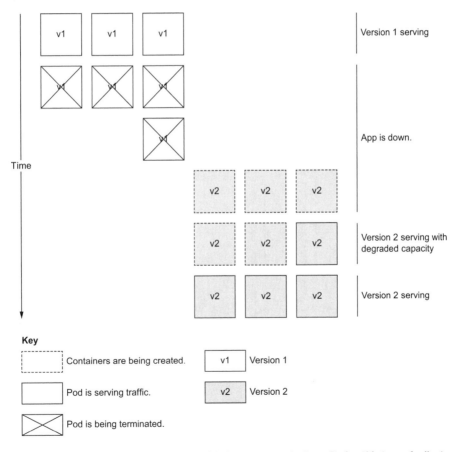

Figure 4.3 A Pod status during a rollout with the re-create strategy. During this type of rollout, the app will experience a period of total downtime and a period of degraded capacity.

first Pod, assuming it can handle the client traffic at that moment in time. The benefit of this strategy is that it does not require compatibility between the new version and the old version (since the two versions won't be running at the same time), and it doesn't require any additional compute capacity (since it's a direct replacement).

This strategy may be useful for development and staging environments to avoid needing to overprovision compute capacity to handle rolling updates, and to increase speed, but otherwise, it should generally be avoided. To use this, in the `strategy` field given in listing 4.6, you would instead declare:

```
strategy:
  type: Recreate
```

4.2.3   *Blue/green strategy*

The blue/green strategy is a rollout strategy where the new application version is deployed alongside the existing version (figure 4.4). These versions are given the names

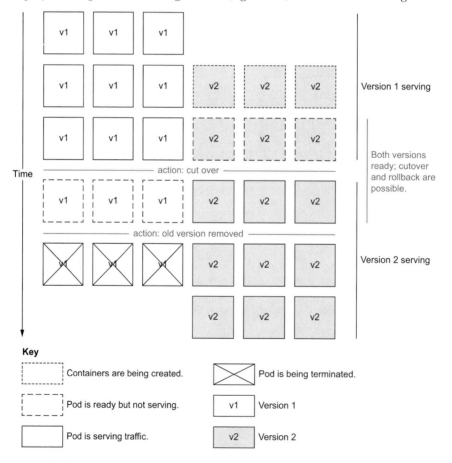

Figure 4.4   A Pod status during a blue/green rollout. Unlike the previous strategies, there are two action points where other systems, potentially including human actors, make decisions.

"blue" and "green." When the new version is fully deployed, tested, and ready to go, the service is cut over. If there's a problem, it can be immediately cut back. After a time, if everything looks good, the old version can be removed. Unlike the prior two strategies, the old version remains ready to serve and is removed only when the new version is validated (and often with a human decision involved).

The benefits of this strategy include the following:

- Only one version of the app is running at a time for a consistent user experience.
- The rollout is fast (within seconds).
- Rollbacks are similarly fast.

The drawbacks include the following:

- It temporarily consumes double the compute resources.
- It is not supported directly by Kubernetes Deployments.

This approach is an advanced rollout strategy, popular with large deployments. There are often several other processes included. For example, when the new version is ready, it can be tested first by a set of internal users, followed by a percentage of external traffic prior to the 100% cutover—a process known as *canary analysis*. After the cutover, there is often a period of time where the new version continues to be evaluated prior to the old version being scaled down (this could last days). Of course, keeping both versions scaled up doubles the resource usage, with the tradeoff that near-instant rollbacks are possible during that window.

Unlike the prior two strategies—rolling updates and re-create—there is no in-built Kubernetes support for blue/green. Typically, users will use additional tooling to help with the complexities of such a rollout. Such tools include Istio, to split traffic at a fine-grained level, and Spinnaker, to help automate the deployment pipeline with the canary analysis and decision points.

Despite the lack of in-built support, it is possible to perform a blue/green rollout in Kubernetes. Without the aforementioned tools to help with the pipeline and traffic splitting, it is a slightly manual process and missing some benefits, like being able to do canary analysis on a tiny percentage of production traffic. However, that doesn't mean it's hard to implement.

Recall the Deployment and Service we deployed in chapter 3. Employing a blue/green strategy for this application simply requires having one extra Deployment. Duplicate the Deployment and give one a suffix of -blue, and the other -green. This suffix should be applied to the name of the Deployment and the Pod's label. You can then direct traffic from your Service by selecting either the -blue or the -green labeled Pods.

The update strategy you would specify in the Deployment configuration in this case is the Recreate strategy. Since only the Pods in the inactive Deployment are updated, deleting all the old versions and creating Pods with the new version won't result in downtime and is faster than a rolling update.

The Service's selector is used to decide which version to route traffic to (figure 4.5). In this two-Deployment system, one version is live, and one is not live at any given time. The Service selects the Pods of the live Deployment with the label selector.

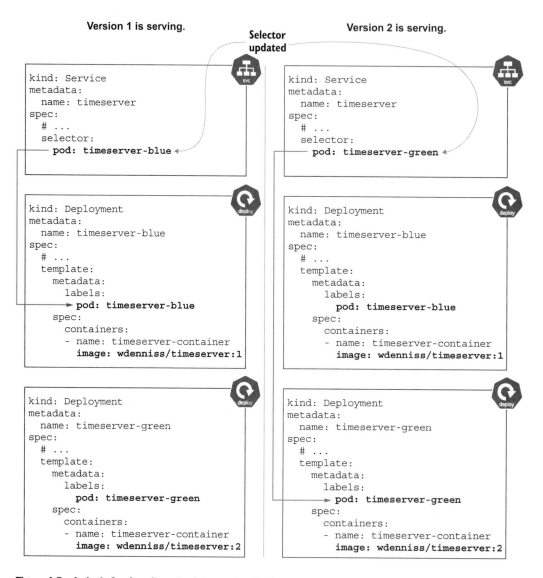

Figure 4.5   A single Service alternates between two Deployments, each with a different version of the container.

The steps to roll out a new version with blue/green are as follows:

1 Identify the nonlive Deployment (the one not selected by the Service).
2 Update the image path of the nonlive Deployment with the new container image version.

3 Wait until the Deployment is fully rolled out (`kubectl get deploy`).

4 Update the Service's selector to point to the new version's Pod labels.

The update steps are performed by modifying the YAML configuration for the resource in question and applying the changes with `kubectl apply`. The next time you want to roll out a change to this application, the steps are the same, but the labels are reversed (if blue was live for the last update, green will be live next time).

As mentioned, this strategy doubles the number of Pods used by the Deployment, which will likely affect your resource usage. To minimize resource costs, you can scale the nonlive Deployment to `0` when you're not currently doing a rollout and scale it back up to match the live version when you're about to do a rollout. You'll likely need to adjust the number of nodes in your cluster as well (covered in chapter 6).

4.2.4 *Choosing a rollout strategy*

For most Deployments, one of the built-in rollout strategies should suffice. Use `RollingUpdate` as an easy way to get zero-downtime updates on Kubernetes. To achieve zero downtime or disruption, you will also need to have a readiness check implemented; otherwise, traffic can be sent to your container before it has fully booted. Two versions of your application can serve traffic simultaneously, so you must design attributes like data formats with that in mind. Being able to support at least the current and previous version is generally good practice anyway, as it also allows you to roll back to the previous version if something goes wrong.

`Recreate` is a useful strategy when you really don't want two application versions running at the same time. It can be useful for things like legacy single-instance services where only one copy can exist at a time.

Blue/green is an advanced-level strategy that requires additional tooling or processes but comes with the advantage of near-instant cutovers while offering the best of both worlds in that only one version is live at a time but without the downtime of the `Recreate` strategy. I recommend getting started with the in-built strategies but keep this one in mind for when you need something more.

Summary

- Kubernetes provides many tools to help you keep your deployments running and updated.
- It's important to define health checks so that Kubernetes has the signals it needs to keep your application running by rebooting containers that are stuck or nonresponsive.
- Liveness probes are used by Kubernetes to determine when your application needs restarting.
- The readiness probe governs which replicas receive traffic from the Service, which is particularly important during updates to prevent dropped requests.
- Kubernetes can also help update your application without downtime.

- `RollingUpdate` is the default rollout strategy in Kubernetes, giving you a zero-downtime rollout while using minimal additional resources.
- `Recreate` is an alternative rollout strategy that does an in-place update with some downtime but no additional resource usage.
- Blue/green is a rollout strategy that isn't directly supported by Kubernetes but can still be performed using standard Kubernetes constructs.
- Blue/green offers some of the highest-quality guarantees but is more complex and temporarily doubles the resources needed by the deployment.

Resource management

Chapter 2 covered how containers are the new level of isolation, each with its own resources, and chapter 3 discussed the schedulable unit in Kubernetes, a Pod (which itself is a collection of containers). This chapter covers how Pods are allocated to machines based on their resource requirements and the information that you need to give the system so that your Pod will receive the resources that it needs. Knowing how Pods are allocated to nodes helps you make better architectural decisions around resource requests, bursting, overcommit, availability, and reliability.

5.1   *Pod scheduling*

The Kubernetes scheduler performs a resource-based allocation of Pods to nodes and is really the brains of the whole system. When you submit your configuration to Kubernetes (as we did in chapters 3 and 4), it's the scheduler that does the heavy lifting of finding a node in your cluster with enough resources and tasks the node with booting and running the containers in your Pods (figure 5.1).

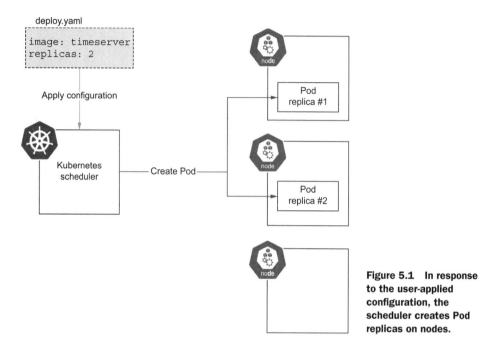

Figure 5.1   In response to the user-applied configuration, the scheduler creates Pod replicas on nodes.

The scheduler and related components' work doesn't stop there. In the case of the Deployment object (what we've been using in the book so far), it continuously monitors the system with the goal of making the system state what you requested it to be. In other words, if your Deployment requests two replicas of your Pod, the scheduler doesn't just create those replicas and then forget about them; it will keep verifying that there are still two replicas running. If something happens (e.g., a node disappeared due to some failure), it would attempt to find a new place to schedule the Pod so that your desired state (in this case, two replicas) is still met (figure 5.2).

The re-creation of Pods due to node failures by the scheduler is a separate behavior from the Pod restarts we covered in the last chapter. Pod restarts due to liveness or readiness failures are handled locally on the node by the kubelet, whereas the scheduler is responsible for monitoring the health of the nodes and reallocating Pods when problems are detected.

Since each node in the cluster is constrained by the available resources and Pods themselves may have different resource requirements, an important responsibility of

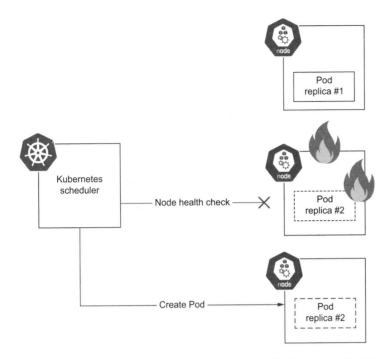

Figure 5.2 If one of the nodes develops a problem, health checks from the Kubernetes control plane fail. So, the scheduler creates a new Pod replica on a healthy node.

the scheduler is finding enough room to run your Pods (figure 5.3). It considers multiple scheduling dimensions when deciding where to place the containers of your Pod in the cluster, both the first time they're deployed and in response to disruption, like the one illustrated in figure 5.2.

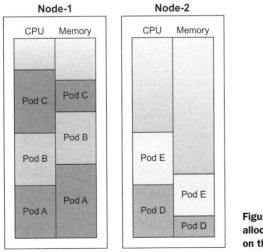

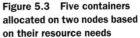

Figure 5.3 Five containers allocated on two nodes based on their resource needs

The scheduler has the task of finding the right place in your cluster to fit the Pod, based on its resource requirements and (as we'll cover in chapter 8) any other placement requirements. Any Pods that can't be placed in the cluster will have the status `Pending` (see the advice titled "Troubleshooting: Stuck in Pending" in chapter 3 if you have Pods that remain in this status for too long).

5.1.1   Specifying Pod resources

You give the scheduler the information it needs to make scheduling decisions by specifying the resource requests in your Deployment manifest (and other workload types that have an embedded Pod specification). So far, the examples in this book have not specified their resource requirements, but for production-grade deployments, this information needs to be added. A Pod that needs 20% of the time for one CPU core and 200MiB of memory would be specified as in the following listing.

> **Listing 5.1   Chapter05/5.1.1_PodResources/deploy_requests.yaml**

```yaml
apiVersion: apps/v1
kind: Deployment
metadata:
  name: timeserver
spec:
  replicas: 3
  selector:
    matchLabels:
      pod: timeserver-pod
  template:
    metadata:
      labels:
        pod: timeserver-pod
    spec:
      containers:
      - name: timeserver-container
        image: docker.io/wdenniss/timeserver:3
        resources:
          requests:
            cpu: 200m          The resource requests
            memory: 250Mi      of this container
```

The `200m` in the example here represents 200 millicores—that is, 20% of one core. You can also use floating-point numbers (e.g., `0.2`); however, it's very common among Kubernetes practitioners to use millicores. The `Mi` suffix for memory indicates mebibytes (MiB), and `Gi` indicates gibibyte (powers of 1,024). `M` and `G` indicate megabyte and gigabyte (powers of 1,000).

Specifying resources is important as it gives Kubernetes the information it needs to match the Pod requirements to the node capacity. Not specifying resources on some Pods will mean that they get placed somewhat randomly on nodes. Compare the side-by-side in figure 5.4. On the left, we have five Pods that have been placed on two nodes based on their requirements, while on the right three of the Pods have no resources specified so are just thrown on the same node as the other Pods. Notice how half the node resources have been allocated for the same 5 Pods when resources were not specified. The risk here is that the Pods with no resource specification could get starved of resources, or evicted if they use more memory than available on the node.

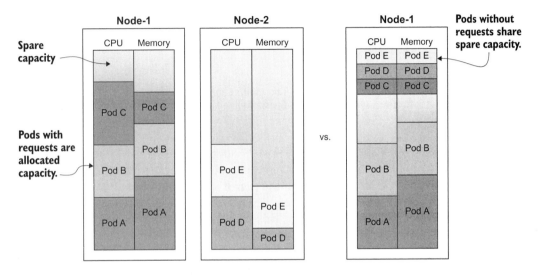

Figure 5.4 Comparison of Pod allocation when all Pods have resource requests and when only some do. Pods without resource requests share the spare capacity on a best-effort basis, without regard to their actual needs.

Kubernetes' Pod placement may sound fairly simple so far—we're just pairing the requests with the resources. It would, in fact, be simple if not for the ability to *burst*—that is, consume more resources than requested. Much of the time, a process may not need all the resources it asks for. Wouldn't it be good if the other Pods on the node could use that capacity on a temporary basis? That's exactly what Kubernetes offers, and it's configured with *limits*. A Pod (like the one in the following listing) declares the resources they request, which are used for scheduling, and sets limits, which constrain the resources used once the Pod is scheduled and running.

Listing 5.2 Chapter05/5.1.1_PodResources/deploy_requests_limits.yaml

```
apiVersion: apps/v1
kind: Deployment
metadata:
  name: timeserver
spec:
  replicas: 3
  selector:
```

```
    matchLabels:
      pod: timeserver-pod
  template:
    metadata:
      labels:
        pod: timeserver-pod
    spec:
      containers:
      - name: timeserver-container
        image: docker.io/wdenniss/timeserver:3
        resources:
          requests:
            cpu: 200m
            memory: 250Mi
          limits:
            cpu: 300m
            memory: 400Mi
```

> **limits:** The resource limits of this container. The container can use up to 30% of a CPU core and 400 MiB memory.

When placing Pods on nodes, the scheduler only takes into account the Pod's resource requests (the limit isn't factored at all when scheduling). Both requests and limits, however, have an impact on the performance of running Pods.

Once running, a Pod that exceeds its memory *limit* will be restarted, and one that exceeds its CPU limit will be throttled. These actions are handled directly on the node, governed by the kubelet.

In times of resource contention, Pods that exceed their memory *request* may be evicted (see section 5.1.3 for how Pods are chosen for eviction), and those exceeding their CPU requests throttled to the requested CPU.

Since these values play such an important role in how the Pod is scheduled and run, it is best practice to have both requests and limits set for the containers in your Pods. But how do you determine what to set them at? Read on to understand how the requests and limits interact to form a quality of service (QoS) class and how you can measure your application's performance to determine what values to set.

5.1.2 Quality of service

Having limits higher than requests, or not set at all, introduces a new problem: what should you do when these Pods consume too many resources (most commonly, too much memory), and they need to be evicted to reclaim the resource? To solve this, Kubernetes ranks Pods to choose which to remove first.

When planning your workloads, consider the qualify of service that they require. Kubernetes offers three quality of service levels: guaranteed, burstable, and best effort.

GUARANTEED CLASS

In guaranteed class Pods, the limits are set equal to the requests. This configuration is the most stable as the Pod is guaranteed the resources it requested—no more, no less. If your Pod has multiple containers, they all must meet this requirement for the Pod to be considered guaranteed.

Guaranteed class Pods will always have the same resources available under varying conditions, and they won't be evicted from the node as it's not possible for them to use more resources than they were scheduled for.

BURSTABLE CLASS

Burstable class Pods have limits set higher than requests and can "burst" temporarily, provided resources are available (i.e., from other Pods that are not using all of their requests or unallocated space on the node). You need to be careful with these Pods as there can be some unforeseen consequences, such as accidentally relying on the bursting. Say a Pod lands on an empty node and can burst to its heart's content. Then, sometime later, it gets rescheduled onto another node with less resources; the performance will now be different. So, it's important to test burstable Pods in a variety of conditions. A Pod with multiple containers is considered burstable if it doesn't meet the criteria for guaranteed class and if any of the containers has a request set. These Pods are safe from eviction unless they exceed their requests of a noncompressible resource like memory.

BEST EFFORT

Pods without any requests or limits set are considered "best effort" and are scheduled wherever Kubernetes wishes. This setup is the lowest of the classes, and I strongly recommend against using this pattern. You can achieve a similar result with the burstable class by setting very low requests, and that is more explicit than just closing your eyes and hoping for the best.

When thinking about the stability of your Pods, it's always best to at least set the resource requests to a value high enough to give them resources to run and avoid not setting any resource requests at all. High-priority, critical workloads should always have limits set to their requests for guaranteed performance. These Pods are the first to be evicted from a node in times of resource contention.

5.1.3   Evictions, priority, and preemption

In times of resource contention of finite resources like memory (e.g., too many Pods trying to burst memory usage at once), Kubernetes will reclaim resources by removing Pods that are using resources beyond their requested allocation through a process known as *evicting*. Thus, it's very important to have a Pod's resources adequately specified. Evicted Pods that belong to a manged workload construct like Deployment will be rescheduled on the cluster, typically on another node. If your Pod is evicted too frequently though, it may reduce the availability of the workload and is a sign you should increase the resource requests.

EVICTION

Guaranteed class Pods are never evicted in times of resource contention, so for a bulletproof deployment, always set your Pods' limits equal to their requests to define them as guaranteed. The rest of this section discusses how the nonguaranteed Pods are ranked when considering eviction and how you can influence the ordering.

When looking for Pods to evict, Kubernetes first considers those Pods that are using more resources than their requests and sorts them by their priority number and then by how many more resources (of the resource in contention) the Pod is using beyond what it requested. Since best effort QoS class Pods have no resource requests, they will be the first evicted (starting with the ones using the most resources). By default, all Pods of the same priority number (0) and for Pods of the same priority, the amount of usage above requests is what's used to rank them, as shown in figure 5.5.

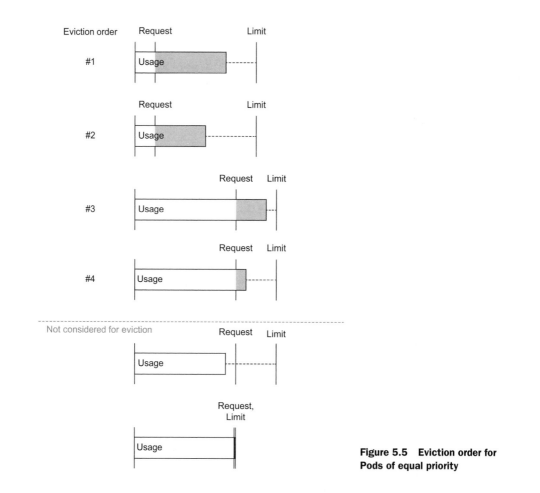

Figure 5.5   Eviction order for Pods of equal priority

EVICTED ERROR STATUS

If you query your Pods and you see a status of `Evicted`, it indicates that the scheduler evicted a Pod because it was using more resources than it requested. This may be acceptable if it happens occasionally, but if you are seeing frequent evictions, increase the resources requested by your containers and review whether you need to add more compute capacity to your cluster.

PRIORITY

Priority is just an integer number (between 0 and 1,000,000,000) that you can assign to Pods via a priority class to change the ranking. Figure 5.6 shows the eviction order when priority numbers are assigned to the Pods from figure 5.5. As you can see, the eviction is first sorted by the priority and then how much the usage is above requests. Pods that are not using more than their requests are not at risk of eviction, regardless of priority.

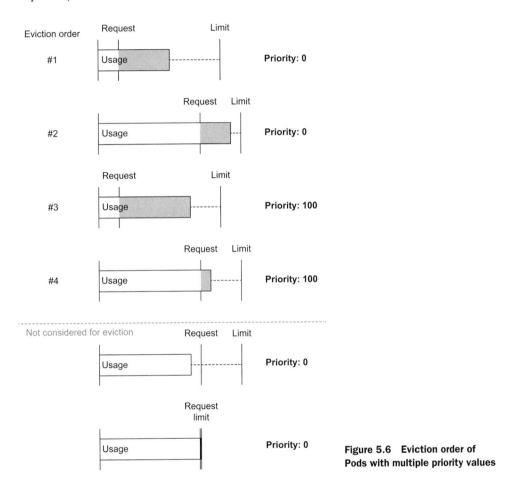

Figure 5.6 Eviction order of Pods with multiple priority values

To create your own priority level, you need to first create a PriorityClass object.

Listing 5.3   Chapter05/5.1.3_Priority/priorityclass.yaml

```
apiVersion: scheduling.k8s.io/v1
kind: PriorityClass
metadata:
  name: high-priority          The priority
value: 1000000                  integer
```

```
preemptionPolicy: Never
globalDefault: false
description: "Critical services."
```

This priority class won't cause eviction of lower priority Pods if there is no available capacity in the cluster.

Whether this priority class should be the default

Then assign the PriorityClass object to a Pod.

Listing 5.4   Chapter05/5.1.3_Priority/deploy.yaml

```
apiVersion: apps/v1
kind: Deployment
metadata:
  name: timeserver
spec:
  replicas: 3
  selector:
    matchLabels:
      pod: timeserver-pod
  template:
    metadata:
      labels:
        pod: timeserver-pod
    spec:
      priorityClassName: high-priority
      containers:
      - name: timeserver-container
        image: docker.io/wdenniss/timeserver:3
        resources:
          requests:
            cpu: 200m
            memory: 250Mi
```

The priority class to use for this Deployment

The priority number is also used during scheduling. If you have many Pods waiting to be scheduled, the scheduler will schedule the highest-priority Pod first. Using priority to govern the scheduling order is particularly useful for ranking which batch jobs should execute first (batch jobs are covered in chapter 10).

PREEMPTION

When used by itself, priority is useful to rank workloads so that more important workloads are scheduled first and evicted last. There can be a situation, however, where the cluster does not have enough resources for a period of time, and high-priority Pods are left stuck in `Pending` while low-priority ones are already running.

If you'd rather have higher-priority workloads proactively bump lower-priority ones rather than waiting for capacity to free up, you can add preemption behavior by changing the `preemptionPolicy` field in your `PriorityClass` as shown in the following listing.

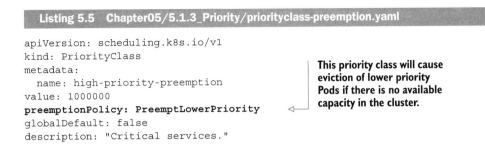

Listing 5.5 Chapter05/5.1.3_Priority/priorityclass-preemption.yaml

```
apiVersion: scheduling.k8s.io/v1
kind: PriorityClass
metadata:
  name: high-priority-preemption
value: 1000000
preemptionPolicy: PreemptLowerPriority
globalDefault: false
description: "Critical services."
```

This priority class will cause eviction of lower priority Pods if there is no available capacity in the cluster.

Fortunately, Kubernetes does not forget about Pods removed from the node due to eviction or preemption provided they belong to a Deployment or other managed workload type. These Pods are returned to the `Pending` state and will be rescheduled on the cluster when there is enough capacity. This is another important reason why you should always use a workload construct like Deployment, as standalone Pods evicted in this way will not be rescheduled.

WHEN TO USE PRIORITY AND PREEMPTION

Priority and preemption are useful Kubernetes features and are important to understand due to their effect on eviction and scheduling. Before spending too much time configuring all your Deployments with a priority, I would prioritize ensuring that your Pod requests and limits are appropriate, as that is the most important configuration.

Priority and preemption really come into play when you're juggling many deployments and looking to save money by squeezing every ounce of compute out of your cluster by overcommitting, which requires that you have a way to signal the relative importance of your Pods to resolve the resource contention. I wouldn't recommend starting with this design, as you're just adding complexity. The simpler way to get started is to allocate enough resources to schedule all your workloads amply and fine-tune things later to squeeze some more efficiency out of your cluster. Once again, the simplest way to guarantee the performance of your critical services is to set the resource requests appropriately and have enough nodes in your cluster for them all to be scheduled.

5.2   Calculating Pod resources

In the previous section, we discussed why it's important to set appropriate resource requests and limits for Pods for the most reliable operational experience. But how do you determine what the best values are? The key is to run and observe your Pods.

Kubernetes ships with a resource usage monitoring tool out of the box, `kubectl top`. You can use it to view the resources used by Pods and nodes. We'll be focusing on Pods as that's what we need to know to set the right resource request.

First, deploy your Pod with an excessively high resource request. This Pod may already be deployed in production—after all, it's generally OK for performance (although not always for budget) to overestimate your resources needed. The goal of this exercise is to start high, observe the Pod's actual usage, and then pair the requests back to provision the right resources and avoid waste.

Until you have a good feel for how many resources the Pod needs, it may be best to leave the limits unset (allowing it to use all the spare resources on the node). This doesn't completely solve the need to set *some* resource requests, as you would prefer to be allocated dedicated capacity above what you need at first.

Listing 5.6   Chapter05/5.2_ResourceUsageTest/deploy.yaml

```
apiVersion: apps/v1
kind: Deployment
metadata:
  name: timeserver            Replicas set
spec:                         to 1 for the
  replicas: 1          ◁──┘   load test
  selector:
    matchLabels:
      pod: timeserver-pod
  template:
    metadata:
      labels:
        pod: timeserver-pod
    spec:
      containers:
      - name: timeserver-container
        image: docker.io/wdenniss/timeserver:3
        resources:        ◁──┐
          requests:           The Pod under test.
            cpu: 200m         Resource limits are not set
            memory: 250Mi     so we can analyze usage.
```

Run `kubectl top pods` (you may need to wait a minute or two for the data to be available) and note the startup resource usage, particularly memory. It's useful to have a snapshot of what resources the Pod needs to boot, as this amount is the lower bound if you choose to use burstable QoS.

NOTE   If you're using Minikube and get an error like `error: Metrics API not available`, you can enable metrics with `minikube addons enable metrics-server`.

Now, direct enough load at the Pod to simulate real-world usage. Performance tools like Apache Bench (installed with Apache[1]) can help here. An example Apache Bench command that will generate 10,000 requests total using 20 threads follows. You typically want to run this test for a while (say, 5 minutes) to make it simpler to observe the high-water mark:

```
kubectl get svc
EXTERNAL_IP=203.0.113.16
ab -n 10000 -c 20 http://$EXTERNAL_IP/
```

---

[1] http://httpd.apache.org/docs/2.4/install.html

You can also observe a Pod receiving a normal production load. Since you don't want to overly constrain a Pod in production until you know what resources it needs, you should start by overestimating the resource requests, and then measuring the actual usage. Once you have a good measure of the actual needs, you can later tune the requests and right-size.

With your Pod under load, run `kubectl top pods` again (remembering that it can take a minute or two to reflect the latest values, so keep your load simulation running). The output will look something like:

```
$ kubectl top pod
NAME                        CPU(cores)      MEMORY(bytes)
timeserver-dd88988f5-tq2d9  145m            11Mi
```

Once your testing is complete for your own Pod, you should have values like those shown in table 5.1 (the data in this table is purely an example).

Table 5.1 Memory and CPU usage from startup and under load

	CPU (cores)	Memory (bytes)
Startup	20m	200Mi
Under normal Load	200m	400Mi

It may be useful to repeat this process a couple more times and get values for your Pod under different loads (e.g., low, normal, and high traffic) and timeframes. Multiple timeframes (e.g., directly after boot, 1 hour after boot, 1 day after boot) are useful to account for potential growth in usage (e.g., memory leaks). So, you might end up with something like what's in table 5.2.

Table 5.2 Memory and CPU usage after testing

	CPU (cores)	Memory (bytes)
Startup	20m	400Mi
Under normal load	200m	500Mi
Under high load	850m	503Mi
After 1 hour	210m	505Mi
After 1 day	200m	600Mi

5.2.1 Setting memory requests and limits

With this data in hand, how should you set your resource requests? For starters, you now have an absolute lower bound for your memory: 400 MiB. Since you're only guaranteed to get your resource request and you know your Pod uses 400 MiB under load, setting it any lower will likely cause your Pod to be OOMKilled (terminated for being out of memory). You may not see it right away if you have a higher resource limit set, but you don't want to rely on spare capacity when you know you'll need it.

Does that make 400 MiB the right request? Probably not. First, you definitely want to have a buffer, say 10%. Also, you can see that after an hour, 505 MiB was used, so this might be a better starting lower bound (before accounting for the buffer). Does it need to be 600 MiB, though? We saw that, after a day, the Pod needed that much, possibly due to a leak somewhere. This answer depends. You certainly could set this higher limit, and then you could have some confidence that your Pod could run for a day. However, thanks to Kubernetes' automatic restarting of crashed containers, having the system reboot a leaky process after a day to reclaim memory may be OK, or even desirable.

When memory leaks are OK

Instagram famously[a] disabled the garbage collection in Python for a 10% CPU improvement. While this is probably not for everyone, it's an interesting pattern to consider. Does it really matter if a process gets bloated over time and is rebooted if it all happens automatically and there are thousands of replicas? Maybe not.

Kubernetes automatically restarts crashed containers (including when that crash is due to the system removing them due to an out-of-memory condition), making it fairly easy to implement such a pattern. I wouldn't recommend this strategy without thorough investigation, but I do think if your application has a slow leak, it may not be your highest priority bug to fix.

Importantly, you need to make sure you at least give the container enough resources to boot and run for a time. Otherwise, you could get caught in an OOMKill crash loop, which is no fun for anyone. Having enough replicas (covered in the next section) is also important to avoid a user-visible failure.

---

[a] https://instagram-engineering.com/dismissing-python-garbage-collection-at-instagram-4dca40b29172

Using the data you gathered, find the lower bound by looking at the memory usage of your Pod under load and add a reasonable buffer (at least 10%). With this example data, I would pick 505 MiB * 1.1 ≈ 555 MiB. You know it's enough to run the Pod under load for at least an hour, with a bit to spare. Depending on your budget and risk profile, you can tune this number accordingly (the higher it is, the lower the risk, but the higher the cost).

So, requests need to at least cover the stable state of the Pod. What about the memory *limit*? Assuming your data is solid and covers all cases (i.e., no high-memory code path that didn't execute while you were observing), I wouldn't set it too much higher than the one-day value. Having an excessive limit (say, twice as high as the limit or greater) doesn't really help much since you already measured how much memory your Pods need over the course of a day. If you do have a memory leak, it may be better for the system to restart the Pod when the limit is hit rather than allow the Pod to grow excessively.

An alternative is to simply set the limit equal to the request for the guaranteed QoS class. This strategy has the advantage of giving your Pod constant performance regardless of what else is running on the node. In this case, you should give the Pod a little extra resource buffer since the Pod will be terminated the moment it exceeds its requested amount.

5.2.2 Setting CPU requests and limits

Unlike memory, CPU is *compressible*. In other words, if the application doesn't get all the CPU resources it needs, it just runs slower. This is quite different from memory: if the application runs out of memory it will crash. You still likely want to give the application enough CPU resources. Otherwise, performance will decrease, but there's not as much need to have a buffer of extra capacity as there is with memory.

In the example data for our application shown in table 5.2, we can see that the stable state is about 200 mCPU of the CPU. That would seem to be a good starting point for your CPU requests. If you want to save money and are OK with degrading performance, you could set it a little lower.

The CPU limit is an area where Kubernetes can improve your resource efficiency, as you can set a limit higher than your requests to enable your application to consume the unused cycles on the node if it needs to burst. As with memory, Kubernetes only guarantees the requested CPU, but often it's nice to allow the Pod to take advantage of unused capacity on the node to run a bit faster. For web applications that spend a lot of time waiting on external dependencies (e.g., waiting for a database to respond), spare CPU capacity is often available on the node, which the active request could take advantage of.

As with memory, the downside of setting limits to higher than requests (i.e., the burstable QoS class) is that your performance won't be constant. A burstable Pod running on an empty node will have a lot more resources than on a node packed with Pods. While, generally, it's nice to be able to handle bursts in traffic by consuming the unused capacity on the node, if constant performance is important, setting limits equal to requests may be preferable.

5.2.3 Reducing costs by overcommitting CPU

One strategy to reduce costs is to overcommit the CPU resources on the node. This overcommitment is achieved by setting the CPU request to a low value (lower than what the Pod actually needs) and therefore cramming more Pods onto the node than you could if you set the CPU request to the actual usage.

This strategy saves money but has an obvious performance drawback. However, in the case of workloads that are considered very *bursty*, it can be a very desirable strategy. Let's say you are hosting hundreds of low-traffic websites. Each may only get a few requests an hour, only needing the CPU for that time. For such a deployment, each application could have a CPU request of 50m (allowing 20 Pods to be scheduled per core) and a limit of 1000m (allowing it to temporarily burst to a full core).

The key to making an overcommitment strategy like this work is being intimately aware of what else is running on the machine. If you are confident that most of the websites will be idle most of the time, this approach could work. However, performance may be degraded if the containers in all Pods need to burst at once. This type of setup means that your containers are not isolated from each other anymore: now, you need to be aware of and plan the makeup of the node accordingly. However, it can be done.

The safest approach, of course, is not to overcommit at all. A sensible compromise is to just not overcommit too much. Giving Pods a little extra CPU (by setting their resource limits higher than their requests) can help reduce latency in an opportunistic fashion. However, you should set the CPU resource *requests* high enough to handle a reasonable base load so that this excess capacity isn't being relied on.

5.2.4 *Balancing Pod replicas and internal Pod concurrency*

Now that you have a handle on how resource requests influence how your Pods are scheduled and the resources they get, it's worth considering concurrency within the Pod. A Pod's concurrency (e.g., how many processes/threads of the application are running) influences the resource size, and there is a tradeoff of efficiency for durability by using concurrency within the Pod over Pod replicas.

If you're coming from an environment where installations of your application were expensive, either in monetary cost for servers or time to configure instances, your application will likely have a lot of internal concurrency configured through the use of threads or forks, often described as the number of workers used to handle incoming requests concurrently. Concurrent workers still have advantages in the Kubernetes world due to their resource efficiency. I wouldn't take a Pod that currently had 10 workers and instead deploy 10 replicas with one worker each. The container's internal concurrency is very efficient memorywise, as forks share some of the memory used by the application binary, and threads share even more. CPU is also pooled between workers, which is useful as a typical web application spends a lot of time waiting on external dependencies—meaning spare capacity is often available to handle many requests at once.

Balancing the benefits of concurrent workers in a single Pod is the fact that the more replicas of a Pod you have, the more durable it is. For example, say you have two replicas of a Pod, with 18 workers each, to handle a total of 36 concurrent connections as shown in figure 5.7. If one of those Pods crashes (or is restarted because it failed the health check you set up in chapter 4), half your capacity would be offline before the Pod restarts. A better approach might be to have six Pods replicas with six workers each, which still maintains some intercontainer concurrency while adding some redundancy.

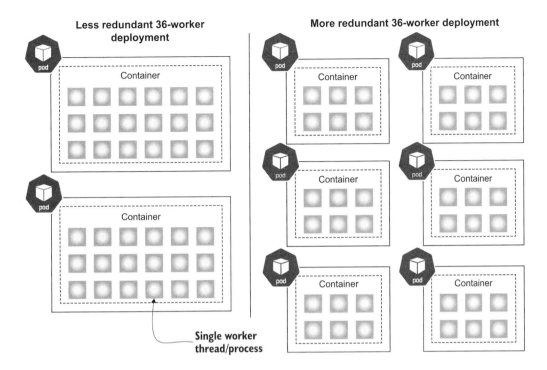

Figure 5.7   Comparison of two possible deployments for a total of 36 workers

To strike the right balance, a simple heuristic can be used. Consider the total number of workers you need to serve your users and, of those, how many can be offline at any given time without noticeable user effect. Once you've calculated how many can be offline—using our previous example, say 16% of the 36 workers can be offline before problems are noticed—then the most number of workers you can concentrate in a single Pod is 16%, or six.

In short, the more Pod replicas you have, the safer the design, but the less efficient in terms of resource usage. Thus, it's worth considering how to balance your own availability and resource requirements.

After balancing the number of Pod replicas you have, another important attribute to increase availability is to ensure that your Pods are spread across multiple nodes. After all, if you design for multiple replicas, but all those replicas run on the same node, you're still at risk from a single point of failure if that node were to become unhealthy. Fortunately, most Kubernetes platforms (including Google Kubernetes Engine) enable default Pod-spreading policies that will spread Pods over all available nodes and across multiple zones (in the case of a regional cluster). To get this default behavior, it's generally enough to ensure that you have a bunch of nodes in your cluster in different zones. If you want to dig more into node placement and Pod spread topologies, chapter 8 has you covered.

Summary

- The Kubernetes scheduler lies at the core of the system and does the heavy lifting of finding the right home for your Deployment's Pods on your infrastructure.
- The scheduler will try to fit as many Pods as it can on a given node, provided the Pod's containers have resource requests set appropriately.
- Kubernetes uses the Pod's resource requests and limits to govern how resources are allocated, overcommitted, and reclaimed.
- Overcommitting resources using bursting can save resources but introduces performance variability.
- The specification of requests and limits by your workloads sets the QoS they receive.
- When designing your workloads, there is an availability/resource-usage tradeoff between the replica count and the Pod's internal thread/process worker count.
- Most platforms enable Pod spreading by default to ensure that replicas are not generally placed on the same node, thus avoiding a single point of failure. Make sure you have a few nodes in your cluster to achieve higher availability.

Part 2

Going to production

Now that you have learned the fundamentals of Kubernetes, such as creating and deploying containers, setting resource limits, and configuring liveness and readiness probes for automation, it is time to take things to the next level. This part covers what you need to know to build production systems on Kubernetes. This includes tasks such as scaling your application up both manually and with automation, including designing the application so it can scale in the first place; connecting multiple services together, potentially managed by different teams; and storing the Kubernetes configuration alongside your code while keeping everything updated and secure.

Additional workload options are introduced beyond the stateless deployment covered in Part 1, including those that require state (attached disks), background queues, batch jobs, and daemon Pods that run on every node. You'll learn how to inform Kubernetes of your scheduling requirements, such as spreading out your Pods or locating them together and how to target specific hardware requirements like Arm architecture, GPU, and Spot compute.

Scaling up

This chapter covers

- Scaling Pods and nodes manually
- Using CPU utilization and other metrics to scale Pod replicas dynamically
- Utilizing managed platforms to add and remove nodes based on the resources your Pods require
- Using low-priority placeholder Pods to provision burst capacity
- Architecting apps so that they can be scaled

Now that we have the application deployed and have health checks in place to keep it running without intervention, it's a good time to look at how you're going to scale up. I've named this chapter "Scaling up," as I think everyone cares deeply about whether their system architecture can handle being scaled up when your application becomes wildly successful and you need to serve all your new users. But, don't worry, I'll also cover scaling down so you can save money during the quiet periods.

The goal is, ultimately, to operationalize our deployment using automatic scaling. That way, we can be fast asleep or relaxing on a beach in Australia, and our application can be responding to traffic spikes dynamically. To get there, we'll need to ensure that the application is capable of scaling, understand the scaling interactions of Pods and nodes in the Kubernetes cluster, and determine the right metrics to configure an autoscaler to do it all for us.

6.1 Scaling Pods and nodes

Getting your application containerized and deployed on Kubernetes is a great step toward building an application deployment that is capable of scaling and supporting your growth. Let's now go over how to actually scale things up when that moment of success arrives and the traffic increases (and scale things down to save some money in the quiet periods).

In Kubernetes, there are essentially two resources that you need to scale: your application (Pods) and the compute resources they run on (nodes). What can make life a bit complicated is that the way you scale these resources is separate, even though the requirements (e.g., more application capacity) are somewhat correlated. It's not enough to just scale Pods as they'll run out of compute resources to run on, nor is it enough to scale up nodes alone as that just adds empty capacity. Scaling both in unison and at the correct ratio is what's needed. Fortunately, there are some tools to make your life easier (and some fully automated platforms that take care of everything for you), which I'll cover in the following discussion.

Firstly, to handle more traffic to your application, you'll need to increase the number of Pod replicas. Starting with the manual approach, you can achieve this by updating your Deployment configuration with the desired number of replicas as follows.

Listing 6.1   Chapter06/6.1_Replicas/deploy.yaml

```
apiVersion: apps/v1
kind: Deployment
metadata:
  name: timeserver              The replicas field specifies how
spec:                           many copies of your Pod you
  replicas: 6        ◁──┘       want to be running.
  selector:
    matchLabels:
      pod: timeserver-pod
  template:
    metadata:
      labels:
        pod: timeserver-pod
    spec:
      containers:
      - name: timeserver-container
        image: docker.io/wdenniss/timeserver:3
        resources:
          requests:
            cpu: 200m
            memory: 250Mi
```

As usual, you can apply changes you make to config with `kubectl apply -f deploy.yaml`.

`kubectl` also offers a convenient imperative command that can achieve the same result:

```
kubectl scale deployment timeserver --replicas=6
```

However, if you try to add too many replicas, you'll soon run out of space in your cluster for those Pods to be scheduled. That's where scaling the nodes come in. You'll know when you've run out of room when you run `kubectl get pods`, and a bunch are listed as `Pending`.

Pods can be in `Pending` for a number of reasons, the most common of which (if the Pod has been in that state for a minute or so) is a lack of resources. Essentially, the lack of resources is an unsatisfied condition, and the Pod remains `Pending` until the condition can be satisfied. There can be other unsatisfied conditions as well if the Pod has dependencies (like requiring to be deployed on a node with another Pod that hasn't been created). To disambiguate, describe the Pod with `kubectl describe pod $POD_NAME` and look at the events. If you see an event, such as `FailedScheduling` with a message like `Insufficient CPU`, you likely need to add more nodes.

Nodeless Kubernetes

I'd like to take a moment to cover nodeless Kubernetes platforms. In my opinion, the ideal cloud Kubernetes platform is one where you don't really need to worry a whole lot about nodes. After all, if you're using the cloud, why not have a platform that provisions the node resources that are needed based on the Pod's requirements so you can focus more on creating great applications and services?

In my role as a product manager at Google Cloud, this is exactly the product I built with my team. We named it *GKE Autopilot*. It's a platform that frees developers from worrying about nodes. With GKE Autopilot, you create standard Kubernetes workloads like Deployments, StatefulSets, and Jobs, specifying the replica counts and the required CPU and memory resources. Autopilot then provisions the necessary compute resources to run your Pods and manages the compute capacity on your behalf. This has two key advantages: it enhances developer efficiency by eliminating the need to define computing requirements twice (in the Pod and the node), and it improves operational efficiency by significantly reducing the burden of node management.

One thing that sets Autopilot apart is that the Kubernetes node concept retains some relevance. Much of the node-related scheduling logic (like spread topologies, affinity, and anti-affinity, covered in chapter 8) is relevant and can still be used. Autopilot is nodeless in the sense that you no longer need to worry about how nodes are provisioned or managed, but it doesn't completely abstract away or hide nodes. After all, there *is* a machine somewhere running your code, and this can have physical relevance around things like failure domains or wanting to co-locate Pods for reduced latency.

(continued)

I believe Autopilot has a best-of-both-worlds design that gives you the node-level controls that you need while still removing the burden of operating and administering those nodes. No need to care anymore about how many nodes you have, their size and shape, whether they are healthy, and whether they are sitting idle or underused.

If you are using GKE Autopilot or a platform like it, you can basically ignore everything in this chapter that talks about scaling *nodes* and focus purely on scaling *Pods*. Scaling Pods manually or automatically (like with a Horizontal Pod Autoscaler) is all you need to do with Autopilot, as the system will provision the necessary node resources for you without any additional configuration.

To scale the nodes, you'll need to consult your Kubernetes provider's platform documentation, as Kubernetes itself doesn't orchestrate nodes. In the case of Google Kubernetes Engine (GKE), if you use Autopilot, nodes are provisioned automatically, and you can skip right ahead to section 6.2. For GKE clusters with node pools, the command looks like this:

```
gcloud container clusters resize $CLUSTER_NAME \
  --node-pool $NODE_POOL_NAME \
  --num-nodes $NODE_COUNT
```

Scaling down is performed with the same commands. When you scale down the nodes, depending on your provider, you should be able to run the same command as to scale up. The cluster will first cordon the nodes to prevent new Pods from being scheduled on them, then drain the nodes, evicting all Pods while giving them time to shutdown gracefully. Pods managed in a Deployment or other higher-order workload construct will be rescheduled on other nodes.

Manually cordoning and draining nodes

If you want to observe what happens when nodes are scaled down, you can manually cordon, drain, and remove nodes with the following commands:

```
$ kubectl get nodes
NAME                                        STATUS  ROLES    AGE  VERSION
gke-cluster-1-default-pool-f1e6b3ef-3o5d    Ready   <none>   7d   v1.27.3-gke.100
gke-cluster-1-default-pool-f1e6b3ef-fi16    Ready   <none>   7d   v1.27.3-gke.100
gke-cluster-1-default-pool-f1e6b3ef-yc82    Ready   <none>   7d   v1.27.3-gke.100

$ NODE_NAME=gke-cluster-1-default-pool-f1e6b3ef-3o5d

$ kubectl cordon $NODE_NAME
node/gke-cluster-1-default-pool-f1e6b3ef-3o5d cordoned

$ kubectl drain $NODE_NAME --ignore-daemonsets --delete-emptydir-data
node/gke-cluster-1-default-pool-f1e6b3ef-3o5d already cordoned
evicting pod default/timeserver-784d5485d9-mrspm
```

(continued)

```
evicting pod kube-system/metrics-server-v0.5.2-66bbcdbffc-78gl7
pod/timeserver-784d5485d9-mrspm evicted
pod/metrics-server-v0.5.2-66bbcdbffc-78gl7 evicted
node/gke-cluster-1-default-pool-f1e6b3ef-3o5d drained
```

Note that deleting the node via `kubectl` does not always delete the underlying VM, meaning you may still be charged for it! If you delete a node with `kubectl delete node $NODE_NAME`, follow up to make sure the VM is also deleted. On GKE in Autopilot mode, cordon and drain is enough to remove the node from use and the system will handle the deletion for you. For GKE node-based clusters, be sure to delete the VM yourself, for example:

```
$ gcloud compute instances delete $NODE_NAME --zone us-west1-c
```

Generally, the cluster will perform these actions automatically as you scale nodes down, so you don't normally need to run them yourself; however, they do come in handy if you ever need to remove a node because it's misbehaving.

So, this is how you scale Pods and nodes by hand. Read on to learn how to automate both these operations with horizontal Pod autoscaling to scale Pods and cluster autoscaling to scale nodes (for cloud providers that offer it).

6.2   *Horizontal Pod autoscaling*

Scaling the number of Pod replicas of your application in Kubernetes is called *horizontal Pod autoscaling*. It's horizontal, as you're increasing the number of replicas to serve increased traffic, rather than vertical, which instead implies increasing the resources available to each replica. Generally, to scale up a system, it's horizontal scaling that you want.

Kubernetes includes a feature called the Horizontal Pod Autoscaler (HPA), a system whereby you specify a Pod *metric* like CPU usage to observe and target, along with some scaling limits (minimum and maximum replicas). The HPA will then attempt to satisfy your metric by creating and removing Pods. In the case of CPU, if your target is, say, 20% CPU utilization, the HPA will add replicas when your average utilization (across all Pods) goes above 20% (of what the Pod requested in its resource requests) and remove them when it goes below 20%. These actions are subject to a minimum and maximum limit you provide, as well as cooldown periods to avoid too much churn. We can create an HPA for our Deployment as in the following listing.

Listing 6.2   Chapter06/6.2_HPA/hpa.yaml

```
apiVersion: autoscaling/v2
kind: HorizontalPodAutoscaler
metadata:
  name: timeserver
spec:
  minReplicas: 1
  maxReplicas: 10
```

Minimum number of replicas

Maximum number of replicas

```
  metrics:
  - resource:
      name: cpu
      target:
        averageUtilization: 20   ◁─── 
        type: Utilization
    type: Resource
  scaleTargetRef:
    apiVersion: apps/v1
    kind: Deployment
    name: timeserver
```

The CPU utilization target. The HPA will create more replicas when the Pod CPU utilization is higher than this value

The Deployment that will be scaled

You can also create it imperatively. As always, I prefer the config approach as it makes it easier to edit things later. But here is the equivalent imperative command for completeness:

```
kubectl autoscale deployment timeserver --cpu-percent=20 --min=1 --max=10
```

To test this, we'll need to make the CPU really busy. Using the following two listings, let's add a really CPU-intensive path to our timeserver application: calculating pi.

Listing 6.3   Chapter06/timeserver4/pi.py

```
from decimal import *

# Calculate pi using the Gregory-Leibniz infinity series
def leibniz_pi(iterations):

  precision = 20
  getcontext().prec = 20
  piDiv4 = Decimal(1)
  odd = Decimal(3)

  for i in range(0, iterations):
    piDiv4 = piDiv4 - 1/odd
    odd = odd + 2
    piDiv4 = piDiv4 + 1/odd
    odd = odd + 2

  return piDiv4 * 4
```

Listing 6.3 is our method to calculate pi, and listing 6.4 shows the addition of a new URL path to server.py, which calls it.

Listing 6.4   Chapter06/timeserver4/server.py

```
from pi import *

# ...

case '/pi':
    pi = leibniz_pi(1000000)
    self.respond_with(200, str(pi))
```

The new HTTP path

The following listing provides a revised Deployment that references the new version of the container with the added path. To work correctly with the HPA, it's important to set resource requests, which we added in chapter 5 and are present here.

> **Listing 6.5 Chapter06/6.2_HPA/deploy.yaml**

```
apiVersion: apps/v1
kind: Deployment
metadata:
  name: timeserver        Replicas
spec:                     initially
  replicas: 1      ◁──┘   set to 1
  selector:
    matchLabels:
      pod: timeserver-pod
  template:
    metadata:
      labels:
        pod: timeserver-pod
    spec:
      containers:
      - name: timeserver-container        The new
        image: docker.io/wdenniss/timeserver:4   ◁──┘   app version
        resources:
          requests:
            cpu: 250m
            memory: 250Mi
```

Resource requests are important for the HPA to work correctly.

We can now create the Deployment, Service, and HPA:

```
$ cd Chapter06/6.2_HPA
$ kubectl create -f deploy.yaml -f service.yaml -f hpa.yaml
deployment.apps/timeserver created
service/timeserver created
horizontalpodautoscaler.autoscaling/timeserver created
$ kubectl get svc -w
NAME         TYPE           CLUSTER-IP      EXTERNAL-IP     PORT(S)         AGE
kubernetes   ClusterIP      10.22.128.1     <none>          443/TCP         6m35s
timeserver   LoadBalancer   10.22.131.179   <pending>       80:32650/TCP    18s
timeserver   LoadBalancer   10.22.131.179   203.0.113.16    80:32650/TCP    26s
```

While you're waiting for the external IP to be provisioned, you can start watching the CPU utilization of your Pods with the following command (I suggest putting it in a new window):

```
kubectl top pods
```

Once you have the external IP, generate some load on the endpoint. Apache Bench, which you can install on most systems, works well for this. The following command will send 50 requests simultaneously to our endpoint, until 10,000 have been sent—that should do it:

```
EXTERNAL_IP=203.0.113.16
ab -n 10000 -c 5 http://$EXTERNAL_IP/pi
```

You can watch the scaling status of the Deployment with the following:

```
kubectl get pods -w
```

The Linux `watch` command is convenient for watching all resources using a single command (which `kubectl` can't do by itself):

```
watch -d kubectl get deploy,hpa,pods
```

If all goes correctly, you should observe the CPU utilization increase as visible with `kubectl top pods`, and more Pod replicas being created. Once you stop sending load to the endpoint (e.g., by interrupting `ab` or waiting for it to finish), you should observe these replicas gradually being removed.

You may observe that replicas are scheduled faster when scaling up in response to the high request load than when they are removed while scaling down when the requests stop. That's just the system being a little cautious when removing capacity to avoid churn in case demand spikes. Here's what it looked like for my sample run:

```
$ kubectl get deploy,hpa,pods
NAME                         READY   UP-TO-DATE   AVAILABLE   AGE
deployment.apps/timeserver   2/6     6            2           7m7s

NAME            REFERENCE               TARGETS    MINPODS  MAXPODS  REPLICAS
hpa/timeserver  Deployment/timeserver   100%/30%   1        6        6
NAME                             READY   STATUS             RESTARTS   AGE
pod/timeserver-b8789946f-2b969   1/1     Running            0          7m7s
pod/timeserver-b8789946f-fzbnk   0/1     Pending            0          96s
pod/timeserver-b8789946f-httwn   1/1     Running            0          96s
pod/timeserver-b8789946f-vvnhj   0/1     Pending            0          96s
pod/timeserver-b8789946f-xw9zf   0/1     ContainerCreating  0          36s
pod/timeserver-b8789946f-zbzw9   0/1     ContainerCreating  0          36s
```

The HPA shown here worked pretty well using the CPU metric, but there's a catch: your workload may not be CPU bound. Unlike the CPU-intensive request used in the demo, many HTTP services spend a lot of time waiting on external services like databases. These deployments may need to scale using other metrics like the number of requests per second (RPS) hitting the service rather than the CPU utilization. Kubernetes offers two built-in metrics: CPU (demonstrated in the previous example) and memory. It doesn't directly support metrics like RPS, but it can be configured by using custom and external metrics exposed by your monitoring service. The next section covers this situation.

What about vertical Pod autoscaling?

Vertical Pod autoscaling (VPA) is a concept whereby Pods are scaled vertically by adjusting their CPU and memory resources. Implementations in Kubernetes achieve VPA by observing the Pods resource usage and dynamically changing the Pod's resource requests over time. Kubernetes doesn't offer a VPA implementation out of the box, although an open source implementation is available,[a] and cloud providers, including GKE, offer their own versions.

As a VPA can determine a Pod's resource requests automatically, it could save you some effort and provide some resource efficiency. It's also the right tool for the job if you need the Pod's resource requests to be adjusted dynamically over time (for Pods that have resource requirements that fluctuate widely).

Using a VPA adds its own complexity and may not always play nicely with the HPA. I would focus first on setting appropriate Pod resource requests and the horizontal scaling of replicas.

---

[a] https://github.com/kubernetes/autoscaler

6.2.1   *External metrics*

One popular scaling metric is requests per second (RPS). The basis of using RPS metrics for scaling is that you measure how many requests an instance of your application can serve every second (the replica's capacity). Then, you divide the current number of requests by this amount, and voila, you have the number of replicas needed:

$$\text{replica\_count} = \text{RPS} \div \text{replica\_capacity}$$

The benefit of the RPS metric is that if you are confident that your application can handle the RPS that you tested it for, then you can be confident that it can scale under load as it's the autoscaler's job to provision enough capacity.

In fact, even if you're not doing *automatic* scaling, this metric is still a really good way to plan your capacity. You can measure the capacity of your replicas, project your traffic, and increase your replicas accordingly. But with Kubernetes, we can also configure an HPA with the RPS metric for automatic scaling.

Now, in this case, we'll be using the *external metric* property of the HPA. One problem with this is that the metric, as its name suggests, is sourced from outside the cluster. So, if you're using a different monitoring solution than the one I use in my example, you'll need to look up what the relevant RPS metric is. Fortunately, RPS is a pretty common metric, and any monitoring solution worth its salt will offer it.

In prior chapters, we discussed a few different ways to get traffic into your cluster via a so-called layer-4 load balancer, which operates at a TCP/IP layer, and a so-called layer-7 Ingress, which operates at the HTTP layer. As *requests* are an HTTP concept, you'll need to be using an Ingress to get this metric. Ingress is covered in the next chapter in depth; for now, it's enough to know that this object sees and inspects your HTTP traffic and thus can expose a metric for the number of requests you are getting.

For this example, as shown in the following two listings, we will use the same Deployment but expose it on an Ingress, via a Service of type `NodePort` (instead of type `LoadBalancer` from the prior chapters).

Listing 6.6   Chapter06/6.2.1_ExternalMetricGCP/service.yaml

```
apiVersion: v1
kind: Service
metadata:
  name: timeserver-internal        ⊲──┐  The name of
spec:                                     this internal
  selector:                               service
    pod: timeserver-pod
  ports:
  - port: 80
    targetPort: 80           ┐  Type NodePort
    protocol: TCP            │  is used for the
  type: NodePort       ⊲──┘  ingress.
```

Listing 6.7   Chapter06/6.2.1_ExternalMetricGCP/ingress.yaml

```
apiVersion: networking.k8s.io/v1
kind: Ingress
metadata:
  name: timeserver-ingress
spec:
  rules:
  - http:
      paths:
      - path: /
        pathType: Prefix
        backend:                          References the
          service:                        internal service
            name: timeserver-internal  ⊲──┘  from listing 6.6
            port:
              number: 80
```

Now if you're using Google Cloud, the following HPA definition can pick up the RPS metric from the Ingress once you replace the forwarding rule name with your own.

Listing 6.8   Chapter06/6.2.1_ExternalMetricGCP/hpa.yaml

```
apiVersion: autoscaling/v2
kind: HorizontalPodAutoscaler
metadata:
  name: timeserver-autoscaler
spec:
  minReplicas: 1
  maxReplicas: 6
```

```
    metrics:
    - type: External
      external:
        metric:
          name: loadbalancing.googleapis.com|https|request_count
          selector:
            matchLabels:
              resource.labels.forwarding_rule_name: "k8s2-fr-21mgs2fl"
        target:
          type: AverageValue
          averageValue: 5
  scaleTargetRef:
    apiVersion: apps/v1
    kind: Deployment
    name: timeserver
```

The external metric — marginal note pointing to the `metric` block.

The `forwarding_rule_name` is how the metric server knows which Ingress object you're talking about. You can omit the `selector` field completely, but then it will match on all Ingress objects—probably not what you want.

Complicating matters this forwarding rule name is a platform-specific resource name and not the Kubernetes object name (in this example, that name is set automatically by GKE). To discover the platform resource name, after waiting a few minutes for your Ingress to be configured, you can describe your Ingress object:

```
$ kubectl describe ingress timeserver-ingress
Name:             timeserver-ingress
Namespace:        default
Address:          203.0.113.16
Default backend:  default-http-backend:80 (10.22.0.202:8080)
Rules:
  Host        Path  Backends
  ----        ----  --------
  *
              /  timeserver-internal:80
        (10.22.0.130:80,10.22.0.131:80,10.22.0.196:80 + 1 more...)
Annotations:  ingress.kubernetes.io/backends:
                {"k8s -be-32730":"HEALTHY","k8s1-a5225067":"HEALTHY"}
              ingress.kubernetes.io/forwarding-rule: k8s2-fr-21mgs2fl
              ingress.kubernetes.io/target-proxy: k8s2-tp-21mgs2fl
              ingress.kubernetes.io/url-map: k8s2-um-21mgs2flEvents:
  Type    Reason  Age                 From                      Message
  ----    ------  ----                ----                      -------
  Normal  Sync    6m28s (x31 over 5h6m)  loadbalancer-controller  Scheduled
      for sync
```

The forwarding rule name — marginal note pointing to the `forwarding-rule` annotation.

Another way to query this information, which is important if you are configuring automated tooling, is to understand where the data is within the object structure and use the JsonPath format of `kubectl`:

```
$ kubectl get ingress -o=jsonpath="{.items[0].metadata.annotations['ingress\.
➥ kubernetes\.io\/forwarding-rule ']}"
k8s2-fr-21mgs2fl
```

TIP   I built the JsonPath expression by first querying the `-o=json` version of the Ingress and then figuring out the path through a combination of looking at the JsonPath docs, Stack Overflow, and trial and error.

Once you have the objects ready, there's one last step, which is to ensure Cloud Monitoring is enabled for the workloads in your cluster, and install some glue that gives the HPA access to the metrics. Follow the instructions[1] to install the Custom Metrics - Stackdriver Adapter.

With our Deployment, Service of type `NodePort`, Ingress, HPA, and metrics adapter all configured, we can now try it out! Generate some requests to the Ingress (replacing the IP of your Ingress, obtained via `kubectl get ingress`):

```
ab -n 100000 -c 100 http://203.0.113.16/
```

And, in a separate window, observe the scale out:

```
$ kubectl get hpa,ingress,pods
NAME                 REFERENCE              TARGETS     MINPODS MAXPODS REPLICAS
hpa/timeserver       Deployment/timeserver  94%/30%     1       6       4

NAME                          CLASS     HOSTS   ADDRESS          PORTS
ingress/timeserver-ingress    <none>    *       203.0.113.16     80

NAME                            READY   STATUS             RESTARTS   AGE
pod/timeserver-b8789946f-8dpmg  1/1     Running            0          5h51m
pod/timeserver-b8789946f-gsrt5  0/1     ContainerCreating  0          110s
pod/timeserver-b8789946f-sjvqb  1/1     Running            0          110s
pod/timeserver-b8789946f-vmhsw  0/1     ContainerCreating  0          110s
```

One thing you may notice is that it's already easier to validate that the system is performing more as expected. Apache Bench allows you to specify concurrent requests; you can see how long they take (and therefore calculate the RPS) and look at the number of replicas to determine whether it's right. This process is a bit harder with the CPU metric, where in order to test, you may have to try to make the Pod as busy as possible, as we did in the previous example. This property of scaling based on *user requests* is one reason why it is a popular metric to use.

OBSERVING AND DEBUGGING

To see what the HPA is doing, you can run `kubectl describe hpa`. Pay particular attention to the `ScalingActive` condition. If it is `False`, it likely means that your metric is not active, which can occur for a number of reasons: (1) the metric adapter wasn't installed (or isn't authenticated), (2) your metric name or selector is wrong, or (3) there just aren't any monitoring samples for the given metric available yet. Note that even with the correct configuration, you will see `False` when there is no monitoring data samples (e.g., there are no requests), so be sure to send some requests to the endpoint and wait a minute or two for the data to come through before investigating further.

---

[1] https://cloud.google.com/kubernetes-engine/docs/tutorials/autoscaling-metrics

AVERAGEVALUE VS. VALUE

In the previous example, we used `targetAverageValue`. `targetAverageValue` is the target *per Pod* value of the metric. `targetValue` is an alternative, which is the target absolute value. As the RPS capacity is calculated at a per-Pod level, it's `targetAverage-Value` we want.

OTHER METRICS

Another popular external metric when dealing with background tasks (covered in chapter 10) is the Pub/Sub queue length. Pub/Sub is a queuing system that allows you to have a queue of work that needs to be performed, and you can set up a workload in Kubernetes to process that queue. For such a setup, you may wish to react to the queue size by adding or removing Pod replicas (workers that can process the queue). You can find a fully worked example on the GKE docs[2] for this; essentially, it boils down to an HPA that looks like the previous one, just with a different metric:

```
metric:
  name: pubsub.googleapis.com|subscription|num_undelivered_messages
  selector:
    matchLabels:
      resource.labels.subscription_id: echo-read
```

This configuration consists of the metric name and the resource identifier for the metric—in this case, the Google Cloud Pub/Sub subscription identifier.

OTHER MONITORING SOLUTIONS

External metrics are something you should be able to configure for *any* Kubernetes monitoring system. While the worked example given previously uses Cloud Monitoring on Google Cloud, the same principles should apply if you're using Prometheus or another cloud monitoring system. To get things going, you'll need to determine (1) how to install the metric adapter for your monitoring solution, (2) what the metric name is in that system, and (3) the right way to select the metric resource.

6.3   Node autoscaling and capacity planning

Using horizontal Pod autoscaling is a great way to automatically scale your Pods based on demand. However, if you have to scale nodes manually to add and remove capacity, it still requires a person in the loop. The common Cluster Autoscaler cluster functionality enables you to scale nodes on demand and pairs well with the HPA to scale Pods.

6.3.1   Cluster autoscaling

Cluster autoscaling is not part of the base Kubernetes API but rather is an optional component. Fortunately, most cloud providers offer it (or something similar) and build it in as a property of the platform that will scale the number of nodes for you, allowing you to focus just on your application and how many replicas it has. As this

---

[2] https://cloud.google.com/kubernetes-engine/docs/tutorials/autoscaling-metrics#pubsub

feature is platform-dependent, the exact implementation will vary (and not all providers offer it). Search for "[product name] Cluster Autoscaler" to find the relevant docs.

In the case of GKE, if you use the Autopilot mode of operation, clusters have built-in node provisioning and autoscaling; no further configuration is required. For GKE clusters with node pools, you can configure autoscaling when creating a node pool or updating an existing node pool.

When using cluster autoscaling, you can focus on scaling your own workloads, having the cluster respond automatically (figure 6.1). This is really convenient, as it can solve the `Pending` Pods problem both when scaling existing workloads and deploying new ones. Read the specific implementation details of your provider, though, to understand what cases are not covered (e.g., how Pods that are too big to fit on current node configurations are handled).

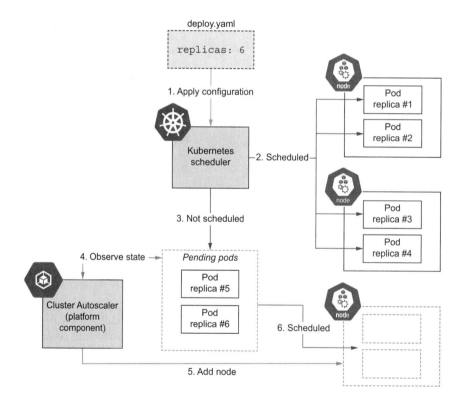

Figure 6.1   The Cluster Autoscaler watches for pending Pods and creates new nodes if needed.

Traditional cluster autoscalers may only add new nodes of an existing predefined configuration, requiring you to define each possible node type you wish to use, so be sure to read the docs. GKE can add new nodes of any type if you use Autopilot (no configuration needed; that's how it works out of the box) or node-based mode with Node Auto Provisioning configured.

Cluster autoscaling and other provider tools that can add and remove nodes automatically make your life easier by allowing you to mostly ignore nodes and focus purely on your own Pods. When paired with Pod-based scaling like HorizontalPodAutoscaler, you can have a fairly hands-off, automated deployment.

6.3.2 Spare capacity with cluster autoscaling

One of the drawbacks of autoscaling nodes compared to manually adding nodes is that sometimes the autoscaler can tune things a little *too* well and result in no spare capacity. This can be great for keeping costs down, but it makes it slower to start new Pods, as capacity needs to be provisioned before the Pod can start up.

Adding new nodes and then starting the Pod is slower than adding new Pods to existing nodes. Nodes have to be provisioned and booted, while Pods that get scheduled onto existing nodes just have to pull the container and boot—and if the container is already in the cache, they can even start booting right away. As shown in figure 6.2, the newly scheduled Pod must wait for capacity to be provisioned before it can begin booting.

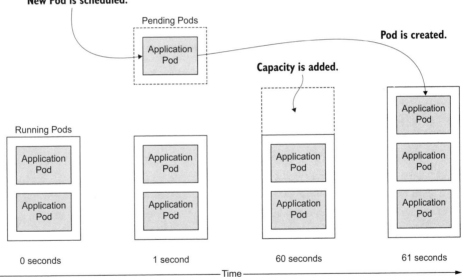

Figure 6.2 Dynamically adding capacity with autoscaling to accommodate newly scheduled Pods

One way to solve both of these problems while still keeping your autoscaler is to use a low-priority placeholder Pod. This Pod does nothing itself other than reserve capacity (keeping additional nodes up and running on standby). This Pod's priority is low, so when your own workloads scale up, they can preempt this Pod and use the node capacity (figure 6.3).

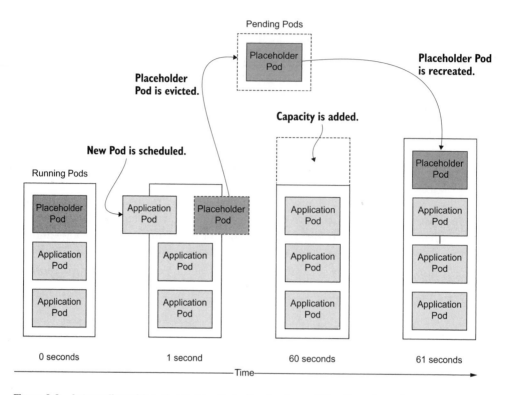

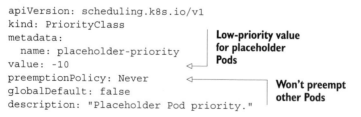

Figure 6.3   Autoscaling with a placeholder Pod, allowing for rapid booting of new Pods using spare capacity

To create our placeholder Pod deployment, first, we'll need a PriorityClass. This priority class should have a priority lower than zero (we want every other priority class to preempt it), as in the following listing.

Listing 6.9   Chapter06/6.3.2_PlaceholderPod/placeholder-priority.yaml

```
apiVersion: scheduling.k8s.io/v1
kind: PriorityClass
metadata:                          Low-priority value
  name: placeholder-priority       for placeholder
value: -10                         Pods
preemptionPolicy: Never
globalDefault: false               Won't preempt
description: "Placeholder Pod priority."   other Pods
```

Now, we can create our "do nothing" container Deployment, as in the following listing.

Listing 6.10   Chapter06/6.3.2_PlaceholderPod/placeholder-deploy.yaml

```
apiVersion: apps/v1
kind: Deployment
```

```
metadata:
  name: placeholder
spec:
  replicas: 10          ◁───   How many replicas do you want? This,
  selector:                    with the CPU and memory requests,
    matchLabels:               determines the size of the headroom
      pod: placeholder-pod     capacity provided by the placeholder Pod.
  template:
    metadata:
      labels:
        pod: placeholder-pod                          Uses the priority
    spec:                                             class we just
      priorityClassName: placeholder-priority   ◁──   created
      terminationGracePeriodSeconds: 0   ◁──┐
      containers:                            We want this Pod to shut
      - name: ubuntu                         down immediately with
        image: ubuntu                        no grace period.
        command: ["sleep"]      │  This is our "do
        args: ["infinity"]      │  nothing" command.
        resources:
          requests:             ┌  The resources that will be reserved by the
            cpu: 200m           ┤  placeholder Pod. This should be equal to the
            memory: 250Mi       └  largest Pod you wish to replace this Pod.
```

When creating this yourself, consider the number of replicas you need and the size (memory and CPU requests) of each replica. The size should be at least the size of your largest regular Pod; otherwise, your workload may not fit in the space when the placeholder Pod is preempted. At the same time, don't increase the size too much; it would be better to use more replicas than replicas that are much larger than your standard workloads, Pods if you wish to reserve extra capacity.

For these placeholder Pods to be preempted by other Pods that you schedule, those Pods will need to have a priority class that both has a higher value and doesn't have a `preemptionPolicy` of `Never`. Fortunately, the default priority class has a `value` of 0 and a `preemptionPolicy` of `PreemptLowerPriority`, so, by default, all other Pods will displace our placeholder Pod.

To represent the Kubernetes default as its own priority class, it would look like listing 6.11. As you don't actually need to change the default, I wouldn't bother configuring this. But, if you're creating your own priority classes, you can use this listing as the reference (just don't set `globalDefault` to `true` unless that's what you really intend). Once again, for the placeholder Pod preemption to work, be sure *not* to set `preemptionPolicy` to `Never`.

> **Listing 6.11   Chapter06/6.3.2_PlaceholderPod/default-priority.yaml**

```
apiVersion: scheduling.k8s.io/v1
kind: PriorityClass
metadata:                      Priority value
  name: default-priority       higher than the
                               placeholder Pods
value: 0             ◁──
```

```
preemptionPolicy: PreemptLowerPriority          ◁─────────────────────────┐
globalDefault: true                                                        │
description: "The global default priority. Will preempt the placeholder Pods."
```
┌▷
│ **Set as the default so other Pods will**   **Will preempt other Pods**
│ **preempt the placeholder Pods.**

Placeholder Pods encapsulated in a Deployment like this are useful for providing constant scaling headroom, giving you a defined amount of capacity ready for quick scheduling. Alternatively, you can encapsulate them in a Job for one-off capacity provisioning, a CronJob to have the capacity provisioned on a schedule, or run them as standalone Pods.

6.4   *Building your app to scale*

Scaling your application up is only part of the equation. The application itself needs to build with scaling in mind. Even though you may not be at the point of your growth where you need to worry about these matters, I believe that *the time when you need to scale is not the time to design how you're going to scale!*

When your application is one with unpredictable growth (e.g., a startup with potentially unlimited users), you really want to plan ahead to avoid the "success failure" scenario. This is where, in a breakout moment of your success, the app fails because it can't handle the scale. Since you don't know when this breakout moment will be, you need to have designed for this ahead of time. Not every startup will have a breakout moment, but if yours does, you want to be ready to capitalize on the opportunity; otherwise, it could all be for naught.

Fortunately, by choosing Kubernetes to orchestrate your containers, you are starting with a really solid foundation for a scalable app. When designing the application, there are some other factors to keep in mind that are largely independent of Kubernetes. Most scalable design principles apply to both Kubernetes and non-Kubernetes environments, but I'll cover a few best practices worth keeping in mind when building a scalable app on Kubernetes. Attending to some scalability principles as you develop your application could matter in the future when your breakout moment arrives and you need to scale it to the moon.

6.4.1   *Avoiding state*

One of the most important aspects of being able to scale is avoiding the local state in your applications. A stateless design is where each replica (instance) of your application that's running can serve any incoming request without reference to any data stored locally on any other instance. Local ephemeral storage can be used for temporary data processing as long as it's not shared between replicas and doesn't need to be available for the next request that comes in.

> **NOTE** The property of the application being stateless is, I believe, the most important factor in the popular Twelve-Factor App design methodology. (https://12factor.net/processes). Stateless apps are easier to scale and maintain as each instance can independently serve any request.

Unlike with a classical host machine, in Kubernetes, all data written to disk by the container is ephemeral (deleted when the container is terminated or restarted) by default. It is possible to create stateful applications using persistent volumes and the StatefulSet construct (see chapter 9), but, by default, containers are treated as stateless, and you generally want to keep it that way so that you can scale.

Rather than storing state on disks that you manage in Kubernetes, use external data stores to store data instead, like SQL and NoSQL databases for structured data, object storage for files, and memory databases like Redis for session state. To support your ability to scale, choose managed services (rather than self-hosting) and ensure the services you choose can handle your potential growth.

This is not to say that all state is bad. After all, you need *somewhere* to store your state, and sometimes this needs to be a self-hosted application. When you do create such an application, be sure to choose highly scalable solutions, like a popular open source solution with a track record of success (e.g., Redis).

Relational database gotchas

If you use a relational database like MySQL or PostgreSQL to store data, there are more than a few potential pitfalls worth paying attention to.

Taming your queries

It goes without saying that inefficient queries will give you inefficient scaling, slowing down as the amount of data increases and the number of requests increase. To keep things under control, I recommend logging and analyzing your queries and starting early in the development process (you don't want to wait until your app is a hit to look at the queries!).

You can't improve what you don't measure, so logging the performance of SQL queries that are performed during each request is the most important first step. Look for requests that generate a lot of queries, or slow queries, and start there.

Both MYSQL and PostgreSQL support the EXPLAIN command, which can help analyze specific queries for performance. Common tactics to improve performance include adding indices for commonly searched columns and reducing the number of JOINS you need to perform. MySQL's documentation "Optimizing SELECT Statements"[a] goes into great detail on many different optimization tactics.

Avoiding N+1 queries

Even if your queries are superefficient, each individual query you make to the database has overhead. Ideally, each request your application processes should perform a constant number of queries, regardless of how much data is displayed.

If you have a request that renders a list of objects, you ideally want to serve this request without generating a separate query for each of those objects. This is commonly referred to as the N+1 query problem (as when the problem occurs, there is often one query to get the list and then one for each item [N items] in the list).

(continued)

This antipattern is particularly common with systems that use object-rational mapping (ORM) and feature lazy loading between parent and child objects. Rendering the child objects of a one-to-many relationship with lazy loading typically results in N+1 queries (one query for the parent and N queries for the N child objects), which will show up in your logs. Fortunately, there is normally a way with such systems to indicate up front that you plan to access the child objects so that the queries can be batched.

Such N+1 query situations can normally be optimized into a constant number of queries, either with a JOIN to return the child objects in the list query or two queries: one to get the record set and a second to get the details for the child objects in that set. Remember, the goal is to have a small constant number of queries per request, and in particular, the number of queries shouldn't scale linearly with the number of records being presented.

Using read replicas for SELECT queries

One of the best ways to reduce the strain on your primary database is to create a read replica. In cloud environments, this is often really trivial to set up. Send all your read queries to your read replica (or replicas!) to keep the load off the primary read/write instance.

To design your application with this pattern in mind before you actually need a read replica, you could have two database connections in your application to the same database, using the second to simulate the read replica. Set up the read-only connection with its own user that only has read permissions. Later, when you need to deploy an actual read replica, you can simply update the instance address of your second connection, and you're good to go!

Incrementing primary keys

If you really hit it big, you may end up regretting using incrementing primary keys. They're a problem for scaling, as they assume a single writable database instance (inhibiting horizontal scaling) and require a lock when inserting, which affects performance (i.e., you can't insert two records at once).

This is really only a problem at very large scale, but worth keeping in mind as it's harder to rearchitect things when you suddenly need to scale up. The common solution to this problem is global UUIDs (e.g., `8fe05a6e-e65d-11ea-b0da-00155d51dc33`), a 128-bit number commonly displayed as a hexadecimal string, which can be uniquely generated by any client (including code running on the user's device).

When Twitter needed to scale up, it opted, instead, to create its own global incrementing IDs to retain the property that they are sortable (i.e., newer tweets have a higher ID number), which you can read about in their post "Announcing Snowflake."[b]

On the other hand, you might prefer to keep incrementing primary keys for aesthetic reasons, like when the record ID is exposed to the user (as in the case of a tweet ID) or for simplicity. Even if you plan to keep your incrementing primary keys for a while, one step you can still take early on is not using auto-incrementing primary keys in

(continued)

places where they wouldn't add any value, like, say, a user session object—maybe not *every* table needs an incrementing primary key.

---

[a] https://dev.mysql.com/doc/refman/8.0/en/select-optimization.html
[b] https://blog.twitter.com/engineering/en_us/a/2010/announcing-snowflake.html

6.4.2 *Microservice architectures*

One way to build up your application is by splitting services into multiple services, often described as using a microservice architecture. This method is basically just creating several internal services to perform separate tasks and using remote procedure calls (an HTTP request, essentially) to call those functions from other services. This contrasts with the monolith service design approach of having the complete program logic in a single container.

While there are some benefits to splitting up a monolith into multiple smaller services, there are some drawbacks as well, so I don't advocate using a microservice architecture just for the sake of it. Benefits include being able to use different programming languages for each service, develop them independently (e.g., by separate teams), and use independent scaling. Drawbacks include more complex debugging and integration testing, as you now have more components and need a way to trace requests through the system.

Microservice vs. monolith

Should you build microservices or a monolith? For the sake of this debate, which I'm not going to litigate in this book, let me share two views on the topic and let you judge for yourself.

David Heinemeier Hansson (DHH) writes in his post "The Majestic Monolith"[a] that microservices are for large tech companies, and most smaller teams are better served by a monolith. His argument is that while microservices can have advantages in certain situations, it's not always clear cut, and the overhead—particularly for smaller teams—is not worth it.

James Lewis and Martin Fowler, in their essay "Microservices,"[b] lay out a well-thought-out and balanced view of microservices. One benefit highlighted is a product mentality, whereby internal teams focus on building and managing their own components, a decentralized approach that allows teams to make their own architectural decisions.

---

[a] https://m.signalvnoise.com/the-majestic-monolith/
[b] http://martinfowler.com/articles/microservices.html

Whether you go all in on microservices or not, the key point I want to focus on here is that if you have multiple services, you can scale them separately. This is true, of course, even if you have just a single internal service in addition to your main application—there's no need to make *every* endpoint its own service to benefit from this architecture. For example, say you have a web application that mostly serves HTML and JSON requests, but one endpoint does some real-time graphics work that uses more memory than your average request. It might be worth creating a separate Deployment (even one using the same container) to serve the graphics endpoint so you can scale it separately and also isolate it a bit.

There are a couple of ways to do this. You can have a single frontend that calls the internal service, as illustrated in figure 6.4, or you can have end users connect to this new service directly, as shown in figure 6.5.

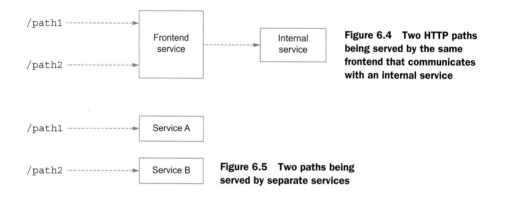

Figure 6.4   **Two HTTP paths being served by the same frontend that communicates with an internal service**

Figure 6.5   **Two paths being served by separate services**

Whether you are going all in on microservices, splitting off a single service to be handled by its own individually scalable Deployment, using multiple programming languages, or running internally developed and open source software to provide your application, you will end up creating *internal services* in Kubernetes. Internal services are provisioned with a private cluster IP address and are called by other services in the cluster to deliver this architecture. The next chapter covers how to configure such internal services.

6.4.3   *Background tasks*

Another important factor to help you scale is to avoid having any heavy inline processing. For example, let's say you have an endpoint that returns a thumbnail of an image and will generate the thumbnail if it doesn't exist in the cache. You could place this logic inline, where the user requests the thumbnail and the service responds by returning the thumbnail from the cache or generating one if the cache is empty. The problem with such a design is that serving the thumbnail from the cache should be very fast while creating the thumbnail is not. If a lot of requests come in, all needing to create a thumbnail, the server could slow down or crash. Plus, it's hard to scale because some requests are lightweight and others are really heavy. You could scale up this service but could still be unlucky and have your load balancer direct all the heavy requests at a single instance.

The solution is to use the background task pattern, covered in detail in chapter 10. Essentially, when heavy processing is needed, rather than doing it in line, you schedule a task and return a status code to the client indicating it should retry the request. There is a container configured to process this task queue, which can be scaled accurately based on the current queue length. So, the request comes in, resulting in a cache miss and a queued task. If things go well, when the client automatically retries the request after a short time, the thumbnail will have been processed by the background queue and be ready for serving—a similar end result for the user, a little extra work to build a background queue and a client with retry logic, but much better scalability.

Summary

- Kubernetes is well-suited to help you scale; some of the largest applications out there run on Kubernetes.
- To make the most of this architecture, design your application from the get-go so that it can scale horizontally.
- HorizontalPodAutoscaler can be used to provision new Pods as needed, working together with cluster autoscaling for a complete autoscaling solution.
- You're not confined to CPU metrics and can scale your Pods based on any metric exported by your monitoring solution.
- Cluster autoscaling feature (if supported by your provider) can be used to provision new nodes as needed.
- Placeholder Pods can be used to add capacity headroom even while autoscaling.
- Consider splitting your application into microservices or simply hosting multiple deployments of the same application to allow for separate scaling groups.

Internal services
and load balancing

Internal services are a way to scale how you develop and serve your application by splitting your application into multiple smaller services. These individual services can be on different development cycles (possibly by different teams) and use completely different programming languages and technology from each other. After all, as long as you can containerize it, you can run it in Kubernetes. No longer do you need to worry whether your application deployment platform can run what you need it to run.

In this chapter, we'll look at how to configure and discover internal services in the cluster, as well as how Kubernetes gives each of these a cluster-local IP address and implements internal network routing to make them addressable by other Pods in the cluster. We'll also look at how you can expose multiple services on a single external IP using Ingress and how Ingress can handle TLS termination so you can offer HTTPS endpoints for your application without needing to configure TLS certificates in your applications.

7.1   Internal services

There are many reasons to create services that are completely internal to your cluster. Perhaps you've adopted a microservice architecture, or you're integrating an open source service, or you just want to connect two applications together that are written in different languages.

In chapter 3, I introduced Services of the type `LoadBalancer` as a way to get external traffic on a public IP. Service is also used to connect internal services but using cluster IP addresses. Kubernetes supports a few different Service types; the two used for internal services are `ClusterIP` and `NodePort`.

The `ClusterIP` type gives you a virtual IP address in the Kubernetes cluster. This IP is addressable from any Pod within your cluster (like from your main application). The `NodePort` type additionally reserves a high port number on each node in the cluster, allowing you to access it from outside the cluster (since the node's IP is directly addressable from the network). Internal cluster communication is typically done with `ClusterIP`, while `NodePort` is used for routing external traffic, including with Ingress. In both cases, Kubernetes configures the network to proxy requests to the Pods that back the service.

> **NOTE**   In fact, three service types get a cluster IP, not just the `ClusterIP` type. The `NodePort` and `LoadBalancer` types are getting *additional* access methods beyond that of the `ClusterIP` type, and are also accessible over a cluster IP.

7.1.1   Kubernetes cluster networking

Now might be a good time for a quick primer on Kubernetes networking. Each Pod gets its own IP address, and can communicate with all other Pods in the cluster directly without needing NAT (Network Address Translation). Containers within the Pod share the same IP. This property of Kubernetes makes Pods behave a bit like VMs, and is convenient as you don't need to worry about port conflict between Pods on the node (i.e., multiple Pods can run a container on port 80). Nodes have their own IP, which is assigned to the network interface of the VM, while the Pod IP uses a virtual network interface where traffic is routed via the node's interface.

Services (other than headless services, covered in Chapter 9) are assigned a virtual IP. The virtual IP isn't routed to a single Pod or node, but rather uses some networking glue on the node to balance traffic to the Pods that back the Service. This networking glue is provided by Kubernetes (using iptables or IP Virtual Service [IPVS]) and handles the traffic routing. A list of Pods that back the Service and their IPs is maintained on the node and is used for this routing.

When a request is made from a Pod to a Service over the cluster IP or node port, that request is first handled by the networking glue on the node, which has an updated list from the Kubernetes control plane of every Pod that belongs to that Service (and which nodes those Pods are on). It will pick one of the Pod IPs at random and route the request to that Pod via its node (figure 7.1). Fortunately, all this happens quite seamlessly; your app can simply make a request like HTTP GET using the IP of the service, and everything behaves as you'd expect.

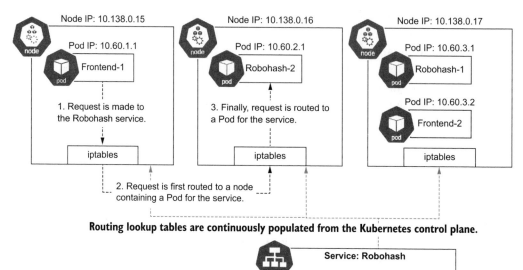

Figure 7.1   IP routing for an internal service named Robohash. The Frontend-1 Pod makes an internal request to the service. The iptables' routing glue on the node has a list of Pods for the Service, which is supplied by the Kubernetes control plane, and selects the Pod named Robohash-2 at random. The request is then routed to that Pod via its node.

What this all means is that when it's time for you to deploy an internal service, you can achieve this by creating a Service of type ClusterIP, thereby obtaining an IP address that the other Pods in your cluster (like your app's frontend) can communicate with seamlessly. This IP address automatically balances the load between all Pod replicas of the internal service. As a developer, you don't typically need to worry about all the networking glue that makes this possible, but hopefully, this section has given you at least a base understanding of how it works.

7.1.2   Creating an internal service

Now that you hopefully understand a bit about how Kubernetes networking works under the hood, let's build an internal service that can be used by other Pods in the cluster. As an example, let's deploy a new internal service to our app. For this, I'm going to use a neat open source library called Robohash that can generate cute robot avatars for users based on a hash (like a hash of their IP). For your own deployments, internal services can be things as simple as avatar generators, other parts of your application, or even entire database deployments. The following listing shows the Deployment for this new container.

Listing 7.1 Chapter07/7.1_InternalServices/robohash-deploy.yaml

```
apiVersion: apps/v1
kind: Deployment
metadata:
  name: robohash
spec:
  replicas: 1
  selector:
    matchLabels:
      app: robohash
  template:
    metadata:
      labels:
        app: robohash
    spec:
      containers:
      - name: robohash-container          The Robohash
        image: wdenniss/robohash:1    ◁─   container
```

This time, instead of exposing this service to the world with a Service of type `Load-Balancer`, we'll keep it internal with a `ClusterIP` type Service. The following listing provides the internal service definition for our Robohash Deployment.

Listing 7.2 Chapter07/7.1_InternalServices/robohash-service.yaml

```
apiVersion: v1
kind: Service
metadata:
  name: robohash-internal
spec:
  selector:
    app: robohash
  ports:
  - port: 80
    targetPort: 80
    protocol: TCP           Defines a local
  type: ClusterIP     ◁─    service
```

Since this isn't a `LoadBalancer`-type Service like we used in chapter 3, it doesn't have an external IP. After creating both resources, to try it out you can use `kubectl` port forwarding:

```
kubectl port-forward service/robohash-internal 8080:80
```

Now you can browse to http://localhost:8080 on your local machine and check out the service. To generate a test avatar, try something like http://localhost:8080/example. You should see an autogenerated robot avatar image like the one in figure 7.2.

Figure 7.2   Example robot avatar (robot parts designed by Zikri Kader, assembled by Robohash.org, and licensed under CC-BY)

Next, let's use this internal service from another service—our frontend—and build out our microservice architecture (figure 7.3)!

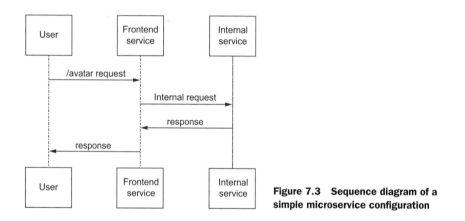

Figure 7.3   Sequence diagram of a simple microservice configuration

To access this internal service from other Pods, you can reference its cluster IP. To view the cluster IP assigned, query the Service:

```
$ kubectl get service
NAME                 TYPE        CLUSTER-IP      EXTERNAL-IP   PORT(S)
robohash-internal    ClusterIP   10.63.254.218   <none>        80/TCP
```

In this case, you can access the service from other Pods on the given cluster IP (seen as `10.63.254.218` in the previous output), such as by making an HTTP GET request to `http://10.63.254.218/example`. This address will only be reachable from other Pods within the cluster.

7.1.3 *Service discovery*

In the previous example, we used `kubectl get service` to look up the internal cluster IP address assigned to our Service. While you could simply take that IP address and hardcode it into your application, doing this isn't great for portability. You may wish to deploy the same application in a few different places, like locally on your development machine, in a staging environment, and in production (how to set up these different environments is covered in chapter 11). If you reference the IP directly, you will need to update your code every time.

It's better to discover the IP address dynamically from the Pod that needs to call the service, much like we discovered the IP address using `kubectl`. Kubernetes offers Pods two ways to perform service discovery: using a DNS lookup, or an environment variable. The DNS lookup works cluster-wide, while the environment variable is only for Pods within the same namespace.

SERVICE DISCOVERY USING ENVIRONMENT VARIABLES

Kubernetes automatically creates an environment variable for each Service, populates it with the cluster IP, and makes the IP available in every Pod created after the Service is created. The variable follows a naming conversion whereby our example `robohash-internal` Service gets the environment variable `ROBOHASH_INTERNAL_SERVICE_HOST`.

Rather than figuring out the correct conversion, you can view a list of all such environment variables available to your Pod by running the `env` command on your Pod with `exec` (with truncated output):

```
$ kubectl get pods
NAME                           READY    STATUS     RESTARTS    AGE
robohash-6c96c64448-7fn24      1/1      Running    0           2d23h

$ kubectl exec robohash-6c96c64448-7fn24 -- env
ROBOHASH_INTERNAL_PORT_80_TCP_ADDR=10.63.243.43
ROBOHASH_INTERNAL_PORT_80_TCP=tcp://10.63.243.43:80
ROBOHASH_INTERNAL_PORT_80_TCP_PROTO=tcp
ROBOHASH_INTERNAL_SERVICE_PORT=80
ROBOHASH_INTERNAL_PORT=tcp://10.63.243.43:80
ROBOHASH_INTERNAL_PORT_80_TCP_PORT=80
ROBOHASH_INTERNAL_SERVICE_HOST=10.63.243.43
```

The benefit of this approach is that it's extremely fast. Environment variables are just string constants, with no dependencies external to the Pod itself. It also frees you to specify any DNS server you like to serve the other requests of the Pod (e.g., `8.8.8.8`). The downside is that only those Services in the same namespace of the Pod are populated in environment variables, and that ordering matters: the Service must be created before the Pod for the Pod to get the Service's environment variable.

If you find yourself in a situation where you need to restart your Deployment's Pods to pick up changes to the Service, you can do so with the following command (no change to the Pod needed):

```
kubectl rollout restart deployment $DEPLOYMENT_NAME
```

One common way to reference these variables is to provide the complete HTTP endpoint of the internal service in its own environment variable defined in the Deployment. This allows your container to be even more portable and able to run outside of Kubernetes (e.g., in Docker Compose). The following listing shows you how to embed the value of the automatically generated environment variable (ROBOHASH_INTERNAL_SERVICE_HOST) in your own custom environment variable (AVATAR_ENDPOINT), which your application will ultimately consume.

Listing 7.3   Chapter07/7.1_InternalServices/timeserver-deploy-env.yaml

```
apiVersion: apps/v1
kind: Deployment
metadata:
  name: timeserver
spec:
  replicas: 1
  selector:
    matchLabels:
      pod: timeserver-pod
  template:
    metadata:
      labels:
        pod: timeserver-pod
    spec:
      containers:
      - name: timeserver-container
        image: docker.io/wdenniss/timeserver:5
        env:
        - name: AVATAR_ENDPOINT
          value: http://$(ROBOHASH_INTERNAL_SERVICE_HOST)   ◁┘ Service discovery
                                                               using environment
                                                               variables
```

Using this additional layer of indirection, where our custom environment variable references the Kubernetes one, is useful as now we can run this container standalone in Docker (just populate AVATAR_ENDPOINT with the endpoint of the internal service wherever it's running) or switch to DNS-based lookups.

In summary, environment variable discovery has a few advantages:

- Superfast performance (they are string constants)
- No dependency on other DNS Kubernetes components

And it has some disadvantages:

- Only available to Pods in the same namespace
- Pods must be created after the Service is created

SERVICE DISCOVERY USING DNS

The other way to discover services is via the cluster's internal DNS service. For Services running in a different namespace than the Pod, this is the only option for discovery. The Service's name is exposed as a DNS host, so you can simply do a DNS lookup on robohash-internal (or use http://robohash-internal as your HTTP path), and it will resolve. When calling the service from other namespaces, append the name-space—for example, use `robohash-internal.default` to call the service `robohash-internal` in the `default` namespace.

The only downside to this approach is that it's a little slower to resolve that IP address, as a DNS lookup is needed. In many Kubernetes clusters, this DNS service will be running on the same node, so it's pretty fast; in others, it may require a hop to the DNS service running on a different node or a managed DNS service, so be sure to cache the result.

Since we previously made the endpoint URL an environment variable of the Deployment, we can easily update the variable, this time giving it the service name (`http://robohash-internal`). The complete Deployment will look like the following listing.

> **Listing 7.4   Chapter07/7.1_InternalServices/timeserver-deploy-dns.yaml**

```
apiVersion: apps/v1
kind: Deployment
metadata:
  name: timeserver
spec:
  replicas: 1
  selector:
    matchLabels:
      pod: timeserver-pod
  template:
    metadata:
      labels:
        pod: timeserver-pod
    spec:
      containers:
      - name: timeserver-container
        image: docker.io/wdenniss/timeserver:5
        env:                                          Service
        - name: AVATAR_ENDPOINT                       discovery
          value: http://robohash-internal   ◁──────  using DNS
```

In summary, DNS-based service discovery has a few advantages:

- Can be called from any namespace in the cluster
- No ordering dependencies

And it has some disadvantages:

- Slightly slower than using an environment variable (which is a constant)
- Dependency on the internal DNS service

So, using environment variables and DNS lookups are two ways that our front-end service can discover the internal service's internal Pod IP, rather than having that IP address hardcoded. Since these discovery methods are Kubernetes-specific, it's recommended that you supply the path as an environment variable to the container as we did in the example. Then, you can easily supply a completely different path when running the container outside of Kubernetes.

PUTTING IT ALL TOGETHER

Let's make a call from the timeserver app to our internal Robohash service on a new endpoint, /avatar. All this new endpoint does is read an image from the internal service and return it.

> **Listing 7.5   Chapter07/timeserver5/server.py**

```python
import urllib.request
import os
import random

# ...

case '/avatar':
    url = os.environ['AVATAR_ENDPOINT'] + "/" + str(random.randint(0, 100))
    try:
        with urllib.request.urlopen(url) as f:
            data = f.read()
            self.send_response(200)
            self.send_header('Content-type', 'image/png')
            self.end_headers()
            self.wfile.write(data)
    except urllib.error.URLError as e:
        self.respond_with(500, e.reason)


# ...
```

Now that our application actually uses the internal service, we can deploy it all to Kubernetes:

```
$ cd Chapter07/7.1_InternalServices
$ kubectl create -f robohash-deploy.yaml
deployment.apps/robohash created
$ kubectl create -f robohash-service.yaml
service/robohash-internal created
$ kubectl create -f timeserver-deploy-dns.yaml
deployment.apps/timeserver created
$ kubectl create -f timeserver-service.yaml
service/timeserver created

$ kubectl get svc/timeserver
NAME            TYPE           CLUSTER-IP      EXTERNAL-IP    PORT(S)        AGE
timeserver      LoadBalancer   10.22.130.155   203.0.113.16   80:32131/TCP   4m25s

$ open "http://203.0.113.16/avatar"
```

Wait for the external IP to be provisioned and then try out the /avatar URL. You should be greeted with a robot avatar. Switch timeserver-deploy-dns.yaml for timeserver-deploy-env.yaml to use the alternative discovery method with the same end result.

We are now using a microservice architecture! Using this technique, you can have multiple internal services that can be deployed and managed separately (perhaps by different teams). You can add separate services using open source tooling or simply bring together different components of your application written in different languages.

7.2 Ingress: HTTP(S) load balancing

So far in the book, we've been creating external IPs using Services of type `Load-Balancer`. This provides you with a so-called layer-4 (L4) load balancer, which balances requests at the network layer and can work with a variety of protocols (e.g., TCP, UDP, SCTP). You configure the Service with your desired protocol and port, and you get an IP that will balance traffic over your Pods. If you expose an HTTP service over a load balancer, you need to implement your own TLS termination handling (i.e., configuring certificates and running an HTTPS endpoint), and all traffic to that endpoint will get routed to one set of Pods (based on the `matchLabels` rules). There is no option for exposing two or more separate services directly on the same load balancer (although one can proxy requests to the other internally).

When you are publishing an HTTP app specifically, you may get more utility from a so-called layer-7 (L7) load balancer, which balances at the HTTP request layer and can do more fancy things, like terminate HTTPS connections (meaning it will handle the HTTPS details for you), and perform path-based routing so that you can serve a single domain host with multiple services. In Kubernetes, an HTTP load balancer is created with an Ingress object.

Ingress lets you place multiple internal services behind a single external IP with load balancing. You can direct HTTP requests to different backend services based on their URI path (`/foo`, `/bar`), hostname (`foo.example.com`, `bar.example.com`), or both (figure 7.4). The ability to have multiple services running on a single IP, and potentially serving different paths under a single domain name, is unique to Ingress, because if you'd exposed them with individual Services of type `LoadBalancer` like in the earlier chapters, the services would have separate IP addresses, necessitating separate domains (e.g., `foo.example.com` to address one, and `bar.example.com` to address the other).

The property of Ingress being able to place multiple services under one host is useful when scaling up your application. When you need to break up your services into multiple services for developer efficiency (e.g., teams wanting to manage their own deployment lifecycle) or scaling (e.g., being able to scale aspects of the application separately), you can use Ingress to route the requests while not altering any public-facing URLs. For example, let's say that your application has a path that is a particularly CPU-intensive request. You might wish to move it to its own service to allow it to be scaled separately. Ingress allows you to make such changes seamlessly to end users.

Listing 7.6 provides an example Ingress where the routes are served by different backends. In this example, we'll expose an internal Timeserver Service on the root path (`/`), and an internal Robohash Service on `/robohash`.

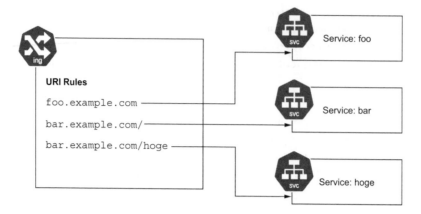

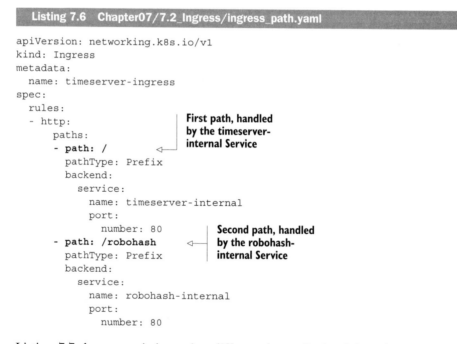

Figure 7.4   The Ingress's rule list, or URL map, allows one HTTP load balancer to handle the traffic for multiple services.

Listing 7.6   Chapter07/7.2_Ingress/ingress_path.yaml

```
apiVersion: networking.k8s.io/v1
kind: Ingress
metadata:
  name: timeserver-ingress
spec:
  rules:
  - http:
      paths:
      - path: /                        First path, handled
        pathType: Prefix               by the timeserver-
        backend:                       internal Service
          service:
            name: timeserver-internal
            port:
              number: 80               Second path, handled
      - path: /robohash                by the robohash-
        pathType: Prefix               internal Service
        backend:
          service:
            name: robohash-internal
            port:
              number: 80
```

Listing 7.7 shows a variation using different hosts. Each of these hosts can also have multiple paths using the format in listing 7.6.

Listing 7.7   Chapter07/7.2_Ingress/ingress_host.yaml

```
apiVersion: networking.k8s.io/v1
kind: Ingress
metadata:
  name: timeserver-ingress
```

```
spec:
  rules:
  - host: timeserver.example.com          ◁——    First host, handled
    http:                                         by the timeserver-
      paths:                                      internal Service
      - path: /
        pathType: Prefix
        backend:
          service:
            name: timeserver-internal
            port:
              number: 80                          Second host, handled
  - host: robohash.example.com            ◁——┤   by the robohash-
    http:                                         internal Service
      paths:
      - path: /
        pathType: Prefix
        backend:
          service:
            name: robohash-internal
            port:
              number: 80
```

The Ingress references internal services that are specified as Services with the type `NodePort`, such as the one in the following listing.

Listing 7.8 Chapter07/7.2_Ingress/timeserver-service-internal.yaml

```
apiVersion: v1
kind: Service
metadata:
  name: timeserver-internal
spec:
  selector:
    pod: timeserver-pod
  ports:
  - port: 80
    targetPort: 80               To use an internal service
    protocol: TCP                with Ingress, it needs to
  type: NodePort          ◁——    be of type NodePort
```

Ingress objects can be configured to perform exact matching (i.e., only requests exactly matching the path given will be routed to the Service) or prefix matching (i.e., all requests matching the path prefix will be routed) with the `pathType` property. I'm not going to go into a lot of detail here, as the official docs do a great job. One facet worth reproducing is the rule on multiple matches:

> *In some cases, multiple paths within an Ingress will match a request. In those cases, precedence will be given first to the longest matching path. If two paths are still equally matched, precedence will be given to paths with an exact path type over prefix path type.*[1]

---

[1] https://kubernetes.io/docs/concepts/services-networking/ingress/#multiple-matches

As you may have seen in listing 7.6, there was a path for / and a second one for /robohash. A request to /robohash will be routed to the second Service, even though it also matches the first path. If you've used other routing mechanisms in the past (like Apache URL rewriting), often the preference would go to the *first* rule matched—not so in Kubernetes, where the longer matched rule gets preference. I find this design convenient, as it matches well with developer intent.

To deploy this example, delete the previous example if it's running (kubectl delete -f Chapter07/7.1_InternalServices), and run the following:

```
$ cd Chapter07/7.2_Ingress
$ kubectl create -f robohash-deploy.yaml
deployment.apps/robohash created
$ kubectl create -f robohash-service.yaml
service/robohash-internal created
$ kubectl create -f timeserver-deploy-dns.yaml
deployment.apps/timeserver created
$ kubectl create -f timeserver-service-internal.yaml
service/timeserver-internal created
$ kubectl create -f ingress_path.yaml
ingress.networking.k8s.io/timeserver-ingress created

$ kubectl get ing -w
NAME                 CLASS    HOSTS    ADDRESS         PORTS   AGE
timeserver-ingress   <none>   *                        80      4s
timeserver-ingress   <none>   *        203.0.113.20    80      100s
```

Once your Ingress has an IP, you can browse to it. Try the /robohash path to connect to the Robohash service via the Ingress. Note that the resources backing the Ingress may take a bit of extra time to be provisioned. Even after you have the IP address and browse to it, you may see a 404 error for a time. I suggest trying again in about 5 minutes to give the cloud provider time to update the Ingress.

To debug problems with the Ingress, you can use kubectl describe ingress. The following is what I saw when I described the Ingress shortly after it had an IP assigned, but before it was ready:

```
$ kubectl describe ingress
Name:             timeserver-ingress
Namespace:        default
Address:          203.0.113.20
Default backend:  default-http-backend:80 (10.22.0.130:8080)
Rules:
  Host        Path  Backends
  ----        ----  --------
  *
              /            timeserver-internal:80 (10.22.0.135:80)
              /robohash    robohash-internal:80 (10.22.1.4:80)
Annotations:  ingress.kubernetes.io/backends:                    Backend status
                {"k8s-be-32730--a52250670846a599":"Unknown",     is unknown
                 "k8s1-a5225067":"Unknown","k8s1-a5225067-default-timeser ...
              ingress.kubernetes.io/forwarding-rule: k8s2-fr-21mgs2f1
```

```
                       ingress.kubernetes.io/target-proxy: k8s2-tp-21mgs2fl
                       ingress.kubernetes.io/url-map: k8s2-um-21mgs2fl
Events:
  Type      Reason      From            Message
  ----      ------      ----            -------
  Normal    Sync        loadbalancer    UrlMap "k8s2-um-21mgs2fl" created
  Normal    Sync        loadbalancer    TargetProxy "k8s2-tp-21mgs2fl" created
  Normal    Sync        loadbalancer    ForwardingRule "k8s2-fr-21mgs2fl" created
  Normal    IPChanged   loadbalancer    IP is now 203.0.113.20
  Normal    Sync        loadbalancer    Scheduled for sync
```

The following shows the status after waiting a few more minutes. Notice how the annotation changed from Unknown to HEALTHY. After that, I was able to browse to the IP and access the service:

```
$ kubectl describe ing
Name:              timeserver-ingress
Namespace:         default
Address:           203.0.113.20
Default backend:   default-http-backend:80 (10.22.0.130:8080)
Rules:
  Host          Path  Backends
  ----          ----  --------
  *
                /             timeserver-internal:80 (10.22.0.135:80)
                /robohash     robohash-internal:80 (10.22.1.4:80)
Annotations:    ingress.kubernetes.io/backends:                              Backend status
                  {"k8s-be-32730--a52250670846a599":"HEALTHY",               is now healthy
                   "k8s1-a5225067":"HEALTHY","k8s1-a5225067-default-timeser...
                ingress.kubernetes.io/forwarding-rule: k8s2-fr-21mgs2fl
                ingress.kubernetes.io/target-proxy: k8s2-tp-21mgs2fl
                ingress.kubernetes.io/url-map: k8s2-um-21mgs2fl
Events:
  Type      Reason      From            Message
  ----      ------      ----            -------
  Normal    Sync        loadbalancer    UrlMap "k8s2-um-21mgs2fl" created
  Normal    Sync        loadbalancer    TargetProxy "k8s2-tp-21mgs2fl" created
  Normal    Sync        loadbalancer    ForwardingRule "k8s2-fr-21mgs2fl" created
  Normal    IPChanged   loadbalancer    IP is now 203.0.113.20
  Normal    Sync        loadbalancer    Scheduled for sync
```

Cost-saving tip: Saving IPs with Ingress

A benefit of Ingress is that by using host-based routing, you can host several services, all with the same external IP address. The Ingress inspects the Host header in the HTTP request and routes traffic accordingly. This contrasts with Services of type LoadBalancer, where each gets its own IP address assigned and performs no HTTP request-based routing.

Cloud providers often charge based on load-balancing rules, which roughly translates into how many load-balancing external IP addresses are assigned. By using an Ingress to combine several services into one, rather than each being exposed with its own IP, you can likely save money.

(continued)

If your cloud provider groups HTTP load balancers (Ingress) and network load balancers (Services of type `LoadBalancer`) separately and has a minimum rule fee (like Google Cloud does at the time of writing), you may want to use one or the other exclusively until you need more than the minimum.

Another trick, but one I don't recommend, is running your own Ingress *controller*. This technique (not covered in this book) means deploying an open source component as a load balancer to implement the Kubernetes Ingress functionality, overriding the default implementation of your cloud provider. This approach means that the Ingress objects and Services objects with type `LoadBalancer` get treated as the same rule types for billing, which can save money if you need both, but there's a sacrifice: you now need to manage this component yourself. Are you an expert at debugging Kubernetes Ingress controllers? In my experience, better to go all-in using standard Ingress objects or stick with pure load balancers if you need to save money.

7.2.1   *Securing connections with TLS*

Another useful property of Ingress is that it will perform TLS encryption for you. Modern web applications are typically hosted as secure HTTPS applications with TLS, which is important for security but comes with some overhead for the application server. Depending on the server middleware you are using, you may see performance gains by letting the Ingress load balancer handle the TLS connection (acting as a so-called TLS terminator) and communicate to the backend only over HTTP—via a secure network like that of your cloud provider, of course (figure 7.5). If you prefer, the Ingress can re-encrypt traffic and connect to your services over HTTPS, but there is no option to pass the unmodified encrypted traffic directly through from the client to the backend For that, you'd use a Service of type `LoadBalancer`, as we did in chapter 3.

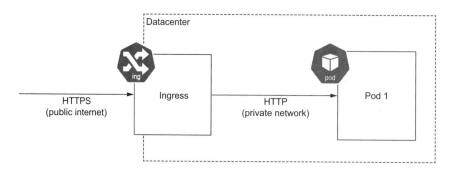

Figure 7.5   The Ingress terminates HTTPS (TLS) traffic and can forward it to the serving Pods over plain HTTP or HTTPS connections.

Now that the Ingress is terminating your TLS connections, you'll need to set it up with certificates. If, like me, you've done this a few times on different systems, you might be dreading this step. Fortunately, Kubernetes makes it a breeze!

You just need to import your certificate and key as a Kubernetes Secret and then reference that secret in your Ingress configuration. A Kubernetes Secret is simply a data object in your cluster used to contain things like TLS keys.

To do this, normally you would follow the instructions of your certificate authority to create a certificate, the end product of which would include the two files we need: the private key that you created and the certificate issued by the certificate authority.

For demonstration purposes, we can create our own self-signed certificate in lieu of a trusted certificate. Note that while this will provide the same encryption for the connection, there is no identity verification, and you'll see scary messages in your browser. The following commands will create such a certificate:

```
# create a private key
openssl genrsa -out example.key 2048

# create a certificate request for 'example.com'
openssl req -new -key example.key -out example.csr \
    -subj "/CN=example.com"

# self-issue an untrusted certificate
openssl x509 -req -days 365 -in example.csr -signkey \
    example.key -out example.crt
```

Once you have your private key and certificate, whether you created them with the previous instructions or by following the instructions of your certificate authority, you can now create the Kubernetes secret:

```
kubectl create secret tls my-tls-cert --cert example.crt --key example.key
```

You may notice the imperative `kubectl create` command here. This is one of the few times I recommend using an imperative command rather than defining the configuration in a file because it's simpler than creating the object manually and Base64-encoding all the data. If you want to see the config that got created with this command, you can easily view it with `kubectl get -o yaml secret my-tls-cert`.

The final step is to reference this secret in our Ingress, as in the following listing.

Listing 7.9   Chapter07/7.2.1_TLS/ingress_tls.yaml

```
apiVersion: networking.k8s.io/v1
kind: Ingress
metadata:
  name: timeserver-tls
spec:
  tls:
  - secretName: my-tls-cert        ⊲——┐ References the
                                        TLS secret
```

```
      rules:
    - host: example.com
      http:
        paths:
        - path: /
          pathType: Prefix
          backend:
            service:
              name: timeserver-internal
              port:
                number: 80
    - http:
        paths:
        - path: /
          pathType: Prefix
          backend:
            service:
              name: robohash-internal
              port:
                number: 80
```

Referencing the Services of type `NodePort` created in the previous section, we can create this new Ingress with a TLS secret:

```
$ cd Chapter07/7.2.1_TLS/
$ kubectl create -f ingress_tls.yaml
ingress.networking.k8s.io/timeserver-tls created
$ kubectl get ing
NAME             CLASS    HOSTS        ADDRESS        PORTS     AGE
timeserver-tls   <none>   example.com  203.0.113.15   80, 443   9m15s
$ open "https://203.0.113.15"
```

Remember that the provisioning step can take a while, even from the point where the Ingress has received an IP. If you use a self-signed certificate, you will see some scary warnings in the browser.

To test out the domain name route in this Ingress (`example.com` in the example), you'll need to configure the DNS for the domain you've used with the IP of the Ingress. To test locally, you can also edit your hosts file and add the IP and domain name (to find instructions on how to do that, a Google search for "update hosts file in <your operating system version>" should do the trick!). The IP of the Ingress can be found with `kubectl get ingress`. The following is what my Ingress object looks like, and the entry I added to my local hosts file:

```
$ kubectl get ingress
NAME             CLASS    HOSTS        ADDRESS        PORTS     AGE
timeserver-tls   <none>   example.com  203.0.113.15   80, 443   82m

$ cat /etc/hosts
# ...
203.0.113.15 example.com
```

Now, provided that you've configured your host, you should be able to browse to https://example.com. If you generate a self-signed certificate, you'll get a scary browser error, which, in this case, is fine to click through. To actually publish your service to the world, you'll want to go back and request a certificate from an actual certificate authority and use that to create the TLS secret instead.

Once again, the nice thing about Kubernetes is that all this configuration is in the form of Kubernetes objects rather than random files on a host, making it straightforward to reproduce the environment elsewhere.

Using GKE? Try managed certificates

The previous instructions are for adding a tried-and-true CA certificate to your Kubernetes Ingress object. If you're using Google Kubernetes Engine (GKE) and want an even simpler approach, you can use a managed certificate instead.

With a managed certificate, you skip the CA signing step and the copying of your private key and certificate into Kubernetes as a Secret. Instead, you need first to prove ownership of the domain to Google (in the Google Cloud console), create a GKE-specific ManagedCertificate object listing the (sub)domains you wish to provision certificates for, and then reference that object in your Ingress. Google will then provision and manage the certificates automatically. It's all pretty straightforward, so I'll let the official docs[a] be your guide for this one.

[a] https://cloud.google.com/kubernetes-engine/docs/how-to/managed-certs

---

Summary

- Kubernetes offers several tools to create, discover, connect, and expose multiple services when your requirements exceed what can be hosted in a single container.
- Internal services are a way to connect a wide range of workloads that can be written in a different language, be on a different release schedule, or simply need to scale independently.
- Internal services can be exposed on a cluster IP that allows them to be called from other Pods in the cluster.
- Kubernetes offers two forms of service discovery to find these internal service IPs: environment variables and DNS.
- Ingress can be used to expose multiple internal services to the internet using a single IP, with routing performed by path or host name.
- Ingress is an HTTP(S) load balancer, which can be configured with multiple TLS certificates to perform TLS termination.
- By performing TLS termination at the load balancer layer, you can save configuration effort in your application and reduce CPU overhead.

Node feature selection 8

This chapter covers

- Selecting nodes with specific hardware properties
- Using taints and tolerations to govern scheduling behavior on nodes with special hardware
- Keeping workloads separated on discrete nodes
- Avoiding a single point of failure with a highly available deployment strategy
- Grouping some Pods together on a node while avoiding nodes that contain specific other Pods

So far, this book has treated the compute nodes in the cluster—the machines responsible for actually running your containers—as equal. Different Pods may request more or less CPU, but they're all running on the same type of nodes under the hood.

One of the fundamental properties of cloud computing is that even when you're using an abstract platform that takes care of much of the low-level compute provisioning for you as Kubernetes platforms are capable of doing, you may still care to some extent about the servers that are actually running your workloads. Serverless is a nice concept, but at the end of the day, the workload is running on a computer, and you can't always escape the properties of that machine, nor do you always want to.

This is where node features selection comes in. In a managed platform, including Google Kubernetes Engine (GKE), there is a great variety of different hardware and configuration options for nodes. The node's CPU can be of the x86 architecture or Arm. It might be AMD or Intel. Nodes can have expensive hardware like a GPU attached if you need it, or they can be run in the low-priced Spot provisioning mode, saving you money while risking disruption. You may not always need to care about these elements, but it can be handy, like to save money with Spot, or critical, like when you need a GPU to run an AI/ML workload.

Another aspect to be aware of is that Kubernetes runs multiple Pods on the same node, a technique known as bin-packing. Running multiple containers on the same hardware can help save you money and is especially useful for bursting, where a Pod can temporarily use another Pod's provisioned capacity if that Pod isn't using it. The downside of bin-packing is the potential for single points of failure. Fortunately, Kubernetes ships with a built-in method called *pod spread topology* to avoid concentrations of replicas of the same Pod on a single node. In this chapter, you'll learn how to select nodes for their features, group Pods together, and spread them apart.

8.1   Node feature selection

Not all compute nodes are equal. You may have workloads that require additional hardware, like higher-performance CPUs and GPUs, or properties, like running in a Spot provisioning model. Some nodes run Linux, while others run Windows. Some CPUs use the x86 architecture; others use Arm and so on. Just as in the past where we might place workloads on machines with specific features, we can do the same in Kubernetes through node selection and affinity.

8.1.1   Node selectors

Node features are differentiated in Kubernetes through node labels. And the way you target specific node features from your Pods is with node selection or node affinity. Node selection and affinity are simply ways to express the desired labels (and therefore features) of the nodes that your Pods require.

Take, for example, a Pod that needs to run on an Arm-based node. Arm-based nodes are labeled with the well-known label `kubernetes.io/arch: arm64` (well-known labels are those that are defined in the open source and are intended to be consistent across different providers). We can use a node selector or node affinity to target that label and ensure our Pod will only run on an Arm-based node. In the following listing, the workload selects the `arm64` architecture to prevent the Pod from being scheduled on any other type of CPU architecture.

Listing 8.1   Chapter08/8.1.1_NodeSelection/deploy_nodeselector.yaml

```
apiVersion: apps/v1
kind: Deployment
metadata:
  name: timeserver
spec:
  replicas: 1
  selector:
    matchLabels:
      pod: timeserver-pod
  template:
    metadata:
      labels:
        pod: timeserver-pod
    spec:
      nodeSelector:                      Selects nodes with the
        kubernetes.io/arch: arm64        arm64 architecture
      containers:
      - name: timeserver-container
        image: docker.io/wdenniss/timeserver:5
```

A more verbose way to express the exact same requirement is through a node affinity.

Listing 8.2   Chapter08/8.1.1_NodeSelection/deploy_nodeaffinity.yaml

```
apiVersion: apps/v1
kind: Deployment
metadata:
  name: timeserver
spec:
  replicas: 1
  selector:
    matchLabels:
      pod: timeserver-pod
  template:
    metadata:
      labels:
        pod: timeserver-pod
    spec:
      affinity:
        nodeAffinity:
          requiredDuringSchedulingIgnoredDuringExecution:
            nodeSelectorTerms:                                    Another way
            - matchExpressions:                                   to select nodes
              - key: kubernetes.io/arch                           with the arm64
                operator: In                                      architecture
                values:
                - arm64
      containers:
      - name: timeserver-container
        image: docker.io/wdenniss/timeserver:5
```

These previous two deployment configurations will achieve the exact same result: a Pod placed only on an Arm-based node (to verify where a Pod lands, you can query with `kubectl get pods -o wide` and then inspect the node with `kubectl describe node $NODE_NAME | grep arch`). The advantage of the node affinity method, and the reason you would use it, is that it allows for more expressive logic, which I will go into more detail in the next section.

Requiring these feature-related node labels in your PodSpecs is the first step, but you need a way to actually have nodes provisioned with that functionality (i.e., having the labels you are selecting). As always, the provisioning of nodes and their associated features is done at the platform level. If you are using a fully managed platform like GKE in Autopilot mode, simply specifying your node selector with your feature labels is enough to get a node that has those capabilities, provided the capability is offered by the platform. On a more traditional Kubernetes platform, you would need to provision nodes that will have those features out of band, for example, by creating a node pool or node group with the desired properties.

To find out what capabilities are supported, the provider's docs are best. However, if you have a node in the cluster with the desired properties you're looking for, you can also inspect it and see what labels are available for selection:

```
kubectl describe nodes
```

Here are some of the labels from that output for an Arm-based node running on GKE:

```
Labels:            cloud.google.com/compute-class=Scale-Out
                   cloud.google.com/gke-boot-disk=pd-standard
                   cloud.google.com/gke-container-runtime=containerd
                   cloud.google.com/gke-image-streaming=true
                   cloud.google.com/gke-max-pods-per-node=32
                   cloud.google.com/gke-nodepool=nap-19wjaxds
                   cloud.google.com/gke-os-distribution=cos
                   cloud.google.com/machine-family=t2a
```
The node label referenced in listings 8.1 and 8.2 ⟶
```
                   kubernetes.io/arch=arm64
                   kubernetes.io/hostname=gk3-autopilot-cluster-4-nap-19wja
                   kubernetes.io/os=linux
                   node.kubernetes.io/instance-type=t2a-standard-4
                   node.kubernetes.io/masq-agent-ds-ready=true
                   topology.gke.io/zone=us-central1-f
                   topology.kubernetes.io/region=us-central1
                   topology.kubernetes.io/zone=us-central1-f
```

8.1.2 Node affinity and anti-affinity

Node affinity is very expressive and can do a lot more than require a set of labels. With the `In` operator, for example, you can specify a list of possible values. Let's say that you want to select either x86 or Arm as the architecture; you can do that using node affinity by providing a list of possible values with the `In` operator as follows.

Listing 8.3 Chapter08/8.1.2_NodeAffinity/deploy_nodeaffinity_multi.yaml

```
apiVersion: apps/v1
kind: Deployment
metadata:
  name: timeserver
spec:
  replicas: 6
  selector:
    matchLabels:
      pod: timeserver-pod
  template:
    metadata:
      labels:
        pod: timeserver-pod
    spec:
      affinity:
        nodeAffinity:
          requiredDuringSchedulingIgnoredDuringExecution:
            nodeSelectorTerms:
            - matchExpressions:
              - key: kubernetes.io/arch
                operator: In
                values:
                - arm64
                - amd64
      containers:
      - name: timeserver-container
        image: docker.io/wdenniss/timeserver:5
        resources:
          requests:
            cpu: 500m
```

> This Pod can run on either arm64 (Arm) or amd64 (x86) architecture.

While the `nodeSelector` field used in listing 8.1 can select on multiple conditions, they all must be satisfied for the Pod to be scheduled. The `In` logic used here to permit scheduling on different values is unique to node affinity. You can require multiple conditions to be satisfied by adding additional expressions under `matchExpressions`.

The `operator` logic can be used to turn the expression into one of anti-affinity (i.e., avoid nodes with the given labels) with `NotIn`, which will ensure the Pod *doesn't* land on a node with the labels specified (table 8.1).

Table 8.1 Operator logic

Operator	Description
In	The value of the node label is one of the options given.
NotIn	The value is not present in the list you supply.
Exists	The label key is present on the node (with any value).
DoesNotExist	The label key is not present on the node.

Table 8.1   Operator logic *(continued)*

Operator	Description
Gt	The value given is greater than that which is in the node label.
Lt	The value given is less than that which is in the node label.

Another benefit of node affinity is that you can create *preferred* rather than *required* rules to express a set of preferences. For example, if your container is multiarchitectural and can run on x86 or Arm, but you prefer to use Arm if possible (e.g., for cost reasons), then you can express that as in the following listing.

Listing 8.4   Chapter08/8.1.2_NodeAffinity/deploy_nodeaffinity_preferred.yaml

```
apiVersion: apps/v1
kind: Deployment
metadata:
  name: timeserver
spec:
  replicas: 6
  selector:
    matchLabels:
      pod: timeserver-pod
  template:
    metadata:
      labels:
        pod: timeserver-pod
    spec:
      affinity:
        nodeAffinity:
          preferredDuringSchedulingIgnoredDuringExecution:
          - weight: 100
            preference:
              matchExpressions:
              - key: kubernetes.io/arch
                operator: In
                values:
                - arm64
      containers:
      - name: timeserver-container
        image: docker.io/wdenniss/timeserver:5
        resources:
          requests:
            cpu: 500m
```

> Prefers to schedule on arm64 but will schedule on any node if arm64 isn't available.

Caveats of preferred affinity

This `preferredDuringSchedulingIgnoredDuringExecution` logic may sometimes yield surprising results. While the preference ordering works when you have existing unallocated capacity on nodes, the way it interacts with cluster autoscaling when

> **(continued)**
>
> there is no unallocated capacity of the preferred type and a new node is needed might be contrary to what you prefer. For example, in the event that there is any unallocated capacity on existing nodes in your cluster, even if it is of the dispreferred type, Kubernetes will actually schedule the Pod there first, before the platform kicks in to add new nodes of your preferred type.
>
> The reason is that the Kubernetes scheduler, responsible for placing Pods on nodes, and the platform autoscaler (a common platform component responsible for adding new nodes), are operating somewhat separately. At the platform level, a typical node autoscaler looks for pending Pods that can be scheduled if more capacity was added. But since the Kubernetes scheduler kicks in first and places the Pod on the dispreferred but available capacity, the autoscaler doesn't have a chance to act.
>
> When using a cloud provider, you can generally just require the functionality you need and rely on the fact that they will have the capacity to serve those needs.

8.1.3   *Tainting nodes to prevent scheduling by default*

Commonly, when you have a group of nodes that have special characteristics you may want to prevent Pods from being scheduled on those nodes by default. Take the Arm architecture, for example: since not all container images support it, you may want to configure your cluster so that Arm architecture nodes will not be used for scheduling by default unless the workload expressly indicates support. Other examples include when you have a node with special hardware like a GPU that you need to reserve only for Pods that will use this hardware or when you have Spot compute that can be shut down abruptly, which not all workloads may respond well to.

While you *could* annotate every other Pod to avoid such nodes using node anti-affinity (i.e., a node affinity rule with the `NotIn` operator), that is laborious. Instead, Kubernetes allows you to "taint" a node to prevent Pods from being scheduled on it by default. How it works is that you taint nodes that have special characteristics and shouldn't be scheduled on by default. Then, you "tolerate" this taint in the PodSpec of just those workloads that are OK to run on these nodes.

By way of example, we can taint nodes individually to see the effect. This isn't how you normally do it in production but it is a decent way to experiment. For this demo, we can use Minikube (introduced in chapter 3) and taint one of the nodes as follows:

```
$ minikube start --nodes 3
Done! kubectl is now configured to use "minikube" cluster

$ kubectl get nodes
NAME            STATUS     ROLES           AGE    VERSION
minikube        Ready      control-plane   77s    v1.24.3
minikube-m02    Ready      <none>          55s    v1.24.3
minikube-m03    NotReady   <none>          19s    v1.24.3
```

```
$ NODE_NAME=minikube-m02
$ kubectl taint nodes $NODE_NAME spot=true:NoSchedule
node/minikube-m02 tainted
```

> **TIP** Later, if you wish to remove the taint, that can be done with `kubectl taint nodes $NODE_NAME spot-`

In this example, `spot=true` is the name we gave to the taint and is used later when marking Pods as able to tolerate this taint. The `NoSchedule` keyword indicates the desired behavior of the effect of this taint (i.e., Pods without the toleration should not be scheduled). There are alternatives to the `NoSchedule` behavior, but I do not recommend them. `PreferNoSchedule` is an option that creates a soft rule, which may sound useful; however, if your primary goal is to avoid scheduling Pods on classes of nodes, a soft rule would not achieve that and may make it harder to debug. Sometimes it's better to have an unscheduled Pod that you need to allocate resources for than having it scheduled on your special tainted machines and cause other unspecified problems.

When you're operating in a hosted Kubernetes platform, it's unlikely that you'll be tainting nodes individually, like in the previous example. Generally, a taint applies to a group of nodes with the same characteristics and nodes are regularly replaced during upgrade or repair events meaning any individual node tainting would be undone. Look for the platform provider's API that allows you to taint groups of nodes so that the taint will be applied to all nodes in the group and persist during upgrades.

Node tainting in GKE

When using GKE in Autopilot mode, node tainting is completely automatic. When you select for a particular (nondefault) feature like Spot compute or Arm architecture, the nodes that are provisioned are automatically tainted. Conveniently, the Pods are also modified to tolerate the automatic taint, so all you need to do is select the feature. This automatic modification of the Pods is done through an admission controller (covered in chapter 12) that is installed and maintained by the platform.

When using GKE with node pools, you can taint node pools when you create them. For example, if you're creating a node pool of VMs, you can configure all the nodes to be tainted as follows:

```
gcloud container node-pools create $NODE_POOL_NAME --cluster $CLUSTER_NAME \
  --spot --node-taints spot=true:NoSchedule
```

If your entire cluster consisted of spot nodes, the taint would not normally be needed, as there would be no need to differentiate the nodes.

Once you have tainted nodes, if you schedule a workload, you'll notice that it won't be scheduled on these nodes (use `kubectl get pods -o wide` to see which nodes the Pod lands on). To make the workload schedulable on the node you just tainted, the workload will need to be updated to tolerate the taint, as shown in the following listing.

Listing 8.5   Chapter08/8.1.3_Taints/deploy_tolerate_spot.yaml

```
apiVersion: apps/v1
kind: Deployment
metadata:
  name: timeserver
spec:
  replicas: 3
  selector:
    matchLabels:
      pod: timeserver-pod
  template:
    metadata:
      labels:
        pod: timeserver-pod
    spec:
      tolerations:          This workload can tolerate nodes with
      - key: spot           the spot=true taint, and therefore
        value: "true"       may be scheduled on them.
      containers:
      - name: timeserver-container
        image: docker.io/wdenniss/timeserver:5
```

The toleration alone won't force the Pod to only be scheduled on a tainted node; it merely *allows* it to be scheduled there. Where the Pod is scheduled will be determined based on a few other factors, like available capacity. Thus, Pods with the toleration can land on untainted nodes, as well as nodes with taints that they tolerate, as shown in figure 8.1.

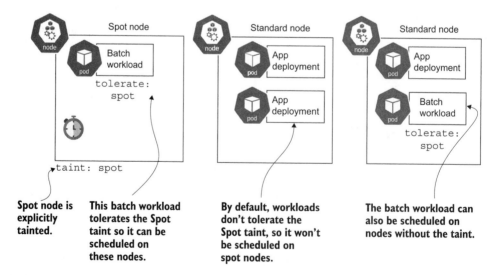

Figure 8.1 This cluster has a lower-availability Spot VM and two standard nodes. The Batch workload Pods tolerate the taint and thus can be scheduled on both, while the App deployment Pods do not, so they will only be scheduled on untainted nodes.

Commonly, you will combine taints and tolerations with node selectors or node affinity to ensure that a particular set of Pods, and only that set of Pods, will be run on the nodes in question. A good example of where this matters is GPU workloads: these workloads must only be run on a node with a GPU, and you don't want non-GPU workloads taking up that valuable space (figure 8.2).

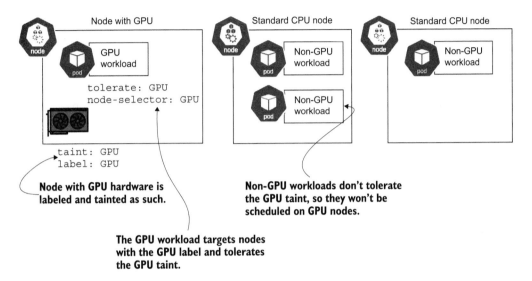

Figure 8.2 This cluster has a special node with a GPU and two standard nodes. The GPU node is tainted to prevent standard workloads from being scheduled on it. The GPU workload tolerates the taint so it can be scheduled on the GPU node and uses a node selector to ensure it is only scheduled on this node.

TOLERATING ALL TAINTS

Some workloads—most commonly, those deployed as DaemonSets (covered in chapter 12)—need to run on every node and must be designed to handle all the configuration of the cluster. Such workloads typically tolerate all taints, as the following listing demonstrates.

Listing 8.6 Chapter08/8.1.3_Taints/daemonset_tolerate_all_taints.yaml

```
apiVersion: apps/v1
kind: DaemonSet
metadata:
  name: example-ds
spec:
  selector:
    matchLabels:
      pod: example-pod
  template:
    metadata:
      labels:
        pod: example-pod
```

```
spec:
  tolerations:
  - effect: NoExecute
    operator: Exists
  - effect: NoSchedule
    operator: Exists
  containers:
  - image: ubuntu
    command: ["sleep", "infinity"]
    name: ubuntu-container
```

Tolerate all taints (annotation pointing to the two toleration blocks)

Just be aware that when you do this, your Pod will actually need to run on all node types that may exist in the cluster now and in the future. This can be a problem when adding a feature like Arm-based nodes that requires containers to be specifically built for the Arm architecture. If a case occurs where you need to have the Pod schedulable on all nodes regardless of taints *except* those with a specific label, such as the Arm architecture, you can do so by combining the tolerations with a node anti-affinity rule, as shown in the next listing.

Listing 8.7   Chapter08/8.1.3_Taints/daemonset_tolerate_antiaffinity.yaml

```
apiVersion: apps/v1
kind: DaemonSet
metadata:
  name: example-ds
spec:
  selector:
    matchLabels:
      pod: example-pod
  template:
    metadata:
      labels:
        pod: example-pod
    spec:
      tolerations:
      - effect: NoExecute
        operator: Exists
      - effect: NoSchedule
        operator: Exists
      affinity:
        nodeAffinity:
          requiredDuringSchedulingIgnoredDuringExecution:
            nodeSelectorTerms:
            - matchExpressions:
              - key: kubernetes.io/arch
                operator: NotIn
                values:
                - arm64
      containers:
      - image: ubuntu
        command: ["sleep", "infinity"]
        name: ubuntu-container
```

Tolerate all taints... (annotation pointing to the two toleration blocks)

...but don't schedule on Arm-based nodes (annotation pointing to the affinity block)

8.1.4 Workload separation

Another use for taints, tolerations, and node selectors is to separate workloads. So far, the use cases for node selection we've covered are around feature-based selection—requiring the Arm architecture, Spot compute, GPU nodes, and the like.

Node selection isn't limited to node features and also can be used to separate workloads from each other on nodes. While you can use Pod anti-affinity (covered in section 8.2.3) to prevent particular Pods from being co-located, sometimes it helps just to keep workloads on their own dedicated groups of nodes.

One requirement for this I've heard multiple times are from people who run batch workloads consisting of coordinator Pods that schedule the work and worker Pods that perform the work. They preferred to keep the Pods for these two roles separate on their own nodes, so that any autoscaling of the nodes for the worker Pods, which tend to come and go, doesn't affect that of the coordinator Pods, which tend to be pretty stable. Another example is the noisy neighbor problem, where two Pods can potentially compete for resources on the node and would work better if separated.

To achieve workload separation, we can combine several of the techniques used so far, along with a custom node label. The node gets a label and a taint, and the workload gets a toleration and selector for that label, which, together, means the workload will be scheduled on a group of nodes by itself (potentially shared with other workloads with the same selector and toleration).

The following listing provides an example Deployment with an arbitrary toleration and node selector to achieve workload separation. For convenience, we will use the same key–value pair (`"group=1"`) for both elements, although note that they are separate concepts in Kubernetes.

> **Listing 8.8   Chapter08/8.1.4_WorkloadSeparation/deploy_group1.yaml**

```
apiVersion: apps/v1
kind: Deployment
metadata:
  name: timeserver1
spec:
  replicas: 5
  selector:
    matchLabels:
      pod: timeserver1-pod
  template:
    metadata:
      labels:
        pod: timeserver1-pod
    spec:
      tolerations:
      - key: group            Tolerate the
        operator: Equal       group=1 taint
        value: "1"
        effect: NoSchedule
```

```
nodeSelector:
    group: "1"                          Select the group=1 label
containers:
- name: timeserver-container
    image: docker.io/wdenniss/timeserver:5
```

And, for demonstration, we can make a copy of this Deployment in the file deploy_group2.yaml using `"group=2"` as the key/value for the toleration and selector:

```
tolerations:
- key: group
    operator: Equal                     Tolerate the
    value: "2"                          group=2 taint
    effect: NoSchedule
nodeSelector:
    group: "2"                          Select the group=2 label
```

To have the Pods for these Deployments deployed on discrete sets of nodes, we'll need to have nodes that are tainted to prevent other Pods from landing on them and labeled so our workloads can target them. If you skip labeling the node, these Deployments won't ever be scheduled, as there won't be a node that meets the node selector requirement. If you label the nodes but don't taint them, these workloads will schedule and be separated from each other by way of the node selector. However, other random Pods might land on them as well since there is no taint to keep them away.

> ### Workload separation on GKE Autopilot
>
> If you deploy the previous workload on GKE in Autopilot mode, nodes with the requested labels and taints will be provisioned automatically! That's because this operationally nodeless platform is actuating on your Pod's requirements and providing nodes that match, so there's nothing more you need to do. In a traditional Kubernetes platform where you are managing nodes, you'll need to create nodes with these properties yourself.

In Kubernetes environments where you manage the nodes, you'll need to provide nodes with the correct taints and labels to achieve workload separation. Using Minikube to demonstrate, we can taint and label nodes directly. Just note that on a managed platform, you typically operate on nodes at a node-pool or group level and would use a platform API to provide the nodes, so look for the label and taint parameters in that API:

```
$ minikube start --nodes 3          ⊲──  Create a new
                                         Minikube cluster.

$ kubectl get nodes
NAME           STATUS   ROLES           AGE   VERSION
minikube       Ready    control-plane   67s   v1.24.3
minikube-m02   Ready    <none>          46s   v1.24.3
minikube-m03   Ready    <none>          24s   v1.24.3
```

View the nodes.

```
$ kubectl taint nodes minikube-m02 group=1:NoSchedule        Taint and label the
$ kubectl label node minikube-m02 group=1                    m02 node for group 1.

$ kubectl taint nodes minikube-m03 group=2:NoSchedule        Taint and label the
$ kubectl label node minikube-m03 group=2                    m03 node for group 2.
```

Both the taint and the label are required (as is the matching toleration and node selector in the Deployment) as they serve different purposes. The taint prevents all but those workloads that tolerate the taint from landing on it, while the label can be used to ensure the workload doesn't land on any other nodes (e.g., nodes without any taints). For convenience, I used the same key–value pair for both the taint and the label (`"group=1"`), but this doesn't have to be the case.

With our cluster configured, we can deploy our workload-separated Deployments and watch the result. Pay particular attention to which node the Pods land on:

```
$ kubectl create -f Chapter08/8.1.4_WorkloadSeparation
deployment.apps/timeserver1 created               Pods for timeserver1 are
deployment.apps/timeserver2 created                  running on the node
                                                         minikube-m02
$ kubectl get pods -o wide
NAME                          READY  STATUS   RESTARTS  AGE   NODE
timeserver1-75b69b5795-9n7ds  1/1    Running  0         2m2s  minikube-m02
timeserver1-75b69b5795-kft64  1/1    Running  0         2m2s  minikube-m02
timeserver1-75b69b5795-mnc4j  1/1    Running  0         2m2s  minikube-m02
timeserver1-75b69b5795-msg9v  1/1    Running  0         2m2s  minikube-m02
timeserver1-75b69b5795-r8r9t  1/1    Running  0         2m2s  minikube-m02
timeserver2-6cbf875b6b-6wm7w  1/1    Running  0         2m2s  minikube-m03
timeserver2-6cbf875b6b-dtnhm  1/1    Running  0         2m2s  minikube-m03
timeserver2-6cbf875b6b-fd6vh  1/1    Running  0         2m2s  minikube-m03
timeserver2-6cbf875b6b-q6fk8  1/1    Running  0         2m2s  minikube-m03
timeserver2-6cbf875b6b-zvk72  1/1    Running  0         2m2s  minikube-m03
```

Pods for timeserver2 are running on the node minikube-m03

Once you're done with the minikube cluster, you can delete all traces of it:

```
minikube delete
```

8.2 Placing Pods

It's good practice to have multiple Pod replicas in case one fails a health check or has a memory leak and needs to be restarted. In addition to how the number of replicas affects availability (discussed in section 5.2.4), it's also important to consider *where* those Pods are placed.

If you have 10 replicas of a Pod, but they're all on a single node, you would be affected by the failure of that node. Expanding on this using typical cloud topologies, if all your *nodes* are in a single availability zone, you're at risk of a zone outage. How much time and money you should spend guarding against these conditions is a choice you need to make based on your own production guarantees and budget since the sky is the limit (e.g., do you even go multicloud?).

I will focus this section on some sensible and affordable strategies for spreading your Pods on the nodes you already have. You can do it for no extra cost, and it gets you some additional availability.

8.2.1   *Building highly available deployments*

So far, we've learned about how resource requests are used to allocate Pods to nodes. However, there are other dimensions to consider. To make your application highly available, it is desirable that the replicas don't all end up on the same node. Say you have a small Pod (100 mCPU, 100 MiB) and three replicas. These three replicas could easily all fit on the same node. But then, if that node were to fail, the deployment would be offline.

Better would be to have the scheduler spread these Pods out across your cluster! Fortunately, Kubernetes has a built-in way to achieve this called a *topology spread constraint* (figure 8.3). A topology spread constraint aims to spread your nodes across a failure domain, such as the node or a whole zone; multiple constraints can be specified, so you can spread across both nodes and zones or any other failure domains defined by your provider.

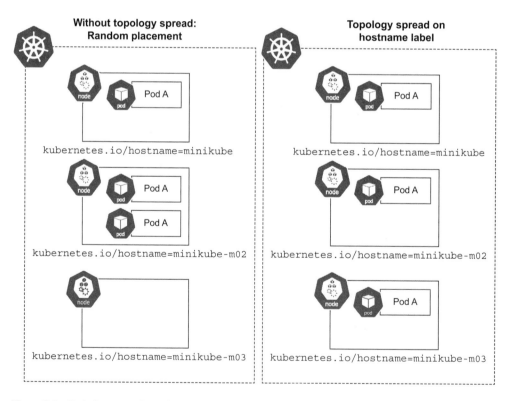

Figure 8.3   Pod placement for a single workload with and without topology constraints

NOTE Many Kubernetes providers have some default topology spread for workload deployments, including GKE. If you trust the default settings to do the right thing in most cases, feel free to skip past this section. I've included this information regardless, as I find it helps to know why things work the way they do, so I think it's important to understand why Pods get spread over nodes. It is also possible to use the techniques in this chapter to modify the default policies, such as to impose something stricter, say, for a mission-critical deployment, and to apply topology spreads to objects that don't get them by default, like Jobs (covered in chapter 10).

To override the spread topology for a particular workload, you can add the `topologySpreadConstraints` key, as I've done in the following listing.

> **Listing 8.9 Chapter08/8.2.1_TopologySpread/deploy_topology.yaml**

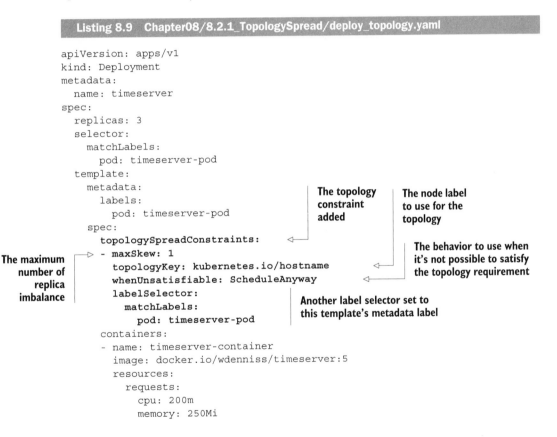

In this example, we're targeting the `kubernetes.io/hostname` topology using the `topologyKey` parameter, which means that Kubernetes will consider all nodes labeled with the same value for the `kubernetes.io/hostname` key to be equal. Since no two nodes should be labeled with the same hostname, this yields a node-level spreading target.

For this configuration to work—and I cannot stress this enough—you must ensure that the nodes in your cluster actually have the label specified in `topologyKey` (`kubernetes.io/hostname` in my example). There are some well-known labels,[1] like the one I'm using here, but there is no guarantee that your Kubernetes platform will use them. So, verify by running `kubectl describe node` and look at the labels that your nodes have.

Going over the rest of the settings in the example, I've used a `maxSkew` of `1`, the smallest possible skew. Thus, there can be, at most, one level of imbalance, which means any node can have, at most, one more Pod than the other nodes.

The `whenUnsatisfiable` parameter governs what happens when the constraint can't be satisfied (say, a node is completely full with other Pods). The choices are `ScheduleAnyway` and `DoNotSchedule`, whose behavior is self-explanatory. `DoNotSchedule` is helpful when testing as it makes it easier to see when the rule is working, but for production, `ScheduleAnyway` is going to be safer. While `ScheduleAnyway` makes the rule a "soft" rule, Kubernetes will still do its best to meet your requirements, which I think is better than leaving the replica unscheduled altogether, especially when our goal is higher availability of our replicas!

The last field is a `labelSelector` with a child `matchLabels` group, which you may recall from chapter 3. It's frustrating that Kubernetes doesn't have a simple self-reference here; that is, why do you even need this at all since it's already embedded in the Pod's specification? In any case, `matchLabels` should be the same as what you specified already in the Deployment.

With that, let's go ahead and deploy this example and verify that the resulting placement is what we expect. To demo this, we'll need a cluster with a few nodes and one without any default spreading behavior. GKE comes with default node and zonal spreading, so this setting isn't as needed on that platform; it's still good to understand that this is what's happening behind the scenes or if you need to fine-tune the behavior. To try this out and see the differences between various topologies, I suggest Minikube configured with three nodes:

```
minikube start --nodes 3
cd Chapter08/8.2.1_TopologySpread
kubectl create -f deploy_topology.yaml
kubectl get pods -o wide
```

Looking at the NODE column in figure 8.4, you should see three separate nodes (assuming you have three nodes in the cluster).

NOTE Topology spread is a scheduling-time constraint; in other words, it's considered only when Pods are placed onto nodes. Once all replicas are running, if the topology changes (e.g., a node is added), the running Pods will not be moved. If needed, you can redeploy the Pods by rolling out a change

[1] https://kubernetes.io/docs/reference/kubernetes-api/labels-annotations-taints/

```
$ kubectl get pods -o wide
NAME                         READY  STATUS   RESTARTS  AGE  IP           NODE
timeserver-754665f45f-6n6bc  1/1    Running  0         39s  10.244.2.46  minikube-m03
timeserver-754665f45f-dkvvp  1/1    Running  0         39s  10.244.0.27  minikube
timeserver-754665f45f-dmqpq  1/1    Running  0         39s  10.244.1.47  minikube-m02
```

Figure 8.4   Deployment with `topologySpreadConstraints`, with the unique nodes shown within the box

to the deployment, which will apply the scheduling rules again, so any topology changes would then be considered.

We can see from the output in figure 8.4 that each of our three Pods was scheduled on a different node. To compare, deploy the same Deployment but without the `topology-SpreadConstraints` field, and you'll notice that Pods can be grouped up on the same node. If you observe Pods being spread out even without a topology being set, then it's likely due to a cluster default.

The `topologySpreadConstraints` field can be used with any node label, so another common strategy is to spread across zones (if you have a multizone cluster). To do so, you can repeat the earlier example but use a zone-based key, with `topology .kubernetes.io/zone` being the standardized, well-known key. But again, do check that your nodes actually have this label; otherwise, it will have no effect or will prevent scheduling entirely depending how you configured the `whenUnsatisfiable` field. Multiple topologies can be specified in the array provided to `topologySpreadConstraints`, so you can have both a node and zonal spread.

8.2.2 Co-locating interdependent Pods

In some cases, you may have tightly coupled Pods where it's desirable to have them be present on the same physical machine (figure 8.5). Services that are particularly "chatty" (i.e., they make a lot of interservice procedure calls) are often candidates for this type of architecture. Say you have a frontend and a backend, and they communicate a lot with each other. You may wish to pair them on nodes together to reduce network latency and traffic.

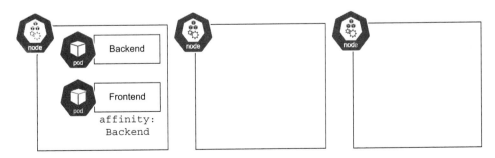

Figure 8.5   Three frontend Pods scheduled on the same node as the backend Pod using Pod affinity

This deployment construct can be achieved through Pod affinity rules. Essentially, one of the Deployments—using the previous example, perhaps the frontend—gets a rule that tells the scheduler, "Only place this Pod on nodes that have a backend Pod." Let's say we have the backend Deployment as in the following listing.

Listing 8.10   Chapter08/8.2.2_Colocation/backend.yaml

```
apiVersion: apps/v1
kind: Deployment
metadata:
  name: mariadb
spec:
  replicas: 1
  selector:
    matchLabels:
      pod: mariadb-pod
  template:
    metadata:
      labels:
        pod: mariadb-pod          The label that will
    spec:                         be used for affinity.
      containers:
      - name: mariadb-container
        image: mariadb
        env:
        - name: MARIADB_RANDOM_ROOT_PASSWORD
          value: "1"
```

There is nothing special about this Deployment at all; it follows the same pattern we've been using. This Pod will be placed on any available space in the cluster.

Now, for the frontend Deployment, where we want to require it to be placed on nodes with instances of a Pod from the backend Deployment, we can use the configuration in the following listing.

Listing 8.11   Chapter08/8.2.2_Colocation/frontend.yaml

```
apiVersion: apps/v1
kind: Deployment
metadata:
  name: timeserver
spec:
  replicas: 3
  selector:
    matchLabels:
      pod: timeserver-pod
  template:
    metadata:
      labels:
        pod: timeserver-pod
    spec:
      containers:
      - name: timeserver-container
        image: docker.io/wdenniss/timeserver:5
```

```
affinity:
  podAffinity:
    requiredDuringSchedulingIgnoredDuringExecution:
    - labelSelector:
        matchExpressions:
        - key: pod
          operator: In
          values:
          - mariadb-pod
        topologyKey: "kubernetes.io/hostname"
```

Pod affinity rule

This specification requires that the scheduler locate this Pod on a node within the specified topology that has an existing Pod with the label `pod: mariadb-pod`. If you create these two objects on the same minikube cluster used in the previous section, you will notice that all four Pods are placed on the same node (being the node where the backend Pod was scheduled). As the topology in the example is a node topology (using the well-known label for hostname), the app will only be scheduled onto a node that has the target Pod. If a zonal topology was used (using the well-known label for zone, as discussed in 8.2.1), the Pod would be placed on any node in the zone that has an existing Pod with the target label.

To make this co-location a soft (or best-effort) requirement so that your Pods will still be scheduled, even if the requirement can't be satisfied, `preferredDuringScheduling-IgnoredDuringExecution` can be used instead of `requiredDuringSchedulingIgnored-DuringExecution`. When using preferred affinity there are a few additional fields to add to the spec, such as the weight of the rule (which is used to rank the priority if multiple preferences are expressed).

As you can see, Kubernetes is really flexible, allowing you to make scheduling rules binding or just guidelines and specify your preferred topology in a myriad of ways (with node and zonal being two common choices). It's so flexible, in fact, that it's possible to get bamboozled by the choices. For most deployments, I would advise *not* using Pod affinities at the outset, but rather keeping these techniques in your back pocket and applying them when you have specific problems you wish to resolve (like wanting to co-locate Pods on a single node to reduce interservice latency).

8.2.3 Avoiding certain Pods

In section 8.2.1, I covered how you can use topology spread to spread out Pods from the *same* workload deployment to avoid single points of failure. What about Pods that are related (so you want them spread out) but are deployed separately (where topology spread will not apply)? As an example, imagine you have a Deployment for a backend service and a separate Deployment for a caching service and would prefer they be spread out.

For this, you can use Pod anti-affinity. This simply throws the Pod affinity rule from the previous section into reverse so that the Pods will be scheduled on other nodes or the topology of your choice.

Listing 8.12   Chapter08/8.2.3_PodAntiAffinity/frontend.yaml

```
apiVersion: apps/v1
kind: Deployment
metadata:
  name: timeserver
spec:
  replicas: 3
  selector:
    matchLabels:
      pod: timeserver-pod
  template:
    metadata:
      labels:
        pod: timeserver-pod
    spec:
      containers:
      - name: timeserver-container
        image: docker.io/wdenniss/timeserver:5
      affinity:
        podAntiAffinity:
          requiredDuringSchedulingIgnoredDuringExecution:
          - labelSelector:
              matchExpressions:
              - key: pod
                operator: In
                values:
                - mariadb-pod
            topologyKey: "kubernetes.io/hostname"
```

The Pod affinity rule from the previous example is reversed, so now this Pod will explicitly avoid nodes that have a Pod with the pod: mariadb-pod label.

All these constructs can be used together, too, so you can have a topology spread that broadly seeks to keep Pods apart, with affinity rules for fine-grained control. Just be careful that your rules can actually be satisfied; otherwise, you'll end up with unscheduled Pods. As with the regular affinity in the previous section, you can also use soft rules by specifying `preferredDuringSchedulingIgnoredDuringExecution` instead of `requiredDuringSchedulingIgnoredDuringExecution`. When doing this, you might want to test it first with the required version of the rule to ensure you have your `labelSelector` field set up correctly before switching to the preferred version. The next section has some more debugging tips for setting these rules.

8.3   *Debugging placement problems*

Pod placement is a pretty complex topic, so don't be surprised if you encounter problems. The most common problem occurs when you require the existence of a label that none of your nodes have or, in the case of a nodeless platform, a label for a feature that isn't supported by the platform. Such Pods will never be scheduled. The following sections highlight some of the common problems you might encounter and how to solve them.

8.3.1   *Placement rules don't appear to work*

If your placement rules don't appear to work in testing, the first thing I'd suggest is to ensure you are not using any soft (preferred) placement rules. These rules mean that the scheduler basically ignores your rule when it can't be satisfied, which isn't so great for testing. It's better to verify that all your rules are working before relaxing them by changing them to soft rules.

Use a small cluster with only a couple of nodes and no soft rules, and you should be able to observe the effect of the placement features. Verify that the rules are enforced by intentionally attempting to schedule Pods that would violate the rules. Their status should be `Pending` because the constraints can't be satisfied.

8.3.2   *Pods are pending*

Pods in the `Pending` state mean that the scheduler can't find a suitable place for them. In chapter 3, we discussed this error in the context of the cluster not having enough resources to place the Pod. Once you configure your placement rules, it's possible the Pod can't be scheduled because the rules can't be satisfied. To find out what the reason is (i.e., which rule couldn't be satisfied), *describe* the Pod. Note that you need to do this at a Pod level—the Deployment itself won't show any error messages, although it will indicate that the desired number of replicas isn't met:

```
kubectl get pods
kubectl describe Pod $POD_NAME
```

The following is an example output for a situation where the available nodes had a taint that the Pod didn't tolerate. Either add the toleration to the Pod or add more nodes without the taint. Some example errors include the following:

```
Events:
  Type      Reason            Age       From               Message
  ----      ------            ----      ----               -------
  Warning   FailedScheduling  4s        default-scheduler  0/1 nodes
are available: 1 node(s) had taints that the pod didn't tolerate.
```

And here's some output for a situation where the Pod's affinity or anti-affinity rules could not be satisfied. Review and revise the rules and try again:

```
  Type      Reason            Age                From               Message
  ----      ------            ----               ----               -------
  Warning   FailedScheduling  17s (x3 over 90s)  default-scheduler  0/1 nodes
are available: 1 node(s) didn't match pod affinity/anti-affinity, 1 node(s)
didn't match pod anti-affinity rules.
```

Summary

- From your Pod specification, you can select or avoid nodes with specific hardware properties.
- Nodes with special characteristics can be tainted to prevent scheduling by default. Pods designed to run on these nodes can be configured to tolerate the taint.
- Taints, tolerations, node labels, and selectors can be combined to keep certain workloads separate from each other.
- Build high-availability deployments with multiple replicas and a well-configured topology spread policy.
- Pods that benefit from being in proximity to each other can be co-located with Pod affinity.
- Pods that you don't wish to co-locate can be configured with Pod anti-affinity.

Stateful applications 9

This chapter covers

- The Kubernetes constructs used to represent disks and state
- Adding persistent storage to Pods
- Deploying a multiple-Pod stateful application with a leader role using StatefulSet
- Migrating and recovering data by relinking Kubernetes objects to disk resources
- Giving Pods large ephemeral storage volumes

Stateful applications (i.e., workloads that have attached storage) finally have a home with Kubernetes. While state*less* applications are often lauded for their ease of deployment and high scalability, helped greatly by avoiding the need to attach and manage storage, that doesn't mean that state*ful* applications don't have their place. Whether you're deploying a sophisticated database or are migrating an old stateful application from a virtual machine (VM), Kubernetes has you covered.

Using persistent volumes, you can attach stateful storage to any Kubernetes Pod. When it comes to multi-replica workloads with state, just as Kubernetes offers

Deployment as a high-level construct for managing a stateless application, StatefulSet exists to provide high-level management of stateful applications.

9.1 Volumes, persistent volumes, claims, and storage classes

To get started with storing state in Kubernetes, there are a few concepts around volume (disk) management to cover before moving on to the higher-level StatefulSet construct. Just like nodes are the Kubernetes representation of a VM, Kubernetes has its own representation of disks as well.

9.1.1 Volumes

Kubernetes offers functionality to Pods that allows them to mount a volume. What's a *volume*? The docs describe it like so:

> At its core, a volume is just a directory, possibly with some data in it, which is accessible to the containers in a Pod. How that directory comes to be, the medium that backs it, and the contents of it are determined by the particular volume type used[1].

Kubernetes ships with some built-in volume types, and others can be added by your platform administrator via storage drivers. One type you may encounter frequently is emptyDir, an ephemeral volume tied to the lifecycle of the node, ConfigMap, which allows you to specify files in Kubernetes manifests and present them to your application as a file on disk, and cloud provider disks for persistent storage.

EMPTYDIR VOLUMES

The built-in volume type emptyDir is an ephemeral volume that is allocated on space from the node's boot disk. If the Pod is deleted or moved to another node or the node itself becomes unhealthy, all data is lost. So what's the benefit?

Pods can have multiple containers, and emptyDir mounts can be shared between them. So when you need to share data between containers, you would define an emptyDir volume and mount it in each container in the Pod (listing 9.1). The data is also persisted between container *restarts*, just not all the other events I mentioned earlier. This is useful for ephemeral data such as that of an on-disk cache, where it is beneficial if the data is preserved between Pod restarts but where long-term storage isn't necessary.

Listing 9.1 Chapter09/9.1.1_Volume/emptydir_pod.yaml

```
apiVersion: v1
kind: Pod
metadata:
  name: emptydir-pod
  labels:
    pod: timeserver-pod
```

---

[1] https://kubernetes.io/docs/concepts/storage/volumes/

```
spec:
  containers:
  - name: timeserver-container
    image: docker.io/wdenniss/timeserver:5
    volumeMounts:
    - name: cache-volume
      mountPath: /app/cache/
  volumes:
  - name: cache-volume
    emptyDir: {}
```

The mount path

The volume definition

Why on earth is this called `emptyDir`? Because the data is stored in an initially empty directory on the node. It's a misnomer, in my opinion, but what can you do?

> **TIP** If you're looking for scratch space for a workload, see section 9.4 on generic ephemeral volumes, a more modern way to get ephemeral storage without relying on the host volume.

For a practical example, see section 9.2.2, in which `emptyDir` is used to share data between two containers in the same Pod, where one of them is an init container that runs first and can perform setup steps for the main container.

CONFIGMAP VOLUME

ConfigMap is a useful Kubernetes object. You can define key–value pairs in one place and reference them from multiple other objects. You can also use them to store entire files! Typically, these files would be configuration files like `my.cnf` for MariaDB, `httpd.conf` for Apache, `redis.conf` for Redis, and so on. You can mount the Config-Map as a volume, which allows the files it defines to be read from the container. ConfigMap volumes are read-only.

This technique is particularly useful for defining a configuration file for use by a public container image, as it allows you to provide configuration without needing to extend the image itself. For example, to run Redis, you can reference the official Redis image and just mount your config file using ConfigMap wherever Redis expects it—no need to build your own image just to provide this one file. See sections 9.2.1 and 9.2.2 for examples of configuring Redis with a custom configuration file specified via a ConfigMap volume.

CLOUD PROVIDER VOLUMES

More applicable for building *stateful* applications, where you don't typically want to use ephemeral or read-only volumes, is mounting disks from your cloud provider as volumes. Wherever you are running Kubernetes, your provider should have supplied drivers into the cluster that allow you to mount persistent storage, whether that's NFS or block-based (often both).

By way of example, the following listing provides the specification for a MariaDB Pod running in Google Kubernetes Engine (GKE) mounting a GCE persistent disk at `/var/lib/mysql` for persistent storage as illustrated in figure 9.1.

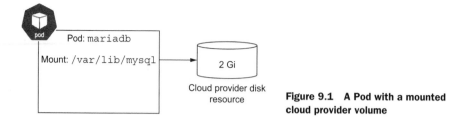

Figure 9.1   **A Pod with a mounted cloud provider volume**

Listing 9.2   Chapter09/9.1.1_Volume/mariadb_pod.yaml

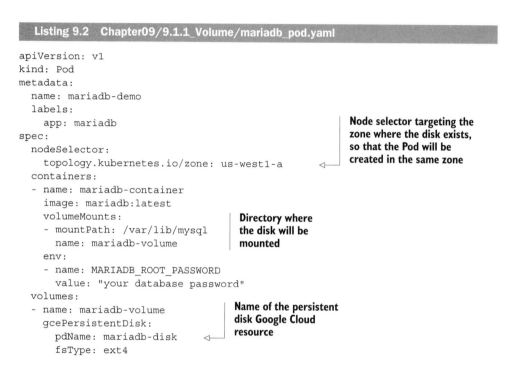

```
apiVersion: v1
kind: Pod
metadata:
  name: mariadb-demo
  labels:
    app: mariadb
spec:
  nodeSelector:
    topology.kubernetes.io/zone: us-west1-a
  containers:
  - name: mariadb-container
    image: mariadb:latest
    volumeMounts:
    - mountPath: /var/lib/mysql
      name: mariadb-volume
    env:
    - name: MARIADB_ROOT_PASSWORD
      value: "your database password"
  volumes:
  - name: mariadb-volume
    gcePersistentDisk:
      pdName: mariadb-disk
      fsType: ext4
```

Node selector targeting the zone where the disk exists, so that the Pod will be created in the same zone

Directory where the disk will be mounted

Name of the persistent disk Google Cloud resource

Unlike the more automated and cloud-agnostic approaches we'll cover next, this method is tied to your cloud provider and requires manual creation of the disk. You need to ensure that a disk with the name specified exists, which you need to create out of band (i.e., using your cloud provider's tools), and that both the disk and the Pod are in the same zone. In this example, I use `nodeSelector` to target the zone of the disk, which is important for any Kubernetes cluster that exists in multiple zones; otherwise, your Pod could be scheduled on a different zone from that of the disk.

Creating the disk used by this example out of band can be achieved using the following command:

```
gcloud compute disks create --size=10GB --zone=us-west1-a mariadb-disk
```

NOTE   This example and the accompanying cloud-provider-specific instructions are provided for completeness, and to illustrate how volumes developed, but it's not the recommended way to use volumes. Read on for a better, platform-agnostic way to create disks with PersistentVolumes and StatefulSet!

Since we're creating this disk manually, pay close attention to the location where the resource is being created. The zone in the previous command and the zone set via the `nodeSelector` configuration need to match. If you see your Pod stuck in `Container Creating`, inspect your event log for the answer. Here's a case where I hadn't created the disk in the right project:

```
$ kubectl get events -w

0s Warning FailedAttachVolume pod/mariadb-demo
AttachVolume.Attach failed for volume "mariadb-volume" : GCE persistent disk
not found: diskName="mariadb-disk" zone="us-west1-a"
```

The downside to mounting volumes directly is that the disks need to be created outside of Kubernetes, which means the following:

- The user creating the Pod must have permissions to create the disk, which is not always the case.
- Steps exist outside of Kubernetes configuration that need to be remembered and run manually.
- The volume descriptors are platform-dependent, so this Kubernetes YAML is not portable and won't work on another provider.

Naturally, Kubernetes has a solution for this lack of portability. By using the persistent volume abstraction provided by Kubernetes, you can simply request the disk resources you need and have them provisioned for you with no need to perform any out-of-band steps. Read on.

9.1.2 Persistent volumes and claims

To provide a way to manage volumes in a more platform-agnostic way, Kubernetes offers higher-level primitives: *PersistentVolume* (PV) and *PersistentVolumeClaim* (PVC). Instead of linking to the volume directly, the Pod references a PersistentVolumeClaim object, which defines the disk resources that the Pod requires in platform-agnostic terms (e.g., "1 gigabyte of storage"). The disk resources themselves are represented in Kubernetes using a PersistentVolume object, much like how nodes in Kubernetes represent the VM resource. When the PersistentVolumeClaim is created, Kubernetes will seek to provide the resources requested in the claim by creating or matching it with a PersistentVolume and binding the two objects together (figure 9.2). Once bound, the PV and PVC, which now reference each other, typically remain linked until the underlying disk is deleted.

This behavior of having the claim, which requests resources, and an object that represents the availability of resources is similar to how a Pod requests compute resources like CPU and memory and the cluster finds a node that has these resources

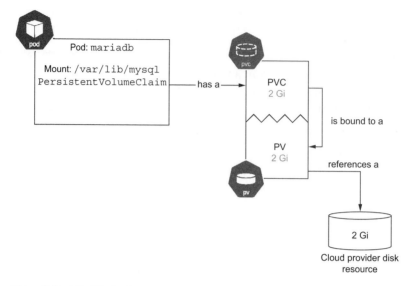

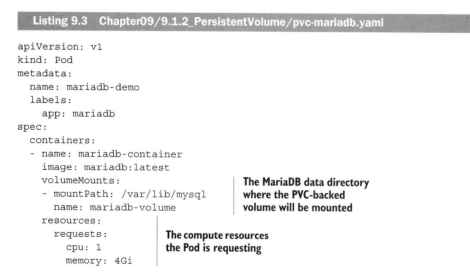

Figure 9.2   A Pod that references a `PersistentVolumeClaim` that gets bound to a `PersistentVolume`, which references a disk

to schedule the Pod on. It also means that the storage requests are defined in a platform-independent manner. Unlike using the cloud provider disk directly, when using PersistentVolumeClaim, your Pods can be deployed anywhere, provided the platform supports persistent storage.

Let's rewrite our Pod from the previous section to use PersistentVolumeClaim to request a new PersistentVolume for our Pod. This Pod will attach an external disk mounted to `/var/lib/mysql`, which is where MariaDB stores its data.

Listing 9.3   Chapter09/9.1.2_PersistentVolume/pvc-mariadb.yaml

```
apiVersion: v1
kind: Pod
metadata:
  name: mariadb-demo
  labels:
    app: mariadb
spec:
  containers:
  - name: mariadb-container
    image: mariadb:latest
    volumeMounts:
    - mountPath: /var/lib/mysql
      name: mariadb-volume
    resources:
      requests:
        cpu: 1
        memory: 4Gi
```

The MariaDB data directory where the PVC-backed volume will be mounted

The compute resources the Pod is requesting

```
    env:
    - name: MARIADB_ROOT_PASSWORD
      value: "your database password"
  volumes:
  - name: mariadb-volume
    persistentVolumeClaim:          ┃  Reference to the persistentVolumeClaim
      claimName: mariadb-pv-claim    ┃  object instead of a disk resource
---
apiVersion: v1
kind: PersistentVolumeClaim    ◁──┨  The PersistentVolumeClaim
metadata:                         ┃  object
  name: mariadb-pv-claim
spec:
  accessModes:
  - ReadWriteOnce
  resources:             ┃  The storage resources
    requests:            ┃  the Pod is requesting
      storage: 2Gi
```

In the PersistentVolumeClaim definition, we're making a request for 2 GiB of storage and specifying the desired `accessMode`. The `ReadWriteOnce` access mode is for a volume that behaves like a traditional hard drive, where your storage is mounted to a single Pod for read/write access and is the most common. The other choices for `accessMode` are `ReadOnlyMany`, which can be used to mount a volume of existing data that's shared across many Pods, and `ReadWriteMany` for mounting file storage (like NFS), where multiple Pods can read/write at the same time (a fairly special mode, only supported by a few storage drivers). In this chapter, the goal is stateful applications backed by traditional block-based volumes, so `ReadWriteOnce` is used throughout.

If your provider supports dynamic provisioning, a PersistentVolume backed by a disk resource will be created to fulfill the storage requested by the PersistentVolumeClaim, after which the PersistentVolumeClaim and PersistentVolume will be bound together. The dynamic provisioning behavior of the PersistentVolume is defined through the StorageClass, which we will cover in the next section. GKE and almost every provider support dynamic provisioning and will have a default storage class, so the previous Pod definition in listing 9.3 can be deployed pretty much anywhere.

In the rare event that your provider *doesn't* have dynamic provisioning, you (or the cluster operator/admin) will need to manually create PersistentVolume yourself with enough resources to satisfy the PersistentVolumeClaim request (figure 9.3). Kubernetes still does the matchmaking of linking the claim to the volume of the manually created PersistentVolumes.

The PersistentVolumeClaim, as defined in the previous example, can be thought of as a request for resources. The claim on a resource happens later when it is matched with, and is bound to, a PersistentVolume resource, and both resources are linked to each other. Essentially, the PersistentVolumeClaim has a lifecycle that starts as a request and becomes a claim when bound.

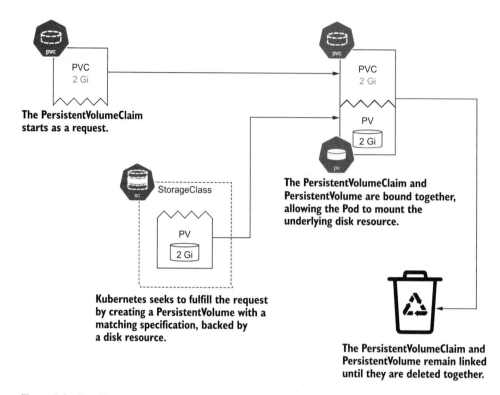

Figure 9.3 The lifecycle of a PersistentVolumeClaim and PersistentVolume in a dynamically provisioned system

We could leave it there, but since your precious data will be stored on these disks, let's dig in to see just how this binding works. If we create the resource in listing 9.3 and then query the YAML of the PersistentVolumeClaim *after* it's bound, you'll see that it's been updated with a volumeName. This volumeName is the name of the Persistent-Volume that it was linked to and now claims. Here's what it looks like (with some superfluous information omitted for readability):

```
$ kubectl create -f Chapter09/9.1.2_PersistentVolume/pvc-mariadb.yaml
pod/mariadb-demo created
persistentvolumeclaim/mariadb-pv-claim created

$ kubectl get -o yaml pvc/mariadb-pv-claim
apiVersion: v1
kind: PersistentVolumeClaim
metadata:
  name: mariadb-pv-claim
spec:
  accessModes:
  - ReadWriteOnce
  resources:
    requests:
```

```
      storage: 2Gi
  storageClassName: standard-rwo
  volumeMode: Filesystem
  volumeName: pvc-ecb0c9ed-9aee-44b2-a1e5-ff70d9d3823a
status:
  accessModes:
  - ReadWriteOnce
  capacity:
    storage: 2Gi
  phase: Bound
```

The PersistentVolume
that this object is
now bound to

We can query the PersistentVolume named in this configuration with `kubectl get -o yaml pv $NAME`, and we'll see that it links right back to the PVC. Here is what mine looked like:

```
$ kubectl get -o yaml pv pvc-ecb0c9ed-9aee-44b2-a1e5-ff70d9d3823a
apiVersion: v1
kind: PersistentVolume
metadata:
  name: pvc-ecb0c9ed-9aee-44b2-a1e5-ff70d9d3823a
spec:
  accessModes:
  - ReadWriteOnce
  capacity:
    storage: 2Gi
  claimRef:
    apiVersion: v1
    kind: PersistentVolumeClaim
    name: mariadb-pv-claim
    namespace: default
  csi:
    driver: pd.csi.storage.gke.io
    fsType: ext4
    volumeAttributes:
      storage.kubernetes.io/csiProvisionerIdentity: 1615534731524-8081-pd.
  csi.storage.gke.io
      volumeHandle: projects/gke-autopilot-test/zones/us-west1-b/disks/pvc-ecb
  0c9ed-9aee-44b2-a1e5-ff70d9d3823a
  persistentVolumeReclaimPolicy: Delete
  storageClassName: standard-rwo
  volumeMode: Filesystem
status:
  phase: Bound
```

The PersistentVolumeClaim that
this PersistentVolume is bound to

The pointer to
the underlying
disk resources

The status is
now bound.

It helps to visualize this side by side, so take a look at figure 9.4.

The PersistentVolumeClaim has really undergone a metamorphosis here, going from a request for resources to being a claim for a specific disk resource that will contain your data. This is not really like any other Kubernetes object I can think of. While it's common to have Kubernetes add fields and perform actions on the object, few changes like these do, starting as a generic request for and representation of storage and ending up as a bound stateful object.

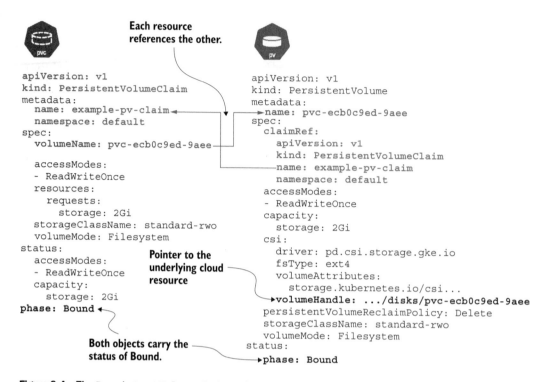

Each resource references the other.

Pointer to the underlying cloud resource

Both objects carry the status of Bound.

Figure 9.4   The `PersistentVolumeClaim` and `PersistentVolume` after the latter was provisioned, and they were bound together

There is one exception to this typical lifecycle of a PersistentVolumeClaim, which is when you have existing data that you wish to mount into a Pod. In that case, you create the PersistentVolumeClaim and the PersistentVolume objects already pointing at each other, so they are bound immediately at creation. This scenario is discussed in section 9.3 on migrating and recovering disks, including a fully worked data recovery scenario.

Testing the MariaDB Pod locally

Want to connect to MariaDB and check everything was setup correctly? It's easy. Just forward to the mariadb container's port to your machine:

```
kubectl port-forward pod/mariadb-demo 3306:3306
```

Then, connect to it from a local mysql client. Don't have a client handy? You can run one via Docker!

```
docker run --net=host -it --rm mariadb mariadb -h localhost -P 3306 \
-u root -p
```

(continued)

The database password can be found in the environment variable of the Pod (listing 9.3). Once you connect you can run a SQL query to test it out, for example:

```
MariaDB [(none)]> SELECT user, host FROM mysql.user;
+-------------+-----------+
| User        | Host      |
+-------------+-----------+
| root        | %         |
| healthcheck | 127.0.0.1 |
| healthcheck | ::1       |
| healthcheck | localhost |
| mariadb.sys | localhost |
| root        | localhost |
+-------------+-----------+
6 rows in set (0.005 sec)

MariaDB [(none)]> CREATE DATABASE foo;
Query OK, 1 row affected (0.006 sec)

MariaDB [(none)]> exit
Bye
```

9.1.3 *Storage classes*

So far, we've relied on the default dynamic provisioning behavior of the platform provider. But what about if we want to change what type of disks we get during the binding process? Or, what happens to the data if the PersistentVolumeClaim is deleted? That's where storage classes come in.

Storage classes are a way to describe the different types of *dynamic* storage that are available to be requested from PersistentVolumeClaims and how the volumes that are requested in this way should be configured. Your Kubernetes cluster probably has a few defined already. Let's view them with `kubectl get storageclass` (some columns in the output have been removed for readability):

```
$ kubectl get storageclass
NAME                    PROVISIONER              RECLAIMPOLICY
premium-rwo             pd.csi.storage.gke.io    Delete
standard                kubernetes.io/gce-pd     Delete
standard-rwo (default)  pd.csi.storage.gke.io    Delete
```

When we created the Pod in the previous section with a PersistentVolumeClaim, the default storage class (`standard-rwo`, in this case) was used. If you go back and look at the bound PersistentVolumeClaim object, you'll see this storage class in the configuration under `storageClassName`.

This is a pretty good start, and you may not need to change much, but there is one aspect that might be worth reviewing. If you read the `RECLAIMPOLICY` column in the output from `kubectl get storageclass` earlier, you may notice it states `Delete`. This means that if the PVC is deleted, the bound PV and the disk resource that backs it will also be deleted. If your stateful workloads are mostly just caching services storing non-critical data, this might be fine. However, if your workloads store unique and precious data, this default behavior is not ideal.

Kubernetes also offers a `Retain` reclaim policy, which means that the underlying disk resource will not be deleted on the deletion of the PVC. This allows you to keep the disk, and bind it to a new PV and PVC, potentially even one that you create in a completely separate cluster (which you might do when migrating workloads). The downside to `Retain`, and why it's typically not the default, is that you'll need to manually delete disks you don't wish to keep, which isn't ideal for testing and development, or workloads with ephermal data (like caches).

To build our own StorageClass, it's simplest to start with an existing one to use as a template, such as the current default. We can export the default StorageClass listed earlier as follows. If your StorageClass name is different than mine, replace `standard-rwo` with the storage class you want to modify:

```
kubectl get -o yaml storageclass standard-rwo > storageclass.yaml
```

Now we can customize and set the all-important `Retain` reclaim policy. Since we want to create a new policy, it's also important to give it a new name and strip the `uid` and other unneeded metadata fields. After performing those steps, I get the following listing.

Listing 9.4   Chapter09/9.1.3_StorageClass/storageclass.yaml

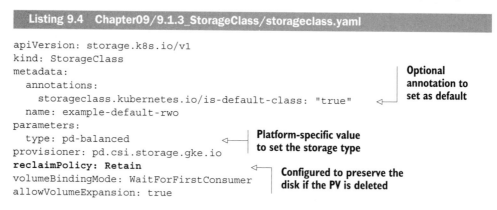

```
apiVersion: storage.k8s.io/v1
kind: StorageClass
metadata:
  annotations:                                              Optional
                                                            annotation to
    storageclass.kubernetes.io/is-default-class: "true"     set as default
  name: example-default-rwo
parameters:
  type: pd-balanced                    Platform-specific value
provisioner: pd.csi.storage.gke.io     to set the storage type
reclaimPolicy: Retain
volumeBindingMode: WaitForFirstConsumer    Configured to preserve the
allowVolumeExpansion: true                 disk if the PV is deleted
```

You can reference your new StorageClass directly in any PersistantVolumeClaim object or template with the `storageClassName` field. This is a great option, say, if you only want to use the retain reclaim policy for a select few workloads.

Optionally, you can set a new default storage class by adding the `is-default-class` annotation shown in listing 9.4. If you want to change the default, you'll need to mark the current default as nondefault. You can edit it with `kubectl edit storageclass standard-rwo`, or patch it with the following one-liner. Again, replace `standard-rwo` with whatever the name of your default class is:

```
kubectl patch storageclass standard-rwo -p '{"metadata": {"annotations":
  {"storageclass.kubernetes.io/is-default-class":"false"}}}'
```

When ready, create the new storage class with `kubectl create -f storageclass.yaml`. If you changed the default, any new PersistentVolume created will use your new StorageClass.

It's typical to have multiple storage classes with different performance and retention characteristics defined for different types of data. For example, you might have critical production data for a database that needs fast storage and to be retained, cache data that benefits from high performance but can be deleted, and ephermal storage for batch processing that can use average performance disks and not be retained. Pick a good default based on your preferences, and reference the others manually by specifying `storageClassName` in the PersistentVolumeClaim.

9.1.4 Single-Pod stateful workload deployments

Utilizing PersistentVolumeClaims, we can provision a one-replica stateful workload by simply enclosing our Pod into a Deployment. The benefit of using a Deployment even for a single-replica Pod is that if the Pod is terminated, it will be re-created.

Listing 9.5 Chapter09/9.1.4_Deployment_MariaDB/mariadb-deploy.yaml

```
apiVersion: apps/v1
kind: Deployment
metadata:
  name: mariadb-demo
spec:
  replicas: 1
  selector:
    matchLabels:
      app: mariadb
  strategy:
    type: Recreate
  template:
    metadata:
      labels:
        app: mariadb
    spec:
      containers:
      - name: mariadb-container
        image: mariadb:latest
        volumeMounts:
        - mountPath: /var/lib/mysql
          name: mariadb-volume
        resources:
          requests:
            cpu: 1
            memory: 4Gi
        env:
        - name: MARIADB_ROOT_PASSWORD
          value: "your database password"
      volumes:
      - name: mariadb-volume
        persistentVolumeClaim:
          claimName: mariadb-pvc
```

Re-create strategy used to prevent multiple replicas attempting to mount the same volume during rollouts.

The Pod template spec is identical to the one shown in section 9.1.2.

```
---
apiVersion: v1
kind: PersistentVolumeClaim
metadata:
  name: mariadb-pvc
spec:
  accessModes:
  - ReadWriteOnce
  resources:
    requests:
      storage: 2Gi
```

So, there we have it. This is a single Pod deployment of a MariaDB database with an attached disk that won't be deleted even if the entire Kubernetes cluster is deleted, thanks to the `Retain` policy in the default storage class we created in the prior section.

If you want to give this database a spin, create a Service for it (Chapter09/9.1.4_ Deployment_MariaDB/service.yaml). Once the Service is created, you can connect to the database from a local client (see the sidebar "Testing the MariaDB Pod locally"), or you can try out a containerized phpMyAdmin (see the Bonus/phpMyAdmin folder in the code repository that accompanies the book).

Running databases in Kubernetes

Before you take the plunge to manage your own MariaDB database in Kubernetes, you probably want to look for a managed solution with your cloud provider. I know it's tempting just to deploy in Kubernetes because it's fairly easy to create such a database, as I demonstrated. However, the operational cost comes later when you have to secure, update, and manage it. Generally, I recommend reserving the stateful workload functionality of Kubernetes for customized or bespoke services or services that your cloud provider doesn't provide as a managed offering.

As demonstrated in this section, we can make our workloads stateful by attaching volumes using PersistentVolumeClaims. Using Pod and Deployment objects for this, however, limits us to single-replica stateful workloads. This might be enough for some, but what if you have a sophisticated stateful workload like Elasticsearch or Redis with multiple replicas? You could try to stitch together a bunch of Deployments, but fortunately, Kubernetes has a high-level construct that is designed to represent exactly this type of workload called the StatefulSet.

9.2   StatefulSet

We've seen how persistent storage can be added to a Pod in Kubernetes—a useful feature because Pods are the basic building block in Kubernetes, and they are used in many different workload constructs, like Deployments (chapter 3) and Jobs (chapter 10). Now, you can add persistent storage to any of them and build stateful Pods wherever you need, provided that the volume specification is the same for all instances.

The limitation of the workload constructs like Deployment is that all Pods share the same specification, which creates a problem for traditional volumes with a `Read-WriteOnce` access method, as they can only be mounted by a single instance. This is OK when there is only one replica in your Deployment, but it means that if you create a second replica, that Pod will fail to be created as the volume is already mounted.

Fortunately, Kubernetes has a high-level workload construct that makes our lives easier when we need multiple Pods where they each get their own disk (a highly common pattern). Just like Deployment is a higher-level construct for managing continuously running services (typically stateless), StatefulSet is the construct provided for managing stateful services.

StatefulSet has a few helpful properties for building such services. You can define a volume template instead of referencing a single volume in the PodSpec, and Kubernetes will create a new PersistentVolumeClaim (PVC) for each Pod (thus solving the problem of using Deployment with volumes, where each instance got the exact same PVC). StatefulSet assigns each Pod a stable identifier, which is linked to a particular PVC and provides ordering guarantees during creation, scaling, and updates. With StatefulSet, you can get multiple Pods and coordinate them by using this stable identifier to potentially assign each a different role.

9.2.1   Deploying StatefulSet

Putting this into practice, let's look at two popular stateful workloads—MariaDB and Redis—and how to deploy them as a StatefulSet. At first, we'll stay with a single-Pod StatefulSet, which is the simplest to demonstrate without multiple roles to worry about. The next section will add additional replicas with different roles to use the power of StatefulSet fully.

MariaDB

First, let's convert the single-Pod MariaDB Deployment we created in the previous section to one using StatefulSet and take advantage of the PVC template to avoid the need to create a separate PVC object ourselves.

Listing 9.6   Chapter09/9.2.1_StatefulSet_MariaDB/mariadb-statefulset.yaml

```
apiVersion: apps/v1
kind: StatefulSet
metadata:
  name: mariadb
spec:
  selector:
    matchLabels:
      app: mariadb-sts
  serviceName: mariadb-service
  replicas: 1
  template:
    metadata:
      labels:
        app: mariadb-sts
```

StatefulSet uses the same match labels pattern as Deployments, discussed in chapter 3.

This is a reference to the headless Service, which is defined at the bottom of the file.

```
  spec:
    terminationGracePeriodSeconds: 10        ◁
    containers:
    - name: mariadb-container
      image: mariadb:latest
      volumeMounts:
      - name: mariadb-pvc                     ◁
        mountPath: /var/lib/mysql
      resources:
        requests:
          cpu: 1
          memory: 4Gi
      env:
      - name: MARIADB_ROOT_PASSWORD
        value: "your database password"
  volumeClaimTemplates:
  - metadata:
      name: mariadb-pvc
    spec:
      accessModes:
      - ReadWriteOnce
      resources:
        requests:
          storage: 2Gi
---
apiVersion: v1
kind: Service
metadata:
  name: mariadb-service
spec:
  ports:
  - port: 3306
  clusterIP: None
  selector:
    app: mariadb-sts
```

StatefulSet requires that a graceful termination period be set. This is the number of seconds the Pod has to exit on its own before being terminated.

The MariaDB data volume mount, now defined in the volumeClaimTemplates section

With StatefulSet, we can define a template of a PersisantVolumeClaim just like we define the template of the Pod replicas. This template is used to create the PersistentVolumeClaims, associating one to each of the Pod replicas.

The headless Service for this StatefulSet

How is this StatefulSet specification different from the Deployment specification of the same MariaDB Pod in the previous section? Other than the different object metadata, there are two key changes. The first difference is how the PersistentVolume-Claim is configured. When used in the previous section, it was defined as a standalone object. With StatefulSet, this is rolled into the definition itself under `volumeClaim-Templates`, much like how a Deployment has a Pod template. In each Pod, the Stateful-Set will have a PersistentVolumeClaim created based on this template. For a single-Pod StatefulSet, you end up with a similar result (but without the need to define a separate PersistentVolumeClaim object), and it becomes critical later when creating multiple replica StatefulSets. Figure 9.5 shows the PersistentVolumeClaim (used in the Deployment) and the `volumeClaimTemplates` (used in the StatefulSet) side by side.

```
apiVersion: v1                          ...
kind: PersistentVolumeClaim             volumeClaimTemplates:
metadata:                               - metadata:
  name: mariadb-pvc                         name: mariadb-pvc
spec:                                     spec:
  accessModes:                              accessModes:
  - ReadWriteOnce                           - ReadWriteOnce
  resources:                                resources:
    requests:                                 requests:
      storage: 2Gi                              storage: 2Gi
```

Figure 9.5 PersistentVolumeClaim vs. `volumeClaimTemplates`

If you query the PVCs after creating the StatefulSet, you'll see that one was created with this template (with some columns removed for readability):

```
$ kubectl get pvc
NAME                       STATUS   VOLUME      CAPACITY   ACCESS MODES
mariadb-pvc-mariadb-0      Bound    pvc-71b1e   2Gi        RWO
```

The main difference is that the PVC created with the template has the Pod name (`mariadb-0`, in the case of the first Pod) appended to it. So, instead of being `mariadb-pvc` (the name of the claim template), it's `mariadb-pvc-mariadb-0` (the claim template name and Pod name combined).

   Another difference compared to Deployment is that a Service is referenced in the StatefulSet with the `serviceName: mariadb-service` line and defined as follows:

```
apiVersion: v1
kind: Service
metadata:
  name: mariadb-service
spec:
  ports:
  - port: 3306
  clusterIP: None
  selector:
    app: mariadb-sts
```

This Service is a bit different from the ones presented in the book so far, as it's what's known as a headless Service (indicated by the `clusterIP: None` in the specification). Unlike the other Service types, there's no virtual cluster IP created to balance traffic over the Pods. If you query the DNS record of this Service (e.g., by execing into a Pod and running `host mariadb-service`), you will notice that it still returns an A record. This record is actually the IP address of the Pod itself, rather than the virtual cluster IP. For a headless Service with multiple Pods (like the Redis StatefulSet; see the next section), querying the Service will return multiple A records (i.e., one for each Pod).

The other useful property of the headless Service is that the Pods in a StatefulSet get their own stable network identities. Since each Pod in the StatefulSet is unique, and each has its own attached volume, it's useful to be able to address them individually. This is unlike Pods in a Deployment, which are designed to be identical, such that it shouldn't matter which one you connect to for any given request. To facilitate direct connections to Pods in the StatefulSet, each is assigned an incrementing integer value known as an ordinal (0, 1, 2, and so on). If the Pod in the StatefulSet is re-created following a disruption, it retains the same ordinal, whereas those replaced in a Deployment are assigned a new random name.

Pods in the StatefulSet can be addressed using their ordinal with the construction `$STATEFULSET_NAME-$POD_ORDINAL.$SERVICE_NAME`. In this example, our single Pod can be referenced using the DNS address `mariadb-0.mariadb-service`. From outside the namespace, you can append the namespace (like with any Service). For example, for the namespace named `production`, the Pod could be addressed with `mariadb-0-mariadb-service.production.svc`.

To try out this MariaDB instance running in a StatefulSet we can forward the port and connect locally with `kubectl port-forward sts/mariadb 3306:3306`, but for something more interesting let's create a MariaDB client using an ephemeral Pod running in the cluster, and connect using the service hostname.

```
kubectl run my -it --rm --restart=Never --pod-running-timeout=3m \
  --image mariadb -- mariadb -h mariadb-0.mariadb-service -P 3306 -u root -p
```

This creates a Pod in the cluster running the MariaDB client configured to connect to the primary Pod in our StatefulSet. It's ephemeral and will be deleted once you exit the interactive session, making it a convenient way to perform one-off debugging from within the cluster. When the Pod is ready, type the database password found in the MARIADB_ROOT_PASSWORD environment variable in listing 9.6, and you can now execute database commands. When you're done type `exit` to end the session.

REDIS

Another example we can use is Redis. Redis is a very popular workload deployment in Kubernetes and has many different possible uses, which often include caching and other real-time data storage and retrieval needs. For this example, let's imagine the caching use case where the data isn't super precious. You still want to persist the data to disk to avoid rebuilding the cache in the event of a restart, but there's no need to back it up. What follows is a perfectly usable single-Pod Redis setup for Kubernetes for such applications.

To configure Redis, let's first define our config file, which we can mount as a volume in the container.

> **Listing 9.7 Chapter09/9.2.1_StatefulSet_Redis/redis-configmap.yaml**

```
apiVersion: v1
kind: ConfigMap
```

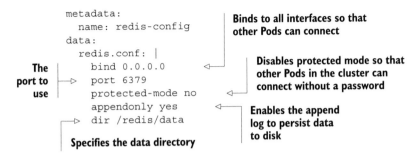

```
metadata:
  name: redis-config
data:
  redis.conf: |
    bind 0.0.0.0
    port 6379
    protected-mode no
    appendonly yes
    dir /redis/data
```

The port to use

Binds to all interfaces so that other Pods can connect

Disables protected mode so that other Pods in the cluster can connect without a password

Enables the append log to persist data to disk

Specifies the data directory

The key to note with this configuration is that we're persisting the Redis state to the /redis/data directory, so it can be reloaded if the Pod is re-created, and we'll next need to configure the volume to be mounted to that directory.

This example does not configure authentication for Redis, which means that every Pod in the cluster will have read/write access. If you take this example and use it in a production cluster, please consider how you wish to configure the cluster.

Now let's go ahead and create a StatefulSet that will reference this config and mount the /redis/data directory as a PersistentVolume.

Listing 9.8   Chapter09/9.2.1_StatefulSet_Redis/redis-statefulset.yaml

```
apiVersion: apps/v1
kind: StatefulSet
metadata:
  name: redis
spec:
  selector:
    matchLabels:
      app: redis-sts
  serviceName: redis-service
  replicas: 1
  template:
    metadata:
      labels:
        app: redis-sts
    spec:
      terminationGracePeriodSeconds: 10
      containers:
      - name: redis-container
        image: redis:latest
        command: ["redis-server"]
        args: ["/redis/conf/redis.conf"]
        volumeMounts:
        - name: redis-configmap-volume
          mountPath: /redis/conf/
        - name: redis-pvc
          mountPath: /redis/data
        resources:
          requests:
            cpu: 1
            memory: 4Gi
```

1 replica, as this is a single-role StatefulSet

Mount the configuration file from listing 9.7 into a directory in the container.

The Redis data volume mount, defined in the volumeClaimTemplates section

```
      volumes:
      - name: redis-configmap-volume
        configMap:
          name: redis-config          References the
  volumeClaimTemplates:               ConfigMap object
  - metadata:                         defined in listing 9.7
      name: redis-pvc
    spec:
      accessModes: [ "ReadWriteOnce" ]
      resources:
        requests:
          storage: 1Gi
---
apiVersion: v1
kind: Service
metadata:
  name: redis-service
spec:
  ports:
  - port: 6379
  clusterIP: None
  selector:
    app: redis-sts
```

Compared to the MariaDB StatefulSet, it's a similar setup, other than the application-specific differences, like the different ports used, the container image, and the mounting of the config map into /redis/conf.

After creating the resources in Chapter09/9.2.1_StatefulSet_Redis, to connect to Redis and verify it's working, you can forward the port to your local machine and connect using the redis-cli tool, like so:

```
$ kubectl port-forward pod/redis-0 6379:6379
Forwarding from 127.0.0.1:6379 -> 6379

$ docker run --net=host -it --rm redis redis-cli
27.0.0.1:6379> INFO
# Server
redis_version:7.2.1
127.0.0.1:6379> exit
```

So that's two examples of a one-replica StatefulSet. Even with just one replica, it's more convenient than using a Deployment for such a workload, as Kubernetes can take care of creating the PersistentVolumeClaim automatically.

If you delete the StatefulSet object, the PersistentVolumeClaim object will remain. If you then re-create the StatefulSet, it will reattach to the same PersistentVolumeClaim, so no data is lost. Deleting the PersistentVolumeClaim object itself *can* delete the underlying data, though, depending on how the storage class is configured. If you care about the data being stored (e.g., not just a cache that can be re-created), be sure to follow the steps in section 9.1.3 to set up a StorageClass that will retain the underlying cloud resources if the PersistentVolumeClaim object is deleted for whatever reason.

If we increased the replicas for this StatefulSet, it would give us new Pods with their own volumes, but it doesn't automatically mean they will actually talk to each other. For the Redis StatefulSet defined here, creating more replicas would just give us more individual Redis instances. The next section goes into detail about how to set up a multiple-Pod architecture within a single StatefulSet, where each unique Pod is configured differently, based on the ordinal of the Pod, and connected together.

9.2.2   Deploying a multirole StatefulSet

The real power of a StatefulSet comes into play when you need to have multiple Pods. When designing an application that will use StatefulSet, Pod replicas within the StatefulSet need to know about each other and communicate with each other as part of the stateful application design. This is the benefit, though, of using the StatefulSet type because each of the Pods gets a unique identifier in a set known as the ordinal. You can use this uniqueness and guaranteed ordering to assign different roles to the different unique Pods in the set and associate the same persistent disk through updates and even deletion and re-creation.

For this example, we'll take the single Pod Redis StatefulSet from the previous section and convert it to a three-Pod setup by introducing the replica role. Redis uses a leader/follower replication strategy, consisting of a primary Pod (in section 9.2.1, this was the only Pod) and additional Pods with the replica role (not to be confused with Kubernetes "replicas," which refer to all of the Pods in the StatefulSet or Deployment).

Building on the example in the previous section, we'll keep the same Redis configuration for the primary Pod and add an additional configuration file for the replicas, which contains a reference to the address of the primary Pod. Listing 9.9 is the ConfigMap where these two configuration files are defined.

Listing 9.9   Chapter09/9.2.2_StatefulSet_Redis_Multi/redis-configmap.yaml

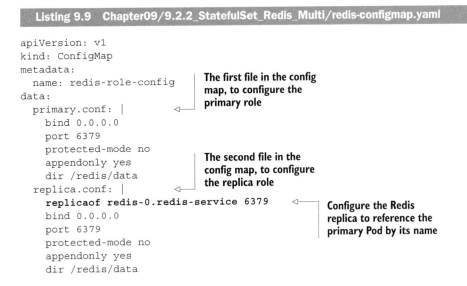

```
apiVersion: v1
kind: ConfigMap
metadata:
  name: redis-role-config          The first file in the config
data:                               map, to configure the
  primary.conf: |          ◁──     primary role
    bind 0.0.0.0
    port 6379
    protected-mode no
    appendonly yes                  The second file in the
    dir /redis/data                 config map, to configure
  replica.conf: |          ◁──      the replica role
    replicaof redis-0.redis-service 6379    ◁──   Configure the Redis
    bind 0.0.0.0                                  replica to reference the
    port 6379                                     primary Pod by its name
    protected-mode no
    appendonly yes
    dir /redis/data
```

ConfigMaps are simply a convenient way for us to define two configuration files, one for each of the two roles. We could equally build our own container using the Redis base image and put these two files in there. But since this is the only customization we need, it's simpler to just define them here and mount them into our container.

Next, we'll update the StatefulSet workload to use an `init` container (i.e., a container that runs during the initialization of the Pod) to set the role of each Pod replica. The script that runs in this `init` container looks up the ordinal of the Pod being initialized to determine its role and copies the relevant configuration for that role—recall that a special feature of StatefulSets is that each Pod is assigned a unique ordinal. We can use the ordinal value of `0` to designate the primary role, while assigning the remaining Pods to the replica role.

This technique can be applied to a variety of different stateful workloads where you have multiple roles. If you're looking for MariaDB, there's a great guide[2] provided with the Kubernetes docs.

> **Listing 9.10 Chapter09/9.2.2_StatefulSet_Redis_Multi/redis-statefulset.yaml**

```
apiVersion: apps/v1
kind: StatefulSet
metadata:
  name: redis
spec:
  selector:
    matchLabels:
      app: redis-sts
  serviceName: redis-service
  replicas: 3                    ◁── 3 replicas for
  template:                          the multi-role
    metadata:                        StatefulSet
      labels:
        app: redis-sts
    spec:                                      The init container that runs once
      terminationGracePeriodSeconds: 10        on boot, to copy the config file
      initContainers:                          from the ConfigMap mount to
      - name: init-redis             ◁─────    the emptyDir mount
        image: redis:latest
        command:          Run the
        - bash            following script.
        - "-c"
        - |
          set -ex
          # Generate server-id from Pod ordinal index.
          [[ `hostname` =~ -([0-9]+)$ ]] || exit 1
          ordinal=${BASH_REMATCH[1]}
          echo "ordinal ${ordinal}"
          # Copy appropriate config files from config-map to emptyDir.
          mkdir -p /redis/conf/
          if [[ $ordinal -eq 0 ]]; then
            cp /mnt/redis-configmap/primary.conf /redis/conf/redis.conf
```

```
            else
              cp /mnt/redis-configmap/replica.conf /redis/conf/redis.conf
            fi
            cat /redis/conf/redis.conf
        volumeMounts:
        - name: redis-config-volume
          mountPath: /redis/conf/
        - name: redis-configmap-volume
          mountPath: /mnt/redis-configmap
      containers:
      - name: redis-container
        image: redis:latest
        command: ["redis-server"]
        args: ["/redis/conf/redis.conf"]
        volumeMounts:
        - name: redis-config-volume
          mountPath: /redis/conf/
        - name: redis-pvc
          mountPath: /redis/data
        resources:
          requests:
            cpu: 1
            memory: 4Gi
      volumes:
      - name: redis-configmap-volume
        configMap:
          name: redis-role-config
      - name: redis-config-volume
        emptyDir: {}
  volumeClaimTemplates:
  - metadata:
      name: redis-pvc
    spec:
      accessModes: [ "ReadWriteOnce" ]
      resources:
        requests:
          storage: 1Gi
---
apiVersion: v1
kind: Service
metadata:
  name: redis-service
spec:
  ports:
  - port: 6379
  clusterIP: None
  selector:
    app: redis-sts
```

Annotations:
- **The main Redis container** → `- name: redis-container`
- **emptyDir mount, shared with the main container** → `mountPath: /redis/conf/`
- **ConfigMap mount with the 2 files from listing 9.9** → `mountPath: /mnt/redis-configmap`
- **emptyDir mount, shared with the init container** → `mountPath: /redis/conf/`
- **The Redis data volume mount, defined in the volumeClaimTemplates section** → `mountPath: /redis/data`
- **References the ConfigMap object defined in listing 9.9** → `name: redis-role-config`
- **Defines the emptyDir volume** → `emptyDir: {}`

There's a bit to unpack here, so let's take a closer look. The main difference to our single-instance Redis StatefulSet is the presence of an init container. This init container, as its name suggests, runs during the initialization phase of the Pod. It mounts two volumes, the ConfigMap and a new volume redis-config-volume:

```
volumeMounts:
- name: redis-config-volume
  mountPath: /redis/conf/
- name: redis-configmap-volume
  mountPath: /mnt/redis-configmap
```

The `redis-config-volume` is of type `emptyDir`, which allows data to be shared between containers but does not persist data if the Pod is rescheduled (unlike Persistent-Volume). We are only using this `emptyDir` volume to store a copy of the config, and it is ideal for that. The `init` container runs a bash script contained in the YAML:

```
command:
- bash
- "-c"
- |
  set -ex
  # Generate server-id from Pod ordinal index.
  [[ `hostname` =~ -([0-9]+)$ ]] || exit 1
  ordinal=${BASH_REMATCH[1]}
  # Copy appropriate config files from config-map to emptyDir.
  mkdir -p /redis/conf/
  if [[ $ordinal -eq 0 ]]; then
    cp /mnt/redis-configmap/primary.conf /redis/conf/redis.conf
  else
    cp /mnt/redis-configmap/replica.conf /redis/conf/redis.conf
  fi
```

This script will copy one of the two different configurations from the ConfigMap volume (mounted at `/mnt/redis-configmap`) to this shared `emptyDir` volume (mounted at `/redis/conf`), depending on the ordinal number of the Pod. That is, if the Pod is `redis-0`, the `primary.conf` file is copied; for the rest, `replica.conf` is copied.

The main container then mounts the same `redis-config-volume` `emptyDir` volume at `/redis/conf`. When the Redis process is started, it will use whatever configuration resides at `/redis/conf/redis.conf`.

To try it out you can connect to the primary Pod using the port-forward/local client combination, or by creating an ephemeral Pod as documented in the previous sections. We can also connect directly with exec to quickly write some data, like so:

```
$ kubectl exec -it redis-0 -- redis-cli
127.0.0.1:6379> SET capital:australia "Canberra"
OK
127.0.0.1:6379> exit
```

Then connect to a replica and read it back:

```
$ kubectl exec -it redis-1 -- redis-cli
Defaulted container "redis-container" out of: redis-container, init-redis (init)
127.0.0.1:6379> GET capital:australia
"Canberra"
```

The replicas are read-only so you won't be able to write data directly:

```
127.0.0.1:6379> SET capital:usa "Washington"
(error) READONLY You can't write against a read only replica.
127.0.0.1:6379> exit
```

9.3 Migrating/recovering disks

Now I know what you're thinking: can I really trust Kubernetes with my precious data? There's a bit too much magic going on here; how can I be confident that my data is safe and recoverable if the Kubernetes cluster goes away?

Time to build some confidence. Let's create a stateful workload in Kubernetes. Then, we'll completely delete every Kubernetes object associated with it and try to re-create that workload from scratch, relinking it to the underlying cloud disk resources.

One thing to be very aware of is that commonly, by default, disk resources that Kubernetes creates are deleted if you delete the associated bound PersistentVolume-Claim because they are configured with a `reclaimPolicy` set to `Delete`. Deleting the StatefulSet itself doesn't delete the associated PersistentVolumeClaim objects, which is useful as it forces you to manually delete those objects if you no longer need the data, but deleting the PersistentVolumeClaim objects *will* delete the underlying disk resources, and it's not that hard to do (e.g., by passing `--all` to the relevant `kubectl delete` command).

So, if you value your data, the first thing is to make sure the StorageClass that's used when creating the disks for your precious data has its `reclaimPolicy` set to `Retain`, not `Delete`. This will preserve the underlying cloud disk when the Kubernetes objects are deleted, allowing you to manually re-create the PersistentVolumeClaim–PersistentVolume pairing in the same or a different cluster (which I will demonstrate).

To run this experiment, deploy the Redis example from section 9.2.2, with either the default or explicit storage class configured to retain data. To verify the status of the PersistentVolumes after creation, use `kubectl get pv` to inspect, and `kubectl edit pv $PV_NAME` to modify, the `persistentVolumeReclaimPolicy` field, if needed.

With our reclaim policy set correctly, we can now add some data that we can use to validate our ability to recover our Kubernetes StatefulSet after we delete it. To add data, first exec into the primary Pod and run the `redis-cli` tool. You can do both with the following command:

```
kubectl exec -it redis-0 -- redis-cli
```

Once connected, we can add some data. If you've not used Redis before, don't worry about this—we're just adding some trivial data to prove we can recover it. This example data is some key–value pairs for world capitals:

```
127.0.0.1:6379> SET capital:australia "Canberra"
OK
127.0.0.1:6379> SET capital:usa "Washington"
OK
```

If you like, at this point, you can delete the StatefulSet and re-create it. Then, exec back into the CLI and test the data. Here's how:

```
$ cd Chapter09/9.2.2_StatefulSet_Redis_Multi/
$ kubectl delete -f redis-statefulset.yaml
service "redis-service" deleted
statefulset.apps "redis" deleted

$ kubectl create -f redis-statefulset.yaml
service/redis-service created
statefulset.apps/redis created

$ kubectl exec -it redis-0 -- redis-cli
127.0.0.1:6379> GET capital:usa
"Washington"
```

This works (i.e., the data is persisted) because when the StatefulSet is re-created. It references the same PersistentVolumeClaim that has our data for Redis to load when it boots, and so Redis picks off right where it left off.

Good so far. Now let's take a more drastic step and delete the PVC and VC and attempt to re-create. The re-creation can optionally be done in a completely new cluster if you like to simulate the entire cluster being deleted. Just be sure to use the same cloud region so the disk can be accessed.

Before we delete those objects, though, let's save their configuration. This isn't strictly necessary; you certainly can re-create them from scratch if needed, but it will help save some time. Use the following commands to list and save the objects (output truncated for readability):

```
$ kubectl get pvc,pv
NAME                                        STATUS    VOLUME
persistentvolumeclaim/redis-pvc-redis-0     Bound     pvc-64b52138
persistentvolumeclaim/redis-pvc-redis-1     Bound     pvc-4530141b
persistentvolumeclaim/redis-pvc-redis-2     Bound     pvc-5bbf6729

NAME                            STATUS    CLAIM
persistentvolume/pvc-4530141b   Bound     default/redis-pvc-redis-1
persistentvolume/pvc-5bbf6729   Bound     default/redis-pvc-redis-2
persistentvolume/pvc-64b52138   Bound     default/redis-pvc-redis-0
$ kubectl get -o yaml persistentvolumeclaim/redis-pvc-redis-0 > pvc.yaml
$ PV_NAME=pvc-64b52138
$ kubectl get -o yaml persistentvolume/$PV_NAME > pv.yaml
```

Now, the nuclear option: delete all StatefulSets, PVCs, and PVs in the namespace:

```
kubectl delete statefulset,pvc,pv --all
```

> **WARNING** Only run that comment in a test cluster! It will delete all objects of that type in the namespace, not just the example Redis deployment.

Due to the `Retain` policy on the StorageClass (hopefully, you used a storage class with `Retain` as instructed!), the cloud disk resource will still exist. Now it's just a matter of manually creating a PV to link to that disk and a PVC to link to that.

Here's what we know (figure 9.6):

- We know (or can find out) the name of the underlying disk resource from our cloud provider
- We know the name of the PVC that the StatefulSet will consume (`redis-pvc-redis-0`)

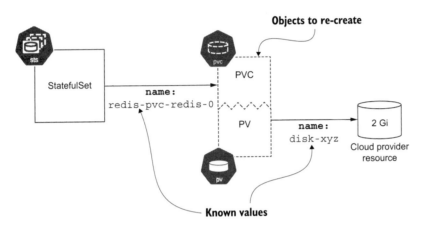

Figure 9.6 The known values and the objects we need to re-create

So, we need to create a PVC with the name `redis-pvc-redis-0` that is bound with a PV that references the disk. Importantly, the PVC needs to name the PV, and the PV needs to define the bound PVC; otherwise, the PVC could bind a different PV, and the PV could be bound by a different PVC.

Creating the objects directly from our saved config with `kubectl create -f pv.yaml` and `kubectl create -f pvc.yaml` unfortunately won't work. That configuration also exported the *state* of the binding, which uses unique identifiers that don't carry over when you delete and create the object from config. If you create those objects without modification, you'll see that the PVC `status` is `Lost`, and the PV status is `Released`—not what we want.

To fix this, we just need to remove the binding status and the `uids` from the saved config:

1. Edit the PV (the configuration we exported to `pv.yaml`) and make two changes:
   a. Remove the `uid` field from the `claimRef` section (the `claimRef` is the pointer to the PVC; the problem is that the PVC's `uid` has changed).
   b. Set the `storageClassName` to the empty string `""` (we're manually provisioning and don't want to use a `storageClass`).

2 Edit to the PVC (the configuration we exported to `pvc.yaml`) and make two
   changes:

   a Delete the annotation `pv.kubernetes.io/bind-completed: "yes"` (this PVC
      needs to be re-bound, and this annotation will prevent that).

   b Set the `storageClassName` to the empty string `""` (same reason as the previ-
      ous step).

Alternatively, if you're re-creating this config from scratch, the key is that the `volume-Name` of the PVC needs to be set to that of the PV, the `claimRef` of the PV needs to reference the PVC's name and namespace, and both have the `storageClassName` of `""`.

It's easier to visualize side by side. Figure 9.7 is based on the configuration I exported when I ran this test and removed the fields as documented as previously outlined.

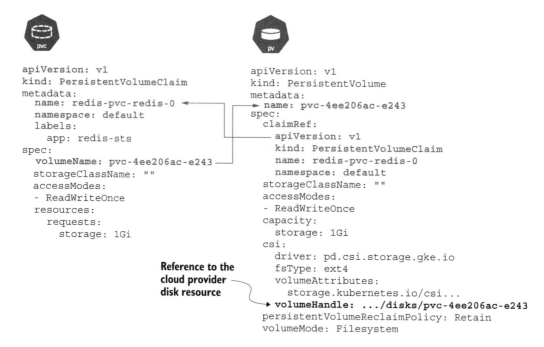

Figure 9.7 Prelinked PVC and PV objects

Once prepared, you can create both configuration files in the cluster and then inspect their status with `kubectl get pvc,pv`.

If it goes correctly, the status for the PV should read `Bound`, and the PVC `Pending` (while it waits for the StatefulSet to be created). If, instead, one or both are listed as `Pending` or `Released`, go back and check that they are linked correctly with all the information needed and without any extra information. Yes, unfortunately, this is a bit of a pain, but it is possible to rebind these objects, provided that the underlying cloud resource is still there (which it will be, since you used the `Retain` policy on your StorageClass, didn't you?). This is what success looks like (with some columns removed for readability):

```
$ kubectl create -f pv.yaml
persistentvolume/pvc-f0fea6ae-e229 created

$ kubectl get pv
NAME                   RECLAIM POLICY   STATUS      CLAIM
pvc-f0fea6ae-e229      Retain           Available   default/redis-pvc-redis-0

$ kubectl create -f pvc.yaml
persistentvolumeclaim/redis-pvc-redis-0 created

$ kubectl get pv,pvc
NAME                      RECLAIM POLICY   STATUS   CLAIM
pv/pvc-f0fea6ae-e229      Retain           Bound    default/redis-pvc-redis-0

NAME                                         STATUS    VOLUME
persistentvolumeclaim/redis-pvc-redis-0      Pending   pvc-f0fea6ae-e229
```

Once you have your manually created PVC and PV objects, it's time to re-create the StatefulSet. As we tested earlier when we deleted and re-created the StatefulSet, as long as the PVC exists with the expected name, it will be reattached to the Pods of the StatefulSet. The name of the PVCs that the StatefulSet creates is deterministic, so when we re-create the StatefulSet, it will see the existing PVC objects and reference them rather than creating new ones. Basically, everything should work the same as when we re-created these objects using the same names as before.

Notice, in this example, that although the StatefulSet has three PVCs and, therefore, three associated disks, we only manually recovered one disk—the one attached to the primary Pod. The Redis replicas will automatically re-create their data from that source. You can, of course, manually re-link all three disks.

```
$ kubectl create -f redis-statefulset.yaml
service/redis-service created
statefulset.apps/redis created

$ kubectl get pv,pvc,pods
NAME                      RECLAIM POLICY   STATUS   CLAIM
pv/pvc-f0fea6ae-e229      Retain           Bound    default/redis-pvc-redis-0
pv/pvc-9aabd1b8-ca4f      Retain           Bound    default/redis-pvc-redis-1
pv/pvc-db153655-88c2      Retain           Bound    default/redis-pvc-redis-2

NAME                                         STATUS    VOLUME
persistentvolumeclaim/redis-pvc-redis-0      Bound     pvc-f0fea6ae-e229
persistentvolumeclaim/redis-pvc-redis-1      Bound     pvc-9aabd1b8-ca4f
persistentvolumeclaim/redis-pvc-redis-2      Bound     pvc-db153655-88c2

NAME          READY   STATUS    RESTARTS   AGE
pod/redis-0   1/1     Running   0          15m
```

```
pod/redis-1   1/1        Running   0                13m
pod/redis-2   1/1        Running   0                11m
```

With the StatefulSet created, all the PV and PVC objects show `Bound`. Once the StatefulSet is deployed, let's exec into one of those replicas and see whether the data we created earlier is still there:

```
$ kubectl exec -it redis-1 -- redis-cli
127.0.0.1:6379> GET capital:australia
"Canberra"
```

If you can read back the data written to Redis earlier, congratulations! You've recovered the StatefulSet from scratch. This same technique can be used to migrate a disk to a StatefulSet in a new cluster. Just follow these steps, but create the objects in a new cluster. Pay attention to the location of the disk as typically the cluster needs to be in the same region.

I hope this section has given you some confidence about the persistence of the data when the `Retain` policy is used. As demonstrated, you can completely delete all the objects (heck, even the entire cluster) and re-create all the links from scratch. It's a bit laborsome, but it's possible. To reduce the toil, it's advisable (but not essential) to export the config for your PVC and PV objects and store them in your configuration repository to make it faster to re-create these objects in the future.

9.4 *Generic ephemeral volume for scratch space*

So far, we've used PersistentVolumes and PersistentVolumesClaims for stateful services. What about when you just need a really big disk to do some temporary calculations—scratch space for tasks like data processing? At the beginning of the chapter, `emptyDir` was mentioned as an option for scratch space, but it has some drawbacks. Namely, you need to preallocate storage on the node to be able to use `emptyDir`, which requires a upfront planning of node boot disk sizes (and which may not be possible at all on platforms that don't expose nodes). Generic ephemeral volumes are a way to get scratch space by mounting an attached volume in the same way we do persistent volumes.

There are numerous benefits of using ephemeral volumes over `emptyDir` when you have large amounts of temporary data to handle. By being independent of the boot disk, you can provision very large volumes of space on the fly without prior planning (e.g., Google Cloud supports up to 64 TB at the time of this writing). You can attach multiple volumes, too, so that limit is a per-volume limit. You can also access different storage classes and configure different attributes on the storage class, like, for example, provisioning a higher-performant SSD disk than the node's own boot disk. The following listing provides an example.

Listing 9.11   Chapter09/9.4_EphemeralVolume/ephemeralvolume_pod.yaml

```
apiVersion: v1
kind: Pod
```

```
metadata:
  name: ephemeralvolume-pod
  labels:
    pod: timeserver-pod
spec:
  containers:
  - name: timeserver-container
    image: docker.io/wdenniss/timeserver:1
    volumeMounts:
    - mountPath: "/scratch"          Mount point for the
      name: scratch-volume           scratch volume
  volumes:
  - name: scratch-volume
    ephemeral:
      volumeClaimTemplate:
        metadata:
          labels:
            type: scratch-volume
        spec:                           Defines a 1TB
          accessModes: [ "ReadWriteOnce" ]   ephemeral
          storageClassName: "ephemeral"       volume
          resources:
            requests:
              storage: 1Ti
```

When using generic ephemeral volumes, you want to ensure that your storage class has a reclaim policy set to `Delete`. Otherwise, the ephemeral storage will be retained, which is not really the point. The following listing provides such a StorageClass.

Listing 9.12 Chapter09/9.4_EphemeralVolume/ephemeral_storageclass.yaml

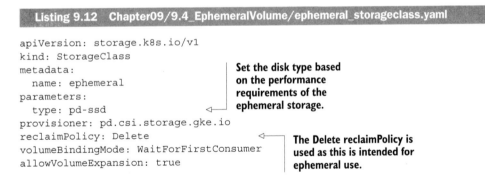

```
apiVersion: storage.k8s.io/v1
kind: StorageClass
metadata:                          Set the disk type based
  name: ephemeral                  on the performance
parameters:                        requirements of the
  type: pd-ssd                     ephemeral storage.
provisioner: pd.csi.storage.gke.io
reclaimPolicy: Delete                    The Delete reclaimPolicy is
volumeBindingMode: WaitForFirstConsumer  used as this is intended for
allowVolumeExpansion: true               ephemeral use.
```

Putting it together, let's run, inspect, and clean up the sample. The following commands (run from the sample root directory) show the Pod being created, with a 1 TB disk attached, and then deleted, which cleans up all the resources (output is truncated for readability):

```
$ kubectl create -f Chapter09/9.4_EphemeralVolume
storageclass.storage.k8s.io/ephemeral created
pod/ephemeralvolume-pod created
```

```
$ kubectl get pod,pvc,pv
NAME                          READY    STATUS     RESTARTS     AGE
pod/ephemeralvolume-pod       1/1      Running    0            34s

NAME                 STATUS    VOLUME    CAPACITY    ACCESS MODES    STORAGECLASS
pvc/scratch-volume   Bound     pvc-a5a2  1Ti         RWO             ephemeral

NAME                 CAPACITY   RECLAIM POLICY    STATUS    CLAIM
pv/pvc-a5a2          1Ti        Delete            Bound     default/scratch-volume

$ kubectl exec -it ephemeralvolume-pod -- df -h
Filesystem      Size   Used  Avail  Use%  Mounted on
overlay          95G   4.6G    90G    5%  /
/dev/sdb        1007G   28K  1007G    1%  /scratch

$ kubectl delete pod ephemeralvolume-pod
pod "ephemeralvolume-pod" deleted

$ kubectl get pod,pvc,pv
No resources found
```

The 1TiB volume is available for use.

As you can see, with ephmeral volumes, deleting the Pod will delete the associated PVC object. This is unlike the StatefulSet where the PVC object needs to be deleted manually when deleting the StatefulSet. You can also wrap this Pod into a Deployment, where each replica will get its own ephemeral volume.

Summary

- Kubernetes isn't just confined to running stateless workloads; it can also deftly handle stateful workloads.
- Kubernetes supports several types of volumes, including the ability to directly mount a persistent disk from a cloud provider resource.
- PersistentVolume and PersistentVolumeClaim, together with StorageClass, are Kubernetes's abstraction layer for dynamically provisioned disk resources and make the workload portable.
- StatefulSet is the high-level workload type designed for running stateful workloads with advantages such as being able to define different roles for each replica.
- PersistentVolume and PersistentVolumeClaim objects have a complex lifecycle, starting as a request and then being bound into a single logical object.
- StorageClasses can be configured to enable dynamic storage with your preferred options—most importantly, the option to retain the cloud provider disk resources should the Kubernetes objects be deleted.
- Data can be recovered even if all objects in the cluster are deleted, provided you use the Retain reclaim policy.
- Generic ephemeral volumes provide a way to use mounted disks for ephemeral scratch space.

Background processing *10*

This chapter covers

- How to process background tasks in Kubernetes
- The Kubernetes Job and CronJob objects
- When to use (and not use) Job objects for your own batch processing workloads
- Creating a custom task queue with Redis
- Implementing a background processing task queue with Kubernetes

In prior chapters, we looked at developing services that are exposed on an IP address, whether it's providing an external service on a public address or an internal service on a cluster local IP. But what about all the other computations that you may need to do that aren't directly part of a request–response chain, like resizing a bunch of images, sending out device notifications, running an AI/ML training job, processing financial data, or rendering a movie one frame at a time? These are typically processed as background tasks, which are processes that take an input and produce an output without being part of the synchronous handling of user requests.

You can process background tasks using Deployment or the Kubernetes Job object. Deployment is ideal for a continuously running task queue like the one

215

most web applications run for tasks such as image resizing. The Kubernetes Job construct is great for running one-off maintenance tasks, periodic tasks (via CronJob), and processing a batch workload when there is a set amount of work to complete.

> **Terminology: task or job**
>
> Practitioners routinely use the terms *task* and *job* interchangeably when referring to a background computation (e.g., job queue, task queue, background job, background task). Since Kubernetes has an object named Job, to reduce ambiguity, I will always use *Job* when referring to the object itself, and *task* (e.g., background task, task queue) when referring to the general concept of background processing regardless of how it is implemented.

This chapter covers using both Deployment and Job for background task processing. By the end, you'll be able to configure a continuous background task processing queue for your web application and define batch workloads with an end state, including periodic and one-off tasks, all in Kubernetes.

10.1   *Background processing queues*

Most web applications deployed in the wild have a major background task processing component to handle processing tasks that can't be completed in the short HTTP request–response time window. User research conducted by Google shows that the longer the page load time is, the higher the chance the user will "bounce" (i.e., leave the page and go somewhere else), observing that "the probability of bounce increases 32% as page load time goes from 1 second to 3 seconds."[1] So, it's generally a mistake to try to do any heavy lifting while the user is waiting; instead, a task should be put on a background queue, and the user should be kept apprised of its progress. Page load speeds need to be on everyone's mind, from the frontend developers to the backend; it's a collective responsibility.

There's a lot that goes into the time it takes to load the page, and many aspects, like image sizes and JavaScript, are out of the scope of Kubernetes. A relevant metric to consider when looking at your workload deployments in Kubernetes is time to first byte (TTFB). This is the time it takes for your web server to complete its processing of the request and the client to start downloading the response. To achieve a low overall page loading time, it's critical to reduce the TTFB time and respond in subsecond times. That pretty much rules out any kind of data processing that happens inline as part of the request. Need to create a ZIP file to serve to a user or shrink an image they just uploaded? Best not to do it in the request itself.

As a result, the common pattern is to run a continuous background processing queue. The web application hands off tasks it can't do inline, like processing data,

---

[1] Google/SOASTA Research, 2017. https://www.thinkwithgoogle.com/marketing-strategies/app-and-mobile/page-load-time-statistics/

which gets picked up by the background queue (figure 10.1). The web application might show a spinner or some other UI affordance while it waits for the background queue to do its thing, email the user when the results are ready, or simply prompt the user to come back later. How you architect your user interaction is up to you. What we'll cover here is how to deploy this kind of background processing task queue in Kubernetes.

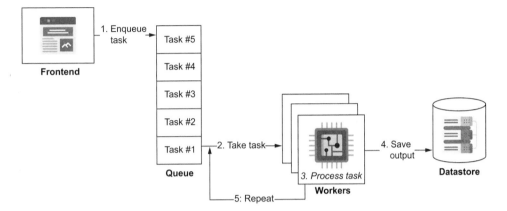

Figure 10.1   Frontend web server with a background task queue

Recall that a Deployment (as covered in chapter 3) is a workload construct in Kubernetes whose purpose is to maintain a set of continuously running Pods. For background task–processing queues, you need a set of continuously running Pods to serve as your task workers. So that's a match! It doesn't matter that the Pods in the Deployment won't be exposed with a Service; the key is that you want at least one worker to be continuously running. You'll be updating this Deployment with new container versions and scaling it up and down just as you do a Deployment that serves your frontend requests, so everything we've learned so far can be applied equally to a Deployment of background task workers.

10.1.1   Creating a custom task queue

The worker Pods that you deploy in your task-processing Deployment have a simple role: take an input and produce an output. But where do they get the input from? For that, you'll need a queue on which other components of the application can add tasks. This queue will store the list of pending tasks, which the worker Pods will process. There are a bunch of off-the-shelf solutions for background queues (some of which I mention in section 10.1.4), but to best understand how these work, let's create our own!

For the queue data store, we'll be using the same Redis workload deployment we created in the previous chapter. Redis includes built-in support for queues, making it perfect for this task (and many off-the-shelf solutions also use Redis). The design of our task processing system is pretty straightforward: the web application role enqueues tasks to Redis (we can emulate this role by manually adding tasks), and worker Pods from our Deployment pop the tasks, perform the work, and wait for the next task.

Queues in Redis

Redis has several convenient data structures out of the box. The one we're using here is a queue. There are two functions we'll be using on this queue structure to achieve FIFO (first-in, first-out) ordering, which is typical of a background queue (i.e., processing items in the order they are added): RPUSH to add items to the back of the queue and BLPOP to pop items from the front of the queue and block if none are available.

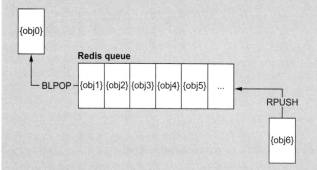

If you think of the queue going from right to left, where the rightmost item is at the back of the queue, and the leftmost item is the front, then the L and R function prefixes will make more sense (RPUSH to push an object on the right and BLPOP to pop the leftmost item in a blocking fashion). The additional B prefix refers to the blocking form of the function (in this case, the blocking version of LPOP), which will cause it to wait for an item in the event the queue is empty rather than returning right away with nil. We could simply use LPOP in our own retry loop, but it's useful to block on the response to avoid a "busy wait," which would consume more resources, and this way, we can leave that task to Redis.

As a concrete but trivial example, our task will take as input an integer n, and calculate Pi using the Leibniz series formula with n iterations (the more iterations when calculating Pi in this way, the more accurate the end result). In practice, your task will complete whatever arbitrary processing you need it to do and will likely take as input a URL or dictionary of key–value parameters. The concept is the same.

CREATING A WORKER CONTAINER

Before we get to the Kubernetes Deployment, we'll need to create our worker container. I'll use Python again for this sample, as we can implement a complete task queue in a few lines of Python. The complete code for this container can be found in the Chapter10/pi_worker folder in the source code that accompanies this book. It consists of three Python files, presented in the following listings.

Listing 10.1 is the work function where the actual computation happens. It has no awareness of being in a queue; it simply does the processing. In your own case, you'd replace this with whatever computation you need to do (e.g., create a ZIP file or resize an image).

Listing 10.1   Chapter10/pi_worker/pi.py

```python
from decimal import *

# Calculate pi using the Gregory-Leibniz infinity series
def leibniz_pi(iterations):

    precision = 20
    getcontext().prec = 20
    piDiv4 = Decimal(1)
    odd = Decimal(3)

    for i in range(0, iterations):
        piDiv4 = piDiv4 - 1/odd
        odd = odd + 2
        piDiv4 = piDiv4 + 1/odd
        odd = odd + 2

    return piDiv4 * 4
```

Then, in listing 10.2, we have our worker implementation that will take the task object at the head of the queue with the parameters of the work needing to be done and perform the work by calling the `leibniz_pi` function. For your own implementation, the object that you queue just needs to contain the relevant function parameters for the task, like the details for a ZIP file to create or image to process. It's useful to separate the queue processing logic from the work function, so that the latter can be reused in other environments.

Listing 10.2   Chapter10/pi_worker/pi_worker.py

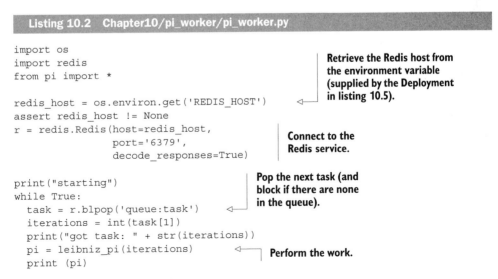

```python
import os
import redis
from pi import *
```
Retrieve the Redis host from the environment variable (supplied by the Deployment in listing 10.5).

```python
redis_host = os.environ.get('REDIS_HOST')
assert redis_host != None
r = redis.Redis(host=redis_host,
                port='6379',
                decode_responses=True)
```
Connect to the Redis service.

```python
print("starting")
while True:
    task = r.blpop('queue:task')
```
Pop the next task (and block if there are none in the queue).

```python
    iterations = int(task[1])
    print("got task: " + str(iterations))
    pi = leibniz_pi(iterations)
```
Perform the work.

```python
    print (pi)
```

To pop our Redis-based queue, we use the Redis BLPOP command, which will get the first element in the list and block if the queue is empty and wait for more tasks to be added. There is more we would need to do to make this production-grade, such as adding signal handling for when the Pod is terminated (covered in section 10.1.2), but this is enough for now.

Lastly, in listing 10.3, we have a little script to add some work to this queue. In the real world, you will queue tasks as needed (by calling RPUSH with the task parameters), such as in response to user actions, like queuing the task to resize an image in response to the user uploading it. For our demonstration, we can seed our task queue with some random values. The following listing will create 10 sample tasks using a random value for our task input integer (with a value in the range of 1 to 10 million).

Listing 10.3   Chapter10/pi_worker/add_tasks.py

```
import os
import redis
import random

redis_host = os.environ.get('REDIS_HOST')
assert redis_host != None
r = redis.Redis(host=redis_host,
                port='6379',
                decode_responses=True)

random.seed()                                        Loop 10 times to
for i in range(0, 10):                               add 10 tasks.
    rand = random.randint(10,100)
    iterations = rand * 100000                       Create a random
    r.rpush('queue:task', iterations)                task parameter.
    print("added task: " + str(iterations))

print("queue depth", str(r.llen('queue:task')))
print ("done")
```

Add the task to the queue. → `r.rpush('queue:task', iterations)`

The rpush method (mapping to RPUSH[2]) adds the given value (in our case, an integer) to the list specified with the key (in our case, the key is `"queue:task"`). If you've not used Redis before, you might be expecting something more complex, but this is all that's needed to create a queue. No preconfiguration or schemas are needed.

Bundling these three Python scripts into a container is pretty simple. As shown in listing 10.4, we can use the official Python base image and add the Redis dependency (see chapter 2 if you need a refresher on how to build such containers). For the default container entry point, we'll run our worker with `python3 pi_worker.py`.

[2] https://redis.io/commands/rpush

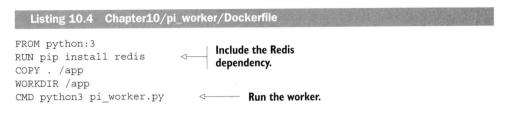

Listing 10.4 Chapter10/pi_worker/Dockerfile

```
FROM python:3
RUN pip install redis          ◁───┐  Include the Redis
COPY . /app                         dependency.
WORKDIR /app
CMD python3 pi_worker.py       ◁─────── Run the worker.
```

With our Python worker container created, we can now get to the fun part of deploying it to Kubernetes!

DEPLOYING TO KUBERNETES

Figure 10.2 shows what the Kubernetes architecture looks like: we have the StatefulSet, which runs Redis, and the Deployment, which runs the worker Pods. There is also the web application role that adds the tasks, but we'll do that manually for this example.

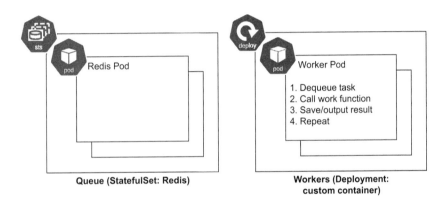

Figure 10.2 Kubernetes architecture of the background processing task queue

Our worker Pods will be deployed in a hopefully now-familiar Deployment configuration (from chapter 3). We'll pass in the location of our Redis host using an environment variable that references the internal service host (as per section 7.1.3).

Listing 10.5 Chapter10/10.1.1_TaskQueue/deploy_worker.yaml

```
apiVersion: apps/v1
kind: Deployment
metadata:
  name: pi-worker
spec:
  replicas: 2
  selector:
    matchLabels:
      pod: pi
  template:
    metadata:
```

```
      labels:
        pod: pi
  spec:
    containers:
    - name: pi-container
      image: docker.io/wdenniss/pi_worker:1
      env:
      - name: REDIS_HOST
        value: redis-0.redis-service
      - name: PYTHONUNBUFFERED
        value: "1"
```

The worker container image →

The Kubernetes Service host name of the primary Redis Pod ←

Env variable to instruct Python to output all print statements immediately ←

Notice that there's nothing special at all about this Deployment when compared with the other Deployments used so far in this book for exposing web services. It's just a bunch of Pods that we happen to have given the role of task workers.

Our worker Pods are expecting a Redis instance, so let's deploy that first. We can use the one from chapter 9; the solutions in the 9.2.1_StatefulSet_Redis and 9.2.2_StatefulSet_Redis_Multi folders both work for our purposes here. From the code sample root folder, simply run:

```
$ kubectl create -f Chapter09/9.2.2_StatefulSet_Redis_Multi
configmap/redis-config created
service/redis-service created
statefulset.apps/redis created
```

```
$ kubectl get pods
NAME      READY   STATUS     RESTARTS   AGE
redis-0   1/1     Running    0          20s
redis-1   1/1     Running    0          13s
redis-2   0/1     Init:0/1   0          7s
```

Now create our worker deployment:

```
kubectl create -f Chapter10/10.1.1_TaskQueue/deploy_worker.yaml
```

Finally, verify everything is working correctly. You should see five running Pods:

```
$ kubectl get pods
NAME                          READY   STATUS    RESTARTS   AGE
pi-worker-55477bdf7b-7rmhp    1/1     Running   0          2m5s
pi-worker-55477bdf7b-ltcsd    1/1     Running   0          2m5s
redis-0                       1/1     Running   0          3m41s
redis-1                       1/1     Running   0          3m34s
redis-2                       1/1     Running   0          3m28s
```

Watching the rollout progress

The get commands I show here, like kubectl get pods, give you a point-in-time status. Recall from chapter 3 that there are two great options for watching your rollout: you can append -w to kubectl commands, which is Kubernetes's built-in watching option (e.g., kubectl get pods -w), or you can use my favorite, the Linux watch

(continued)

command. I use `watch -d kubectl get pods`, which will refresh the status every 2 seconds, and highlight changes. You can also customize the refresh rate. To keep the syntax simple in the book, I won't add watches to every command I share, but remember that they are available to use.

Now that our app is deployed, we can look at the logs to see what it's doing. There's no built-in way in Kubernetes to stream logs from multiple Pods (like our two workers) at the same time, but by specifying the Deployment, the system will randomly pick one and follow its logs:

```
$ kubectl logs -f deployment/pi-worker
Found 2 pods, using pod/pi-worker-55477bdf7b-7rmhp
starting
```

If you want to view the logs for all pods in the deployment but not stream them, that can also be done by referencing the metadata labels from the PodSpec, which in our case is `pod=pi`:

```
$ kubectl logs --selector pod=pi
starting
starting
```

Whichever way you view the logs, we can see that the Pod has printed `starting` and nothing else because our Pod is waiting on tasks to be added to the queue. Let's add some tasks for it to work on.

ADDING WORK TO THE QUEUE

Normally, it will be the web application or another process that will be adding work for the background queue to process. All that the web application need do is call `redis.rpush('queue:task', object)` with the object that represents the tasks.

For this example, we can run the `add_tasks.py` script that we included in our container (listing 10.3) for scheduling some tasks. We can execute a one-off command on the container in one of our Pods:

```
$ kubectl exec -it deploy/pi-worker -- python3 add_tasks.py
added task: 9500000
added task: 3800000
added task: 1900000
added task: 3600000
added task: 1200000
added task: 8600000
added task: 7800000
added task: 7100000
added task: 1400000
added task: 5600000
queue depth 8
done
```

Note that when we pass in `deploy/pi-worker` here, `exec` will pick one of our Pods randomly to run the actual command on (this can even be a Pod in the `Terminating` state, so be careful!). You can also run the command directly on the Pod of your choice with `kubectl exec -it $POD_NAME -- python3 add_tasks.py`.

VIEWING THE WORK

With tasks added to the queue, we can observe the logs of one of our worker pods to see how they're doing:

```
$ kubectl logs -f deployment/pi-worker
Found 2 pods, using pod/pi-worker-54dd47b44c-bjccg
starting
got task: 9500000
3.1415927062213693620
got task: 8600000
3.1415927117293246813
got task: 7100000
3.1415927240123234505
```

This worker is getting the task (being to calculate Pi with n iterations of the Gregory–Leibniz infinity series algorithm) and performing the work.

10.1.2 *Signal handling in worker Pods*

One thing to note is that the previous worker implementation has no SIGTERM handling, which means it won't shut down gracefully when the Pod needs to be replaced. There are a lot of reasons why a Pod might be terminated, including if you update the deployment or if the Kubernetes node is upgraded, so this is a very important signal to handle.

In Python, we can implement this with a SIGTERM handler that will instruct our worker to terminate once it finishes its current task. We'll also add a timeout to our queue-pop call so the worker can check the status more frequently. For your own work, look up how to implement SIGTERM signal handling in your language of choice. Let's add termination handling in the following listing to shut down the worker when SIGTERM is received.

> ### Listing 10.6   Chapter10/pi_worker2/pi_worker.py

```
import os
import signal
import redis
from pi import *

redis_host = os.environ.get('REDIS_HOST')
assert redis_host != None
r = redis.Redis(host=redis_host,
                port='6379',
                decode_responses=True)
running = True
```

Instead of looping indefinitely, exit the loop if this variable is set to false by the signal handler.

```
def signal_handler(signum, frame):
  print("got signal")
  running = False

signal.signal(signal.SIGTERM, signal_handler)
```

> Register a signal handler to set the running state to false when SIGTERM is received.

```
print("starting")
while running:
  task = r.blpop('queue:task', 5)
  if task != None:
    iterations = int(task[1])
    print("got task: " + str(iterations))
    pi = leibniz_pi(iterations)
    print (pi)
```

> Pops the next task but now only waits for 5 seconds if the queue is empty (to allow the running condition to be checked)

Then, deploy this revision in an updated Deployment, specifying the new image along with `terminationGracePeriodSeconds` to request 2 minutes to handle that SIGTERM by wrapping up the current work and exiting.

Listing 10.7   Chapter10/10.1.2_TaskQueue2/deploy_worker.yaml

```
apiVersion: apps/v1
kind: Deployment
metadata:
  name: pi-worker
spec:
  replicas: 2
  selector:
    matchLabels:
      pod: pi
  template:
    metadata:
      labels:
        pod: pi
    spec:
      containers:
      - name: pi-container
        image: docker.io/wdenniss/pi_worker:2
        env:
        - name: REDIS_HOST
          value: redis-0.redis-service
        - name: PYTHONUNBUFFERED
          value: "1"
        resources:
          requests:
            cpu: 250m
            memory: 250Mi
      terminationGracePeriodSeconds: 120
```

> New app version with SIGTERM handling

> Resource requests added so that it can work with HPA

> Request a 120-second graceful termination period to give the container time to shutdown after SIGTERM.

Together, the signal handling in the Pod and the termination grace period means that this Pod will stop accepting new jobs once it receives the SIGTERM and will have 120 seconds to wrap up any current work. Adjust the `terminationGracePeriodSeconds` value as needed for your own workloads.

There are a few more things we didn't consider here. For example, if the worker crashes while processing a task, then that task would be lost as it will be removed from the queue but not completed. Also, there's only minimal observability and other functions. The goal of the previous sample is not to provide a complete queue system but, rather, to demonstrate conceptually how they work. You could continue to implement fault tolerance and other functionality or adopt an open source background task queue and have it do that for you. That choice is yours.

10.1.3 *Scaling worker Pods*

Scaling the worker Pods is the same technique for any Deployment, as covered in chapter 6. You can set the replica count manually or with a Horizontal Pod Autoscaler (HPA). Since our example workload is CPU-intensive, the CPU metric works well for scaling using an HPA, so let's set one up now.

> **Listing 10.8   Chapter10/10.1.3_HPA/worker_hpa.yaml**

```
apiVersion: autoscaling/v2
kind: HorizontalPodAutoscaler
metadata:
  name: pi-worker-autoscaler
spec:
  scaleTargetRef:
    apiVersion: apps/v1        References the
    kind: Deployment           Deployment from
    name: pi-worker            listing 10.7
  minReplicas: 2
  maxReplicas: 10
  metrics:
  - type: Resource
    resource:
      name: cpu
      target:
        type: Utilization
        averageUtilization: 20
```

This code will scale our deployment to between 2 and 10 Pods, aiming for the Pods to be using 20% of their requested CPU resources on average. Create the HPA like so:

```
kubectl create -f Chapter10/10.1.3_HPA
```

With the HPA in place, you can repeat the "add tasks" step from section 10.1.1 and watch the HPA do its thing. The `kubectl get` command supports multiple resource types, so you can run `kubectl get pods,hpa`, which I generally prefix with the Linux `watch` command, to observe all the components interacting:

```
$ kubectl exec -it deploy/pi-worker -- python3 add_tasks.py
$ kubectl get pods,hpa
```

NAME	READY	STATUS	RESTARTS	AGE
pod/pi-worker-54dd47b44c-22x9b	1/1	Running	0	2m42s
pod/pi-worker-54dd47b44c-9wppc	1/1	Running	0	2m27s
pod/pi-worker-54dd47b44c-bjccg	1/1	Running	0	13m
pod/pi-worker-54dd47b44c-f79hx	1/1	Running	0	2m42s
pod/pi-worker-54dd47b44c-fptj9	1/1	Running	0	2m27s
pod/pi-worker-54dd47b44c-hgbqd	1/1	Running	0	2m27s
pod/pi-worker-54dd47b44c-lj2bk	1/1	Running	0	2m27s
pod/pi-worker-54dd47b44c-wc267	1/1	Running	0	2m10s
pod/pi-worker-54dd47b44c-wk4dg	1/1	Running	0	2m10s
pod/pi-worker-54dd47b44c-x2s4m	1/1	Running	0	13m
pod/redis-0	1/1	Running	0	56m
pod/redis-1	1/1	Running	0	56m
pod/redis-2	1/1	Running	0	56m

NAME	REFERENCE	TARGETS	MINPODS	MAXPODS	REPLICAS
pi-worker-autoscaler	Deployment/pi-worker	66%/20%	2	10	10

10.1.4 *Open source task queues*

So far, we've been building our own task queue. I find it best to get hands-on to understand how things work. However, you likely don't need to implement a task queue yourself from scratch since others have done the work for you.

For Python, RQ[3] is a popular choice that allows you to basically enqueue a function call with a bunch of parameters. There's no need to even wrap this function in an object that conforms to a required protocol.

For Ruby developers, Resque,[4] created by the team at GitHub, is a popular choice. Tasks in Resque are simply Ruby classes that implement a `perform` method. The Ruby on Rails framework makes Resque particularly easy to use with its Active Job framework, which allows Resque (among other task queue implementations) to be used as the queuing backend.

Before going out and building your own queue, I'd recommend looking at these options and more. If you have to build something yourself or the off-the-shelf options just don't cut it, I hope you saw from the earlier examples that it's at least pretty straightforward to get started.

10.2 *Jobs*

Kubernetes offers a way to define a finite set of work to process with the Job construct. Both Job and Deployment can be used for handling batch jobs and background processing in Kubernetes in general. The key difference is that Job is designed to process a finite set of work and can potentially be used without needing a queue data structure like Redis, while Deployment is for a continuously running background queue that will need some kind of queue structure for coordination (as we did in section 10.1). You can also use Jobs to run one-off and periodic tasks like

---

[3] https://python-rq.org/

[4] https://github.com/resque/resque

maintenance operations, which wouldn't make sense in a Deployment (which would restart the Pod once it finishes).

You may be wondering why a separate construct is needed in Kubernetes to run something once since standalone Pods could do that as well. While it's true that you can schedule a Pod to perform a task and shut down once it's complete, there is no controller to ensure that the task actually completes. That can happen, for example, if the Pod was evicted due to a maintenance event before it had a chance to complete. Job adds some useful constructs around the Pod to ensure that the task will complete by rescheduling it if it fails or is evicted, as well as the potential to track multiple completions and parallelism.

At the end of the day, Job is just another higher-order workload controller in Kubernetes for managing Pods, like Deployment and StatefulSet. All three create Pods to run your actual code, just with different logic around scheduling and management provided by the controller. Deployments are for creating a set of continuously running Pods; StatefulSet, for Pods that have a unique ordinal and can attach disks through persistent volume templates; and Jobs, for Pods that should run to completion, potentially multiple times.

10.2.1 *Running one-off tasks with Jobs*

Jobs are great for running one-off tasks. Let's say you want to perform a maintenance task like clearing a cache or anything else that is essentially just running a command in your container. Instead of using `kubectl exec` on an existing Pod, you can schedule a Job to run the task as a separate process with its own resources, ensure that the action will complete as requested (or report a failure status), and make it easily repeatable.

The `exec` command should really only be used for debugging running Pods. If you use `exec` to perform maintenance tasks, your task is sharing the resources with the Pod, which isn't great. The Pod may not have enough resources to handle both, and you are affecting the performance. By moving tasks to a Job, they get their own Pod with their own resource allocation.

> **Configuration as code for maintenance tasks**
>
> Throughout this book, I've been espousing how important it is to capture everything in configuration. By capturing routine maintenance tasks as Jobs, rather than having a list of shell commands to copy/paste, you're building a repeatable configuration. If you follow the GitOps approach, where production changes go through Git (covered in the next chapter), your maintenance tasks can go through your usual code review process to be rolled out into production.

In the previous section, we needed to execute a command in the container to add some work to our queue, and we used `kubectl exec` on an existing Pod to run `python3 add_tasks.py`. Let's upgrade the process of adding work to be a proper Job

with its own Pod. The following Job definition can be used to perform the `python3`
`add_tasks.py` task on our container named `pi`.

Listing 10.9   Chapter10/10.2.1_Job/job_addwork.yaml

```
apiVersion: batch/v1
kind: Job
metadata:
  name: addwork
spec:
  backoffLimit: 2
  template:
    spec:
      containers:
      - name: pi-container
        image: docker.io/wdenniss/pi_worker:2
        command: ["python3", "add_tasks.py"]
        env:
        - name: REDIS_HOST
          value: redis-0.redis-service
        - name: PYTHONUNBUFFERED
          value: "1"
      restartPolicy: Never
```

References the same
container image as
the worker...

...but specifies a different
command to run for the
addwork Job

The `spec` within the `template` within the `spec` pattern may look familiar, and that's
because this object embeds a PodSpec template just as Deployment and StatefulSet do
(see figure 10.3 for a visual representation of the object composition). All the parameters of the Pod can be used here, like resource requests and environment variables,
with only a couple of exceptions for parameter combinations that don't make sense in
the Job context.

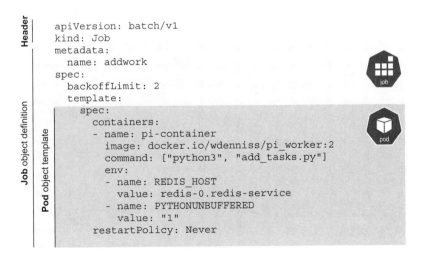

Figure 10.3   Object composition of a Job

Our PodSpec for the Job has the same environment variables as our PodSpec from the Deployment. That's great thing about Kubernetes object composition: the specification is the same wherever the Pod is embedded. The other differences are the `restartPolicy` and the `backoffLimit` fields.

The Pod `restartPolicy`, a property of the PodSpec embedded in the Job, governs whether or not the node's kubelet will restart containers that exit with an error. For Jobs, this can be set to `OnFailure` to restart the container if it fails or `Never` to ignore failures. The `Always` option doesn't make sense for Jobs, as this would restart a successful Pod, which is not what Jobs are designed to do (that's more in the domain of Deployment).

The backoff limit is part of the Job and determines how many times to try to run the Job. This encompasses both crashes and node failures. For example, if the Job crashes twice and then is evicted due to node maintenance, that counts as three restarts. Some practitioners like to use `Never` during development as it's easier to debug and see all the failed Pods and query their logs.

Create the Job like any other Kubernetes object and then observe the progress:

```
$ kubectl create -f Chapter10/10.2.1_Job/job_addwork.yaml
job.batch/addwork created

$ kubectl get job,pods
NAME                  COMPLETIONS   DURATION   AGE
job.batch/addwork     1/1           3s         9s

NAME                                   READY   STATUS      RESTARTS   AGE
pod/addwork-99q5k                      0/1     Completed   0          9s
pod/pi-worker-6f6dfdb548-7krpm         1/1     Running     0          7m2s
pod/pi-worker-6f6dfdb548-pzxq2         1/1     Running     0          7m2s
pod/redis-0                            1/1     Running     0          8m3s
pod/redis-1                            1/1     Running     0          7m30s
pod/redis-2                            1/1     Running     0          6m25s
```

If the Job succeeds, we can watch our worker Pods, which should become busy with newly added work. If you deployed the HPA earlier, then you'll soon see new containers created, as I did here:

```
$ kubectl get pods,hpa
NAME                             READY   STATUS              RESTARTS   AGE
pod/addwork-99q5k                0/1     Completed           0          58s
pod/pi-worker-6f6dfdb548-7krpm   1/1     Running             0          7m51s
pod/pi-worker-6f6dfdb548-h6pld   0/1     ContainerCreating   0          8s
pod/pi-worker-6f6dfdb548-pzxq2   1/1     Running             0          7m51s
pod/pi-worker-6f6dfdb548-qpgxp   1/1     Running             0          8s
pod/redis-0                      1/1     Running             0          8m52s
pod/redis-1                      1/1     Running             0          8m19s
pod/redis-2                      1/1     Running             0          7m14s

NAME                    REFERENCE               TARGETS    MINPODS MAXPODS REPLICAS
pi-worker-autoscaler    Deployment/pi-worker    100%/20%   2       10      2
```

One thing to note about Jobs is that whether the Job has completed or not, you won't be able to schedule it again with the same name (i.e., to repeat the action) without deleting it first. That's because even though the work is now finished, the Job object still exists in Kubernetes. You can delete it like any object created through configuration:

```
kubectl delete -f Chapter10/10.2.1_Job/job_addwork.yaml
```

To recap, Job is for when you have some task or work to complete. Our example was to execute a simple command. However, this could equally have been a long and complex computational task. If you need to run a one-off background process, simply containerize it, define it in the Job, and schedule it. When the Job reports itself as `Completed` (by terminating with an exit status of success), the work is done.

Two parameters of Job that we didn't use to run a one-off task are `completions` and `parallelism`. These parameters allow you to process a batch of tasks using a single Job object description, which is covered in section 10.3. Before we get to that, let's look at how to schedule Jobs at regular intervals.

10.2.2 Scheduling tasks with CronJobs

In the previous section, we took a command that we had executed manually on the cluster and created a proper Kubernetes object to encapsulate it. Now, any developer on the team can perform that task by creating the Job object rather than needing to remember a complex `exec` command.

What about tasks that you need to run repeatedly on a set interval? Kubernetes has you covered with CronJob. CronJob encapsulates a Job object and adds a frequency parameter that allows you to set a daily or hourly (or any interval you like) frequency to run the Job, as in the following listing. This is a popular way to schedule tasks like a daily cache cleanup and the like.

Listing 10.10 Chapter10/10.2.2_CronJob/cronjob_addwork.yaml

```
apiVersion: batch/v1
kind: CronJob
metadata:
  name: addwork
spec:
  schedule: "*/5 * * * *"          ◁┐  The cron schedule
  jobTemplate:                         to run the Job on
    spec:
      backoffLimit: 2
      template:
        spec:
          containers:
          - name: pi-container
            image: docker.io/wdenniss/pi_worker:2
            command: ["python3", "add_tasks.py"]
            env:
            - name: REDIS_HOST
              value: redis-0.redis-service
```

The Job specification, similar to listing 10.9

```
      - name: PYTHONUNBUFFERED
        value: "1"
  restartPolicy: Never
```

You might notice that we just copied the entire specification of the Job (i.e., the `spec` dictionary) from listing 10.9 under this CronJob's `spec` dictionary as the `jobTemplate` key and added an extra spec-level field named `schedule`. Recall that the Job has its own template for the Pods that will be created, which also have their own spec.

So, the CronJob embeds a Job object, which, in turn, embeds a Pod. It can be helpful to visualize this through object composition, so take a look at figure 10.4.

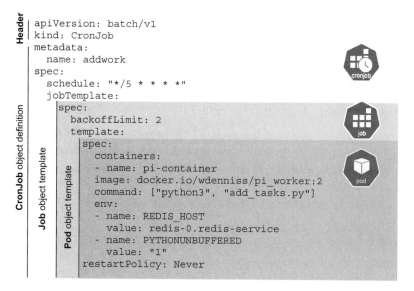

Figure 10.4   Object composition of CronJob

Object Composition in Kubernetes

With all the specs and templates embedding other templates and specs, sometimes it feels like turtles all the way down in Kubernetes. Here we have a CronJob whose spec contains the template for the Job that gets run on the schedule, which itself contains the template of a Pod with its own spec. This may seem confusing and repetitive, or both, but there is a huge benefit to this approach. When looking at the API docs, you can use any field of Job in the `jobTemplate`, just as you can use any field of Pod in the `spec` section. Kubernetes objects are built from the composition of other objects.

Some nomenclature is worth learning: when a Pod is embedded in another object, we refer to the specification of the embedded Pod as a *PodSpec* (e.g., a Deployment contains a PodSpec). When the controller for that higher-level object then creates the Pod in the cluster, that Pod is equal to any other, including ones that were created directly with their own specification. The only difference is that the Pods created by a controller

(continued)
(like Job or Deployment) continue to be observed by that controller (i.e., re-creating them if they fail, and so forth).

So that's how it's composed. What about the `schedule` field, which is CronJob's contribution to the specification? `schedule` is where we define the frequency in the age-old Unix cron format. The cron format is extremely expressive. In listing 10.10, `*/5 * * * *` translates to "every 5 minutes." You can configure schedules like "run every 30 minutes" (`*/30 * * * *`), run daily at midnight (`0 0 * * *`), run Mondays at 4:00 p.m. (`0 16 * * 1`), and many, many more. I recommend using a visual cron editor (a Google search for "cron editor" should do the trick) to validate your preferred expression rather than waiting a week to verify that the Job you wanted to run weekly actually ran.

Create the new CronJob:

```
$ kubectl create -f Chapter10/10.2.2_CronJob/cronjob_addwork.yaml
cronjob.batch/addwork created

$ kubectl get cronjob,job
NAME                     SCHEDULE       SUSPEND   ACTIVE   LAST SCHEDULE   AGE
cronjob.batch/addwork    */5 * * * *    False     0        <none>          58s
```

Wait a couple of minutes (for this example, the Job is created every 5 minutes, i.e., :00, :05, and so forth), and then you can see the Job and the Pod that it spawned:

```
$ kubectl get cronjob,job,pods
NAME                     SCHEDULE       SUSPEND   ACTIVE   LAST SCHEDULE   AGE
cronjob.batch/addwork    */5 * * * *    False     0        2m38s           3m11s

NAME                          COMPLETIONS   DURATION   AGE
job.batch/addwork-27237815    1/1           107s       2m38s

NAME                              READY   STATUS      RESTARTS   AGE
pod/addwork-27237815-b44ws        0/1     Completed   0          2m38s
pod/pi-worker-6f6dfdb548-5czkc    1/1     Running     5          14m
pod/pi-worker-6f6dfdb548-gfkcq    1/1     Running     0          7s
pod/pi-worker-6f6dfdb548-pl584    1/1     Running     0          7s
pod/pi-worker-6f6dfdb548-qpgxp    1/1     Running     5          25m
pod/redis-0                       1/1     Running     0          14m
pod/redis-1                       1/1     Running     0          33m
pod/redis-2                       1/1     Running     0          32m
```

CronJob will spawn a new Job on a schedule, which, in turn, will spawn a new Pod. You can inspect these historic jobs, as they remain with the `Complete` status. The `successfulJobsHistoryLimit` and `failedJobsHistoryLimit` options in the CronJobSpec[5] can be used to govern how many of those historic Jobs will be kept.

---

[5] https://kubernetes.io/docs/reference/kubernetes-api/workload-resources/cron-job-v1/#CronJobSpec

> **Time zones**
>
> Be aware that the CronJob will run on the time zone of your cluster, which for many platforms, including Google Kubernetes Engine (GKE), will be UTC. The time zone used is that of the system Kubernetes controller component, which runs on the control plane. If you're on a managed platform, it may not be possible to query the control plane nodes directly, but it is possible to check the worker nodes, which likely use the same time zone. Here's how to create a one-off Pod to run the Linux `date` command and then exit with the output in bold:
>
> ```
> $ kubectl run date --restart=Never -it --rm --image ubuntu -- date +%Z
> UTC
> pod "date" deleted
> ```

10.3 *Batch task processing with Jobs*

What if you have a batch of work that you want to process as a regular or one-off event? As covered in section 10.1, if a *continuously running* task queue is what you want, then Deployment is actually the right Kubernetes object. But, if you have a finite batch of work to process, then Job is the ideal Kubernetes construct to use.

If you have a dynamic work queue data structure like we did in section 10.1 but want your workers to shut down completely when the queue is empty, that's something that Job can do. With a Deployment, you need a separate system (like a `HorizontalPod-Autoscaler`) to scale the worker Pods up and down, for example, when there is no more work in the queue. When using Job, the worker Pods themselves can signal to the Job controller when the work is complete and they should be shut down and the resources reclaimed.

Another way to use Job is to run it on a static work queue in such a way that a database is not needed at all. Let's say you know you need to process 100 tasks in a queue. You could run the Job 100 times. The catch, of course, is that each Pod instantiation in the Job series needs to know which of those 100 tasks to run on, which is where the indexed Job comes in.

In this section, I'll cover both the dynamic and static approaches to task processing.

10.3.1 *Dynamic queue processing with Jobs*

Let's redesign the dynamic queue from section 10.1 to use a Job instead of a Deployment. Both a Deployment and a Job allow the creation of multiple Pod workers, and both will re-create Pods in the event of failure. Deployment, however, doesn't have the notation of a Pod "completing" (i.e., terminating with an exit status of success). Whatever replica count you give the Deployment is what it will strive to keep running at all times. On the other hand, when a Pod managed by a Job terminates with the success exit code (e.g., `exit 0`), it indicates to the Job controller that the work has completed successfully, and the Pod won't be restarted.

This property of a Job that allows the individual workers to signal when the work is finished is what makes Jobs useful. If you're using a dynamic Kubernetes environment such as one with autoscaling (including GKE in Autopilot mode), then a Job allows you to "set and forget" the work, where you schedule it, and once it's done, the resource consumption goes to zero. Note that you can't scale the Job back up once it's completed, but you can delete and re-create it, which essentially starts a new processing queue.

For our task worker container to work correctly in a Job environment, we need to add a success exit condition for when the queue becomes empty. The following listing shows what our revised worker code looks like.

Listing 10.11 Chapter10/pi_worker3/pi_worker.py

```python
import os
import signal
import redis
from pi import *

redis_host = os.environ.get('REDIS_HOST')
assert redis_host != None
r = redis.Redis(host=redis_host,
                port='6379',
                decode_responses=True)
running = True

def signal_handler(signum, frame):
  print("got signal")
  running = False

signal.signal(signal.SIGTERM, signal_handler)

print("starting")
while running:
  task = r.blpop('queue:task', 5)
  if task != None:
    iterations = int(task[1])
    print("got task: " + str(iterations))
    pi = leibniz_pi(iterations)
    print (pi)
  else:
    if os.getenv('COMPLETE_WHEN_EMPTY', '0') != '0':
      print ("no more work")
      running = False

exit(0)
```

When configured with **COMPLETE_WHEN_EMPTY=1**, don't wait for new tasks when the queue is empty.

The 0 exit code indicates to Kubernetes that the Job completed successfully.

With our worker container set up to behave correctly in the Job context, we can create a Kubernetes Job to run it. Whereas in the deployment we use the `replica` field to govern the number of Pods that are running at once, with a Job, it's the `parallelism` parameter, which basically does the same thing.

Listing 10.12   Chapter10/10.3.1_JobWorker/job_worker.yaml

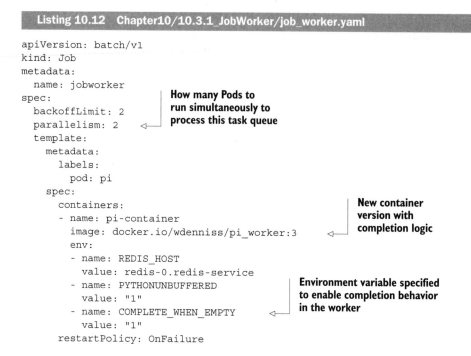

```
apiVersion: batch/v1
kind: Job
metadata:
  name: jobworker
spec:
  backoffLimit: 2
  parallelism: 2          ⊲──┘   How many Pods to
  template:                      run simultaneously to
    metadata:                    process this task queue
      labels:
        pod: pi
    spec:
      containers:                        New container
      - name: pi-container               version with
        image: docker.io/wdenniss/pi_worker:3   ⊲──┘  completion logic
        env:
        - name: REDIS_HOST
          value: redis-0.redis-service
        - name: PYTHONUNBUFFERED          Environment variable specified
          value: "1"                      to enable completion behavior
        - name: COMPLETE_WHEN_EMPTY  ⊲──  in the worker
          value: "1"
      restartPolicy: OnFailure
```

If you compare the PodSpec of the worker created as a Job in listing 10.12 to the Pod-Spec of the worker created as a Deployment in listing 10.7, you'll notice that the embedded PodSpec (the fields under `template`) is identical other than the addition of the `COMPLETE_WHEN_EMPTY` environment variable and the `restartPolicy` field. The restart policy is added because the default of `Always` for Pods doesn't apply to Jobs that are designed to terminate. With the `OnFailure` restart policy, the worker Pod will be restarted only if it crashes without returning success, which is generally desirable. We don't strictly need the labels metadata for the Job version of this worker, but it can be useful to query the logs of multiple Pods at the same time as discussed earlier (i.e., with `kubectl logs --selector pod=pi`).

Preparing

Before running the Job-based version of the task worker, delete the previous Deployment version of the worker and remove the old "addwork" Job and CronJob so they can be run again:

```
$ cd Chapter10

$ kubectl delete -f 10.1.2_TaskQueue2
deployment.apps "pi-worker" deleted

$ kubectl delete -f 10.2.1_Job
job.batch "addwork" deleted
```

(continued)

```
$ kubectl delete -f 10.2.2_CronJob
cronjob.batch "addwork" deleted
```

Since our Redis-based queue may have some existing jobs, you can reset it as well using the LTRIM Redis command:

```
$ kubectl exec -it pod/redis-0 -- redis-cli ltrim queue:task 0 0
OK
```

You can also run the `redis-cli` interactively if you prefer to reset the queue:

```
$ kubectl exec -it pod/redis-0 -- redis-cli
127.0.0.1:6379> LTRIM queue:task 0 0
OK
```

Let's take this Job-based worker for a spin. First, we can add some work to our Redis queue, using a one-off Job like before:

```
$ cd Chapter10

$ kubectl create -f 10.2.1_Job
job.batch/addwork created

$ kubectl get job,pod
NAME                   COMPLETIONS   DURATION   AGE
job.batch/addwork      0/1           19s        19s

NAME                   READY   STATUS              RESTARTS   AGE
pod/addwork-19fgg      0/1     ContainerCreating   0          19s
pod/redis-0            1/1     Running             0          19h
pod/redis-1            1/1     Running             0          19h
pod/redis-2            1/1     Running             0          19h
```

> **TIP** You can't create the same Job object twice, even if the first instance already ran and completed. To rerun a Job, delete it first before creating again.

Once this `addwork` Job has completed, we can run our new Job queue to process the work. Unlike previously, the order matters here since the Job workers will exit if there is no work in the queue, so make sure that `addwork` completed before you run the Job queue. Observe the status like so:

```
$ kubectl get job,pod
NAME                   COMPLETIONS   DURATION   AGE
job.batch/addwork      1/1           22s        36s

NAME                   READY   STATUS      RESTARTS   AGE
pod/addwork-19fgg      0/1     Completed   0          37s
pod/redis-0            1/1     Running     0          19h
pod/redis-1            1/1     Running     0          19h
pod/redis-2            1/1     Running     0          19h
```

Once we see `Completed` on our `addwork` task, we can go ahead and schedule the Job queue:

```
$ kubectl create -f 10.3.1_JobWorker
job.batch/jobworker created

$ kubectl get job,pod
NAME                    COMPLETIONS   DURATION   AGE
job.batch/addwork       1/1           22s        3m45s
job.batch/jobworker     0/1 of 2      2m16s      2m16s

NAME                    READY   STATUS      RESTARTS   AGE
pod/addwork-19fgg       0/1     Completed   0          3m45s
pod/jobworker-swb6k     1/1     Running     0          2m16s
pod/jobworker-tn6cd     1/1     Running     0          2m16s
pod/redis-0             1/1     Running     0          19h
pod/redis-1             1/1     Running     0          19h
pod/redis-2             1/1     Running     0          19h
```

What should happen next is that the worker Pods will process the queue, and when the queue is empty, the workers will complete the task they are currently working on and then exit with success. If you want to monitor the queue depth to know when the work should wrap up, you can run `LLEN` on the Redis queue to observe the current queue length:

```
$ kubectl exec -it pod/redis-0 -- redis-cli llen queue:task
(integer) 5
```

When it gets to zero, you should observe the Pods entering the `Completed` state. Note that they won't enter this state right away but rather after they wrap up the last task they are processing:

```
$ kubectl get job,pod
NAME                    COMPLETIONS   DURATION   AGE
job.batch/addwork       1/1           22s        3m45s
job.batch/jobworker     0/1 of 2      2m16s      2m16s

NAME                    READY   STATUS      RESTARTS   AGE
pod/addwork-19fgg       0/1     Completed   0          10m09s
pod/jobworker-swb6k     1/1     Completed   0          8m40s
pod/jobworker-tn6cd     1/1     Completed   0          8m40s
pod/redis-0             1/1     Running     0          19h
pod/redis-1             1/1     Running     0          19h
pod/redis-2             1/1     Running     0          19h
```

Remember that if you want to rerun any of the Jobs, you need to delete them first and create them again, even if the Jobs have completed and there are no Pods running. To run the previous demo a second time, delete both Jobs (the one that adds the work and the one that runs the workers) and create them afresh:

```
$ kubectl delete -f 10.2.1_Job
job.batch "addwork" deleted
```

```
$ kubectl delete -f 10.3.1_JobWorker
job.batch "jobworker" deleted
$ kubectl create -f 10.2.1_Job
job.batch/addwork created
$ kubectl create -f 10.3.1_JobWorker
job.batch/jobworker created
```

10.3.2 Static queue processing with Jobs

There are a number of ways to run Jobs with a static queue instead of using a dynamic queue like Redis, as we did in the previous section to store the task list. When using a static queue, the queue length is known ahead of time and is configured as part of the Job itself, and a new Pod is created for each task. Instead of having task workers running until the queue is empty, you are defining up front how many times to instantiate the worker Pod.

The main reason for doing this is to avoid the container needing to understand how to pull tasks from the dynamic queue, which for existing containers often means effort to add that functionality. The drawback is that there is generally additional configuration on the Kubernetes side. It essentially shifts the configuration burden from the worker container to Kubernetes objects.

Note that even if you have the requirement that you can't modify the container that performs the work, this doesn't mean you have to use a static queue. You can have multiple containers in a Pod and have one container that performs the dequeuing, passing the parameters on to the other container.

So how do you represent a static work queue in Kubernetes configuration? There are a few different options, three of which I'll outline here.

STATIC QUEUE USING AN INDEX

Indexed Jobs are the most interesting static queue option, in my opinion. They are useful when you know ahead of time how many tasks to process and the task list is one that is easily indexed. One example is rendering an animated movie. You know the number of frames (queue length) and can easily pass each instantiation the frame number (i.e., index into the queue) of the frame to render.

Kubernetes will run the Job the total number of times (`completions`) you specify, creating a Pod for each task. Each time it runs, it will give the Job the next index (supplied in the environment variable $`JOB_COMPLETION_INDEX`). If your work is naturally indexed (e.g., rendering frames in an animated movie), this works great! You can easily instruct Kubernetes to run the Job 30,000 times (i.e., render 30,000 frames), and it will give each Pod the frame number. Another obvious approach is to give each Job the full list of work using some data structure (e.g., an array of tasks encoded in YAML or just plain text, one per line), and Kubernetes supplies the index. The Job can then look up the task in the list using the index.

The following listing provides an example configuration of an Indexed Job that simply outputs a frame number. You can sub in the actual movie rendering logic yourself.

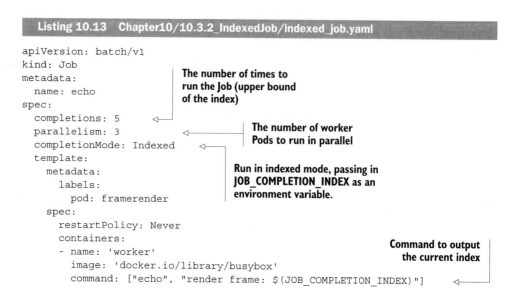

Listing 10.13   Chapter10/10.3.2_IndexedJob/indexed_job.yaml

```
apiVersion: batch/v1
kind: Job
metadata:
  name: echo
spec:
  completions: 5
  parallelism: 3
  completionMode: Indexed
  template:
    metadata:
      labels:
        pod: framerender
    spec:
      restartPolicy: Never
      containers:
      - name: 'worker'
        image: 'docker.io/library/busybox'
        command: ["echo", "render frame: $(JOB_COMPLETION_INDEX)"]
```

The number of times to run the Job (upper bound of the index)

The number of worker Pods to run in parallel

Run in indexed mode, passing in **JOB_COMPLETION_INDEX** as an environment variable.

Command to output the current index

Run and observe this Job:

```
$ kubectl create -f 10.3.2_IndexedJob
job.batch/echo created

$ kubectl get job,pods
NAME              COMPLETIONS    DURATION    AGE
job.batch/echo    5/5            20s         58s

NAME                READY    STATUS        RESTARTS    AGE
pod/echo-0-r8v52    0/1      Completed     0           58s
pod/echo-1-nxwsm    0/1      Completed     0           58s
pod/echo-2-49kz2    0/1      Completed     0           58s
pod/echo-3-9lvt2    0/1      Completed     0           51s
pod/echo-4-2pstq    0/1      Completed     0           45s
```

To inspect the logs, do the following:

```
$ kubectl logs --selector pod=framerender
render frame: 0
render frame: 1
render frame: 2
render frame: 3
render frame: 4
```

Your application can use this environment variable directly, or you can use an init container to take the index and perform any configuration steps needed for the main container to perform the work—for example, by building a script that will be run.

STATIC QUEUE WITH A MESSAGE QUEUE SERVICE

Another approach that doesn't require modification of the container is to populate a message queue and have each Pod pull the work from that. As the containers can be configured to get the required parameters through environment variables in the Kubernetes configuration, it's possible to build a Job where the container is unaware of the queue. It's still "static" since you have to declare upfront how many tasks there are and run one worker Pod per task, but it also requires a data structure (i.e., the message queue). The Kubernetes docs do a great job of demonstrating this approach using RabbitMQ for the message queue.[6]

STATIC QUEUE VIA SCRIPTING

Another option is to use scripting to simply create a separate Job for each task in the queue. Basically, if you have 100 tasks to complete, you'd set up a script to iterate over your task definition and create 100 individual Jobs, giving each the specific input data it needs. This is personally my least-favorite option as it's a bit unwieldy to manage. Imagine you queue all this work up and then want to cancel it. Instead of just deleting a single Job, as in all the other examples in this section, you'd have to delete 100, so you'd likely need more scripting to do that, and on it goes. Again, the Kubernetes docs have a good demo of this, so if it interests you, check it out.[7]

10.4   *Liveness probes for background tasks*

Just like containers that serve HTTP traffic, containers that perform tasks (whether configured as a Deployment or Job) should also have liveness probes. A liveness probe provides Kubernetes the information it needs to restart containers that are running but not performing as expected (for example, the process has hung or an external dependency has failed). The kubelet will automatically restart *crashed* containers (unless the PodSpec's `restartPolicy` field is set to `Never`), but it has no way of knowing if your process has hung or is otherwise not performing as expected without a liveness probe.

In chapter 4, we covered readiness and liveness probes in the context of HTTP serving workloads. For background tasks, we can ignore readiness as background tasks don't have a Service that they can be added to or removed from based on readiness, and focus just on liveness. As with serving workloads, liveness can be used to detect stuck or hung containers in background tasks so Kubernetes can restart them.

As background tasks don't have an HTTP or a TCP endpoint to use for a liveness probe, that leaves the command-based probe option. You can specify any command to run on the container, and if it exits with success, the container is considered live. But what command should you use? One approach is for the task to write the current timestamp to a file periodically and then have a script that checks the recency of that timestamp, which can be used as the liveness command.

Let's go ahead and configure such a liveness probe for our task worker container. First, we need a function to write the current time (as a Unix timestamp) to a file. The following listing implements exactly that.

---

[6] https://kubernetes.io/docs/tasks/job/coarse-parallel-processing-work-queue/
[7] https://kubernetes.io/docs/tasks/job/parallel-processing-expansion/

Listing 10.14   Chapter10/pi_worker4/liveness.py

```
import os
import time

def update_liveness():

    timestamp = int(time.time())
    with open("logs/lastrun.date", "w") as myfile:
        myfile.write(f"{timestamp}")
```

The current time as a Unix timestamp

Write the timestamp to the file logs/lastrun.date.

Then, we need to call this `update_liveness()` method at various points during the worker run loop to indicate that the process is still live. The obvious place to put it is right in the main loop. If you have a very long running task, you might want to add it in a few more places as well. The following listing shows where this method was added to pi_worker.py (see the source that accompanies the book for the unabridged file).

Listing 10.15   Chapter10/pi_worker4/pi_worker.py

```
from liveness import *

# ...

while running:
  update_liveness()
  task = r.blpop('queue:task', 5)

# ...
```

Mark the task "live" during the main run loop.

Next, we need a bash script in the container that can be referenced by the liveness command to determine the freshness of this timestamp. Listing 10.16 is such a script. It takes two parameters: the file to read (variable `$1`) and the number of seconds to consider the result live (variable `$2`). It compares the contents of the file to the current time and returns success (exit code `0`) if the timestamp is considered fresh, or fail (a nonzero exit code) if it's not. Example usage is `./health_check.sh logs/lastrun .date 300`, which will return success if the timestamp written to the lastrun.date file is within 300 seconds (5 minutes) of the current time. See the source that accompanies the book for the complete file including input validation.

Listing 10.16   Chapter10/pi_worker4/check_liveness.sh

```
#!/bin/bash

# ...

if ! rundate=$(<$1); then
  echo >&2 "Failed: unable to read logfile"
  exit 2
fi
```

Reads the timestamp file (specified by input parameter $1), exit with an error if it doesn't exist

```
curdate=$(date +'%s')          ⟵⎯⎤  Get the current timestamp.

time_difference=$((curdate-rundate))      ⟵⎯⎤  Compares the two timestamps

if [ $time_difference -gt $2 ]
then                                          Return an error status code
  echo >&2 "Liveness failing, timestamp too old."   if the process, timestamp is
  exit 1                                      older than the threshold
fi                                            (parameter $2).
        ⎡ Return a success
        ⎢ exit status.
exit 0  ⟵⎯⎤
```

With the task worker writing the timestamp and a bash script to check it, the final step is to update our workload definition to add the liveness probe via the `livenessProbe` field. This field is part of the PodSpec, so it can be added to either the Deployment or Job version of the task worker. The following listing updates the worker Deployment from listing 10.7 to add a liveness probe.

Listing 10.17   Chapter10/10.4_TaskLiveness/deploy_worker.yaml

```yaml
apiVersion: apps/v1
kind: Deployment
metadata:
  name: pi-worker
spec:
  replicas: 2
  selector:
    matchLabels:
      pod: pi
  template:
    metadata:
      labels:
        pod: pi
    spec:
      containers:                              New container
      - name: pi-container                     version with the
        image: docker.io/wdenniss/pi_worker:4  ⟵  liveness probe logic
        env:
        - name: REDIS_HOST
          value: redis-0.redis-service
        - name: PYTHONUNBUFFERED
          value: "1"
        livenessProbe:                         ⟵ The new
          initialDelaySeconds: 60                 liveness
          periodSeconds: 30                       probe
          exec:
            command: ["./check_liveness.sh", "logs/lastrun.date", "300"]
          successThreshold: 1
          timeoutSeconds: 1
      terminationGracePeriodSeconds: 120
```

Putting it all together, we now have a process to detect hung processes in the task worker. If the worker fails to write an updated timestamp into the file in the required freshness time threshold (set to 300 seconds in the example), the liveness probe command will return a failure status, and the Pod will be restarted.

Make sure your worker is updating this timestamp more frequently than the time specified. If you have a very long running task, either increase the freshness time threshold or update the timestamp file multiple times during the task processing instead of just in the loop as we did in listing 10.15. Another consideration is to ensure the timestamp is only written when the worker is behaving normally. You probably wouldn't call `update_liveness()` in an exception handler, for example.

> **NOTE** In this example, the threshold for being considered stale (not live) is unrelated to how *often* the liveness probe is run (the `periodSeconds` field). If you need to increase the threshold, increase the number of seconds given as the third value to the liveness probe—that is, the `"300"` in `["./check_liveness.sh", "logs/lastrun.date", "300"]`.

With this liveness probe configured to the background task, now Kubernetes has the information it needs to keep your code running with less intervention from you.

Summary

- Kubernetes has a few different options for handling background task queues and batch jobs.
- Deployments can be used to build a continuously running task queue, utilizing a queue data structure like Redis for coordination.
- The background processing that many websites run to offload computationally heavy requests would typically be run as a Deployment.
- Kubernetes also has a dedicated Job object for running tasks.
- Jobs can be used for one-off tasks, such as a manual maintenance task.
- CronJob can be used to schedule Jobs to run, for example, a daily cleanup task.
- Jobs can be used to process a task queue and self-terminate when the work is completed, such as when running one-off or period batch jobs.
- Unlike a Deployment-based background queue, Job can be used to schedule work on a static queue, avoiding the need for a queue data structure like Redis.
- Liveness checks are still relevant for Pods that process background tasks to detect stuck/hung processes and can be configured using a command-based liveness check.

GitOps:
Configuration as code

This chapter covers

- Using namespaces and configuration files to replicate environments
- The benefits of treating Kubernetes workload configuration like source code
- Using Git pull requests to drive operations
- Handling secrets without storing them in plain text in version control

You may have noticed in this book so far that we've been writing a lot of YAML configuration files. It is possible to interact with most Kubernetes objects without writing configuration files using imperative `kubectl` commands such as `kubectl run`, and these are arguably easier to learn. So why did I use the declarative configuration-based approach throughout? One reason is that as you take an app to production, you can start treating the configuration like code, with version control and code reviews.

Another reason is it allows you to easily spin up multiple environments with the same configuration. Let's say you want a staging and a production environment that are as similar as possible for better testing. With your workloads defined in configuration files, it's possible to replicate the environments easily.

Kubernetes has a namespaces feature that makes this possible without needing to worry about name collisions.

11.1 Production and staging environments using namespaces

As you prepare your application for production, you'll likely want to create a staging environment where changes can be tested before the live production application is updated. Kubernetes makes this easy with namespaces.

Namespaces, as their name suggests, provide name uniqueness within a single logical space. So you can set up a production namespace and a staging namespace and have the Deployment `foo-deployment` and Service `foo-service` in each of them (figure 11.1). This avoids the need to excessively modify your configuration for the different environments, like creating a differently named `foo-staging-deployment` and `foo-staging-service`, and provides some protection against accidental changes as, by default, `kubectl` commands only apply to the namespace that's currently active.

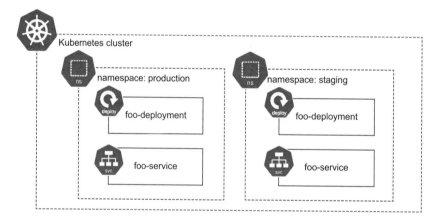

Figure 11.1   A Kubernetes cluster with two namespaces. Note that the Deployment and Service objects in these namespaces have the same name in both.

The main configuration differences between your production and staging are typically things like the scale (number of replicas) and any external service credentials for services not deployed as part of the namespace.

> **TIP**   As the complexity of your application workloads or the number of differently configured environments increases, you may wish to consider using a templating engine such as Kustomize or Helm.

To create a namespace named `staging` to host a new instance of the application, you can run

```
kubectl create namespace staging
```

To interact with this namespace, you can either add `--namespace staging` (or `-n staging` for short) to every `kubectl` command you run or change the `kubectl` context so that all commands will run in this new namespace. I highly recommend the latter, as you don't want to forget the `-n` flag and accidentally run a command in the wrong namespace. Better to switch contexts each time. You can list the available namespaces with `kubectl get namespace` and then set the context to be the namespace of your choosing:

```
kubectl config set-context --current --namespace=staging
```

When listing the namespaces, you may notice that Kubernetes comes with a few namespaces out of the box. `kube-system` is where the system Pods go—best not to touch this one unless you know what you're doing. `default` is the default user namespace which is fine to use, but I recommend creating your own dedicated ones, one for each application environment.

I find the `kubectl` context setting command tedious and highly recommend setting up your shell with a utility to make it simpler to switch. The one I use is `kubectx` + `kubens`.[1] With `kubens` installed, you can run `kubens` to list the namespaces, and the following to set the context:

```
kubens staging
```

The other included utility, `kubectx,` can be used to quickly switch between different clusters entirely. These scripts are just shorthand for the longer `kubectl config set-context` commands, so you can go back to using `kubectl` as normal once the context is set.

11.1.1 Deploying to our new namespace

Once you have the namespace created, you can deploy your application easily from the configuration. This is why this book has been using configuration files in every case. Instead of rerunning a bunch of imperative commands to re-create your workloads, you can simply run the following command from the folder with your configuration:

```
kubectl apply -f .
```

And if you make any changes to the configuration or need to deploy it to yet another namespace, you just rerun that command each time to roll out your changes.

In fact, creating new environments with namespaces in Kubernetes is so trivial to configure that if you were sharing a single staging environment in the past on other platforms, you may see some benefit to having a lot of different environments. You can have a namespace per developer or team, one for staging, another for integration testing, and so forth. Generally, the namespaces are free (of course, the compute resources used by duplicating your Pods are not).

---

[1] https://github.com/ahmetb/kubectx

11.1.2 Syncing mutations from the cluster

But what about any changes that were made imperatively, outside of configuration? Perhaps you scaled a workload with `kubectl scale`, changed the image with `kubectl set-image`, or created a Deployment with `kubectl run`. It happens; I won't judge.

Kubernetes lets you view and export configuration with the `--output` parameter (`-o` for short) on any `get` request. For example, to get the latest YAML configuration for a Deployment use the following:

```
kubectl get deploy timeserver -o yaml          ◁─┐  View the Deployment
                                                  as YAML.

kubectl get deploy timeserver -o yaml > timeserver-exported.yaml   ◁──────┐

                                Pipe the Deployment YAML config to a file.
```

The catch is that Kubernetes adds a lot of extra fields that you don't really want in your on-disk configuration, like status messages, and so forth. There used to be a handy `--export` option that would strip these, but sadly it was deprecated. So it's a bit of an art to figure out which lines you can delete and which you need to keep. But you can compare the YAML files you get this way to the ones in this book to see which lines are important.

If you plan to use the configuration in multiple namespaces, which is common, you will definitely want to delete the `metadata → namespace` field. Removing it will allow you to deploy the configuration in the current namespace (keeping it will mean any changes will update the object in whatever namespace was specified). The danger I see in keeping the namespace is you might accidentally have some configuration in your staging folder set to the production namespace. Section 11.3 discusses some tactics on safety around rollouts to different namespaces, but it relies on *not* specifying the namespace in resource objects directly.

Other fields to consider for removal for cleanliness are from the `metadata` section, the fields `uid`, `resourceVersion`, `generation`, `creationTimestamp`, and the entire `status` section. These fields won't prevent you from reusing the configuration in other namespaces or clusters but don't really have meaning outside their deployed context, so best to keep it out of version control to avoid confusion.

11.2 Configuration as code the Kubernetes way

When you have a bug in your source code, you can inspect the version history to see when the code was changed (such as with `git log` and `git blame`) and might occasionally roll back a commit to get back to the previous working state. When you treat your configuration as code (by committing it to your version control system), you can perform similar actions but with your production systems.

If you have a code review process, you can use the same process for Kubernetes configuration. After all, the configuration affects the running system just as much as the code does. Code review on configuration repositories can help to catch errors before they are rolled out. For example, if you accidently delete all the replicas of a Deployment in a configuration change, your colleague has a chance to catch the mistake during the code review.

You'll find this pattern used at all major internet companies. Most Google services, for example, are developed and deployed out of a single code repository,[2] so the service configuration sits right beside the code. The exact same code review practices are followed for code and service configuration, although the list of owners (the engineers that can approve the changes for merging) may differ.

There's no obligation to store the configuration in the same repository as the code like Google, though. This is mostly a matter of taste (and endless technical debate). The model I'll present here for storing Kubernetes configuration in Git is just an example of what I've found works for me, but you should adapt it to your own engineering practices.

I use a single Git repository to represent all the Kubernetes objects deployed in a single cluster. In this repo is a folder for each Kubernetes namespace, and in those folders are the YAML files for the objects in the namespace (figure 11.2). An alternative

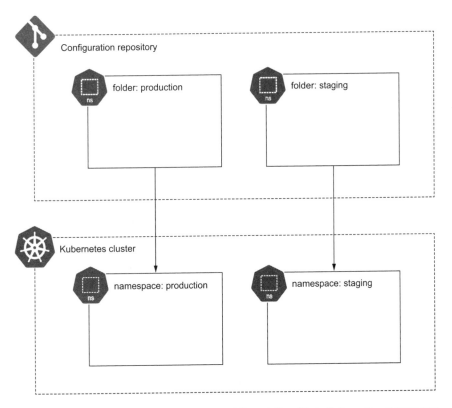

Figure 11.2   Git repository folder structure and the relationship to Kubernetes namespaces

[2] https://research.google/pubs/pub45424/

is to use a separate branch for each namespace, which has some nice properties, like being able to merge changes as they go from staging to production. However, as there are likely some changes you *don't* want to merge, it can get messy (e.g., you wouldn't want to accidentally merge your staging-only changes to production).

Here's an example directory layout:

A directory for any debug scripts you wish to store for all developers

The cluster configuration (e.g., the namespace configuration files). These are only used during cluster creation.

```
/_debug
/_cluster
/staging
/production
```

The environment configuration folders

Each directory in this repository is mapped to a Kubernetes namespace. The beauty of such a 1:1 mapping is that it allows you to confidently execute a `kubectl apply -f .` command to roll out all changes in the directory to the active namespace. Cloning the environment is as simple as duplicating the entire folder and then deploying it to its own namespace.

It's common—particularly for smaller-scale workload deployments—to share a cluster with multiple environment namespaces. Sharing a cluster can reduce the direct costs and operational overhead of managing multiple clusters, and allow workloads to share a common pool of compute resources. As the deployments get larger, it may be desirable to separate environments into their own clusters to provide an extra level of access control and resource isolation (figure 11.3). The good news is that the configuration repository doesn't care where these namespaces are; it's totally fine for them to exist in different clusters.

Once your configuration repository is set up, the development process looks like this:

1 Make changes to the configuration for the desired environment.
2 Commit those changes.
3 Update the live state by setting the current namespace context with `kubectl` and then running `kubectl apply -f .` on the matching directory.

With this, you're following a configuration as code pattern, but there is more you can do. One danger with the setup as described so far is that you can accidently roll out the configuration from one folder to the wrong namespace. The next sections cover how to roll out safely and avoid this problem and how to level up to a full GitOps-style process where the `git push` on the configuration repository triggers the rollout automatically.

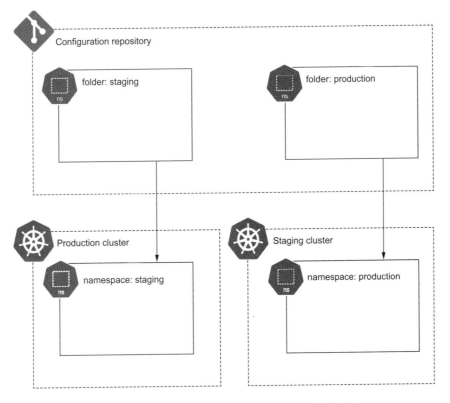

Figure 11.3   Configuration repository with environments in multiple clusters

11.3   *Rolling out safely*

With your configuration as a code repository set up, there is now a question of how best to roll out the changes in the repo. Sure, you can simply check out the repository and run `kubectl apply -f .` as we did earlier, but this can be dangerous. You could accidentally deploy the wrong configuration into the wrong namespace. Since we're reusing object names in multiple environments, this could be quite bad, indeed. Also, there's nothing to stop you from changing the live cluster state directly without committing the configuration change to the repository.

To tackle the wrong-namespace problem, I recommend putting some guardrails in place to avoid accidentally deploying the wrong configuration to the wrong namespace. Instead of simply running `kubectl apply -f .` as we did earlier, wrap it up in a script that performs a check to ensure you're deploying into the right namespace. If we name our folders the same as the namespace, then the check is simple: if the current namespace is equal to the folder name, deploy; otherwise, don't. The following listing provides an example script that compares the current directory name to the current namespace and exits with an error status if they don't match.

Listing 11.1   Chapter11/gitops/gitops_check.sh

```
#! /bin/bash                    Get the last directory
                            component of the current path.

CURRENT_DIR=`echo "${PWD##*/}"`          ◁
CURRENT_NAMESPACE=`kubectl config view --minify          Retrieve the current
➥ -o=jsonpath='{.contexts[0].context.namespace}'`       namespace.

if [ "$CURRENT_DIR" != "$CURRENT_NAMESPACE" ]; then
    >&2 echo "Wrong namespace (currently $CURRENT_NAMESPACE but" \
            "$CURRENT_DIR expected)"
    exit 1
fi
                        Otherwise,
exit 0      ◁           exit with the          Exit with error if this script was run from a
                        success status.        directory that doesn't match the namespace name.
```

You can then use this in any other scripts, like the following rollout script. Instead of running `kubectl apply -f .` directly, you would run this script, which verifies the correct directory/namespace combination.

Listing 11.2   Chapter11/gitops/production/rollout.sh

```
#! /bin/sh                          Verify that the directory name
                                    matches the namespace.

if [ $(../gitops_check.sh; echo $?) != 0 ]; then exit 1; fi          ◁

kubectl apply -f .      ◁      Run kubectl apply
                               as normal.
```

A full GitOps folder structure, including these scripts, is provided in the samples in Chapter11/gitops.

This isn't the only option, of course. Another approach would be to set the desired namespace in your rollout script and then deploy. Just be sure that if the `set namespace` step fails, the whole thing will bail out.

For these scripts to work, though, you'll need to ensure that none of your configuration files specify a `metadata → namespace` field directly. If they have a namespace set, it will ignore the current context, so the script won't prevent updates in that case.

To really follow the GitOps methodology, you'll want to add an additional guarantee that the configuration deployed at all times is what is actually in the repository. The best way to solve that is to remove the human from the loop completely and configure a deployment pipeline or a GitOps operator.

11.3.1 Deployment pipelines

A deployment pipeline is simply a set of functions that run based on a code repository trigger—for example, "When a code is pushed to the configuration repository, deploy the configuration to a Kubernetes cluster" (figure 11.4). Using pipelines guarantees that the configuration being deployed matches what was committed. If the operator needs to make additional changes after the deployment (e.g., to correct an error),

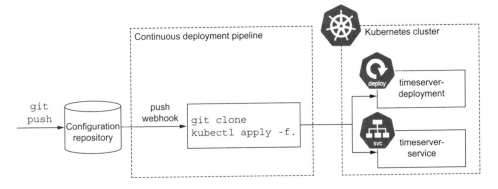

Figure 11.4 A continuous deployment pipeline to Kubernetes

they make them in the configuration code repository like normal: push the change and trigger the pipeline rollout once again.

With your pipeline configured, you can push to producing by merging a code on your Git repo (i.e., Git-driven operations, or GitOps). The key is to not make any changes on the cluster directly; all changes go through the configuration repository and the continuous deployment pipeline.

11.3.2 *Continuous deployment with Cloud Build*

To implement a deployment pipeline in practice, there are many products on the market. For Google Kubernetes Engine (GKE) users, one option is Cloud Build. You can set up a trigger so that when your configuration repository is pushed, it will run `kubectl apply -f .`

To set it up, use the following steps:

1 Configure IAM permissions[3] for the Cloud Build service account to give it permission to act on your GKE cluster.
2 Create a new trigger (set to fire when your configuration repository is pushed).

Add a Cloud Build configuration file to your repository such as the one in the following listing, and reference it in the trigger.

Listing 11.3 Chapter11/11.3.2_CloudBuild/cloudbuild-deploy.yaml

```
steps:
- name: 'gcr.io/cloud-builders/kubectl'
  id: Deploy
  args:
  - 'apply'
  - '-f'
  - '$FOLDER'
```

---

[3] https://cloud.google.com/build/docs/securing-builds/configure-access-for-cloud-build-service-account

```
env:
- 'CLOUDSDK_COMPUTE_REGION=us-west1'
- 'CLOUDSDK_CONTAINER_CLUSTER=my-cluster'
```

This is just scratching the surface of continuous delivery. If you're using Cloud Build, you can consult the excellent "GitOps-Style Continuous Delivery with Cloud Build" guide,[4] which goes further and sets up a complete end-to-end CI/CD flow.

> **Continuous reconciliation**
>
> The method described here can be further improved by using a GitOps operator. This is a control loop that runs in the cluster and constantly reconciles what is running in the cluster to what is present in the configuration repository. The end result is similar to the previously described event-driven pipeline with the advantage that it can perform additional reconciliation if there is ever a divergence, while the pipeline approach relies on the Git push event to trigger. Flux (https://fluxcd.io/) is one such GitOps operator.

11.4   Secrets

A Git repo is a great place to store your Kubernetes configuration, but there is some data that probably shouldn't be stored there: secret values like database passwords and API keys. If such secrets are embedded in the code itself or in environment variables, it means that anyone with access to your source code will have the secret. An improvement would be that only those who can access your production system would have access to this data. You can go further, of course, but in the context of this chapter on GitOps, I'll focus on how to separate your secrets from your code and config repositories.

Kubernetes actually has an object for storing secrets, aptly named Secrets. These objects are a way to provide information such as credentials and keys to workloads in a way that separates them from the configuration of the workload itself.

11.4.1   String-based (password) secrets

If you've been embedding secrets like passwords in plain environment variables in the workload configuration, now would be a good time to migrate them to Secrets. Let's say we have a secret with a value of secret_value (in reality, this might be a key obtained from your cloud provider). We can encapsulate our secret_value into a Kubernetes Secret object like in the following listing.

Listing 11.4   Chapter11/11.4.1_StringSecrets/secret.yaml

```
apiVersion: v1
kind: Secret
```

---

[4] https://cloud.google.com/kubernetes-engine/docs/tutorials/gitops-cloud-build

```
metadata:
  name: secrets-production
type: Opaque
stringData:
  SECRET_KEY: secret_value
  ANOTHER_KEY: another_secret_value
```

Secrets can be provided to Pods as a file mounted into the container or as an environment variable. You would use the file method for secret data that your application will access as a configuration file (e.g., a private SSL key), and the environment variable for items like database passwords. Since our secret in listing 11.4 is a simple string, we'll use the environment variable method to reference it in a Deployment in the following listing (see section 11.4.3 for an example of a file-based secret).

Listing 11.5   Chapter11/11.4.1_StringSecrets/deploy.yaml

```
apiVersion: apps/v1
kind: Deployment
metadata:
  name: timeserver
spec:
  replicas: 1
  selector:
    matchLabels:
      pod: timeserver-pod
  template:
    metadata:
      labels:
        pod: timeserver-pod
    spec:
      containers:
      - name: timeserver-container
        image: docker.io/wdenniss/timeserver:5
        env:
        - name: AVATAR_ENDPOINT          A regular plain-text
          value: http://robohash-internal   environment variable
        - name: SECRET_KEY
          valueFrom:                     An environment
            secretKeyRef:                variable populated
              name: secrets-production   from a Secret
              key: SECRET_KEY
```

To verify that everything worked correctly, create the Secret and Deployment objects in the Chapter11/11.4.1_StringSecrets folder and run

```
$ kubectl exec deploy/timeserver -- env
SECRET_KEY=secret_value
```

You should see the secret in the output. Our application now has access to the secret via the SECRET_KEY environment variable.

11.4.2 *Base64 encoded secrets*

You may encounter Kubernetes documentation and other resources that demonstrate secrets where the value is base64 encoded (using the `data` field rather than `stringData`). This isn't done for security (base64 is an encoding, not encryption) but rather so that you can represent data that can't easily be defined in YAML.

I don't routinely base64 encode secrets by default, as I find that this mostly serves to obfuscate the data without adding much value. However, if you have a string that you can't easily represent in YAML, like if your secret is an entire file, then it makes sense to base64-encode the data. The following listing provides an equivalent base64 encoded representation of the `SECRET_KEY` secret shown in listing 11.4.

> **Listing 11.6   Chapter11/11.4.2_Base64Secrets/secret-base64.yaml**

```
apiVersion: v1
kind: Secret
metadata:
  name: secrets-production
type: Opaque
data:
  SECRET_KEY: c2VjcmV0X3ZhbHVlCg==
```

To do the encoding and decoding, on any Unix-like system, you can do the following:

```
$ echo "secret_value" | base64
c2VjcmV0X3ZhbHVlCg==

$ echo "c2VjcmV0X3ZhbHVlCg==" | base64 -d
secret_value
```

You can include both `data` and `stringData` in the same configuration file if you have some values that need base64-encoding and others that don't. You can also store multiple secrets in each Kubernetes Secret object (one per line). The following listing provides an example that defines three secrets, two using plain text and one using base64.

> **Listing 11.7   Chapter11/11.4.2_Base64Secrets/secrets-multiple.yaml**

```
apiVersion: v1
kind: Secret
metadata:
  name: secrets-production
type: Opaque
stringData:
  SECRET_KEY: secret_value
  ANOTHER_KEY: another_value
data:
  ENCODED_KEY:
    VGhpcyBzdHJpbmcKbWlnaHQgYmUgaGFyZCB0byByZXByZXNlbnQgaW4gWUFNTCDwn5iFCg==
```

If you are retrieving secrets from the server via the command line, you'll get the base64 encoded form and will need to decode them to view the plain-text values (they are provided to your application code already decoded, however).

I personally have one secret object for each of my namespaces, each with multiple secrets. However, I store them in a separate repo from the rest of my config. In section 11.4.4, I'll discuss some options for how to store secrets apart from your main configuration repository while still using a GitOps approach.

11.4.3   File-based secrets

Sometimes you'll be dealing with secrets that you want to access from your application as files rather than strings from environment variables. Kubernetes has you covered here as well. Creating the secret is actually the same, but I'll provide a fresh example of a multiline text file since how such data is represented in YAML has some nuance.

Say we have a private key to store. Here's one I generated using `openssl genrsa 256 -out example.key` (normally you'd use a 2048 bit key or higher, but for brevity, I'll use 256):

> **Listing 11.8   Chapter11/11.4.3_FileSecrets/example.key**

```
-----BEGIN RSA PRIVATE KEY-----
MIGsAgEAAiEA4TneQFg/UMsVGrAvsm1wkonC/5jX+ykJAMeNffnlPQkCAwEAAQIh
ANgcs+MgClkXFQAP0SSvmJRmnRze3+zgUbN+u+rrYNRlAhEA+K0ghKRgKlzVnOxw
qltgTwIRAOfb8LCVNf6FAdD+bJGwHycCED6YzfO1sONZBQiAWAf6Am8CEQDIEXI8
fVSNHmp108UNZcNLAhEA3hHFV5jZppEHHHLy4F9Dnw==
-----END RSA PRIVATE KEY-----
```

This file's data can be represented in YAML in the following way. Note the all-important pipe character, which will preserve the line endings in the data value.

> **Listing 11.9   Chapter11/11.4.3_FileSecrets/secret_file.yaml**

```
apiVersion: v1
kind: Secret
metadata:
  name: secret-files
type: Opaque
stringData:
  example.key: |
    -----BEGIN RSA PRIVATE KEY-----
    MIGsAgEAAiEA4TneQFg/UMsVGrAvsm1wkonC/5jX+ykJAMeNffnlPQkCAwEAAQIh
    ANgcs+MgClkXFQAP0SSvmJRmnRze3+zgUbN+u+rrYNRlAhEA+K0ghKRgKlzVnOxw
    qltgTwIRAOfb8LCVNf6FAdD+bJGwHycCED6YzfO1sONZBQiAWAf6Am8CEQDIEXI8
    fVSNHmp108UNZcNLAhEA3hHFV5jZppEHHHLy4F9Dnw==
    -----END RSA PRIVATE KEY-----
```

If you're tired of wrestling with YAML syntax by now, you can base64-encode the file data instead by using `cat example.key | base64` and represent it like in the following listing (with the data truncated for readability). Note that the entire base64 string is placed on one line (no line breaks!).

Listing 11.10   Chapter11/11.4.3_FileSecrets/secret_file_base64.yaml

```
apiVersion: v1
kind: Secret
metadata:
  name: secret-files
type: Opaque
data:
  example.key: LS0tLS1CRUdJTiBSU0EgUFJJVk...U0EgUFJJVkFURSBLRVktLS0tLQo=
```

It's a bit tedious creating these configuration files for secrets by hand. A more automated approach is to use `kubectl` to create the files for you. The following command will create the same functional output (note that the base64 string is truncated for readability):

```
$ cd Chapter11/11.4.3_FileSecrets
$ kubectl create secret generic secret-files \
      --from-file=example.key=./example.key --dry-run=client -o yaml

apiVersion: v1
data:
  example.key: LS0tLS1CRUdJTiBSU0EgUFJJVk...U0EgUFJJVkFURSBLRVktLS0tLQo=
kind: Secret
metadata:
  creationTimestamp: null
  name: secret-files
```

The `--dry-run=client -o yaml` part means that you won't actually create the secret on the server and, instead, output it as YAML (for you to place in a configuration file, to be later applied to the server with `kubectl apply -f secret.yaml`). Omitting the `--dry-run`, would create the secret directly on the cluster (i.e., the imperative style of creating Kubernetes objects). In fact, every example given in this section could have been written as an imperative `kubectl` command, but there are durable benefits to a declarative, configuration-driven approach to operating your cluster, including those covered earlier in this chapter.

Once created, you can mount all the files in the Secret as a folder in your container. The following listing mounts our `secret-files` Secret to the location `/etc/config`. Each of the data keys is mounted as its own file. In our case, there was only one: `example.key`.

Listing 11.11   Chapter11/11.4.3_FileSecrets/deploy.yaml

```
apiVersion: apps/v1
kind: Deployment
metadata:
  name: timeserver
```

```
spec:
  replicas: 1
  selector:
    matchLabels:
      pod: timeserver-pod
  template:
    metadata:
      labels:
        pod: timeserver-pod
    spec:
      containers:
      - name: timeserver-container
        image: docker.io/wdenniss/timeserver:5
        volumeMounts:
        - name: secret-volume              The path the file
          mountPath: "/etc/config"    ⊲─┤  secrets will be
          readOnly: true                   mounted at.
      volumes:
      - name: secret-volume
        secret:                            Reference to the
          secretName: secret-files         Secrets object
```

To verify that everything worked correctly, create the Secret and Deployment objects and use `exec` to list the directory. You should see our file `example.key`:

```
$ kubectl exec deploy/timeserver -- ls /etc/config
example.key
```

To view the file itself, replace the `ls` command with `cat /etc/config/example.key`. Now you can point your code to this file, just like any other file on the system.

11.4.4 Secrets and GitOps

Using Secrets is only one part of the equation. Now, you'll need to figure out how to store them. If you place them in the same configuration repository, you may as well have just used plain environment variables and skipped the step in the previous section. There's no silver bullet to this problem, but here are a few ideas, presented in increasing order of complexity.

SEPARATE REPOSITORY

A simple option is to have a separate configuration repository for your secrets with fewer users granted access than your regular repos. You still have all the benefits of configuration as code (e.g., code reviews, rollback, and so forth) but can limit the audience. If you operate a repository with granular access control, you could place the secrets in an access-controlled folder of that repo.

One logical place for this repository to be located would be together with your production resources at your cloud provider, with the same access control as your production environment. Since anyone with access to your production environment has the secrets anyway, this model doesn't provide any additional access if someone compromises the account.

SEALED SECRETS

The Sealed Secrets[5] project has an interesting approach: you encrypt your secrets before storing in Git (so nobody can read them), and they're decoded by a controller in the cluster using a private key. While you still end up with the same problem of where to store that private key, it means that the encrypted secrets can be included in the main configuration repository with all the benefits that this entails, like rollback.

SECRETS SERVICE

Another option is to run a separate service that can inject secrets into your cluster. Vault by HashiCorp[6] is a popular implementation of this concept and is available as open source if you wish to run it yourself.

Summary

- Use namespaces to separate different environments, like production and staging, and different applications.
- Treating configuration as code allows you to easily duplicate and maintain multiple environments.
- Follow the configuration as code methodology by storing Kubernetes configuration in version control as you would code (including conducting code reviews if you do them).
- Instead of making changes directly to the live cluster, make the changes to configuration first, commit to version control, then apply them.
- A deployment pipeline can be used to automatically roll out changes when they are committed and pushed to the configuration repository.
- A GitOps operator like Flux can be used to provide continuous reconciliation of the configuration repository.
- Utilize Kubernetes Secrets to store sensitive information such as database keys in separate Kubernetes objects. Store that configuration in a way that limits access.

---

[5] https://github.com/bitnami-labs/sealed-secrets
[6] https://www.vaultproject.io/

Securing Kubernetes

So far, this book has focused on deploying different types of software into Kubernetes clusters. In this last chapter, I'll cover some key topics when it comes to keeping everything secure. Security is a huge area in general, and Kubernetes is no exception. If you deploy code to a Kubernetes cluster managed by another team, then lucky you—you may not need to worry about some of these topics. For developers who are also responsible for operations or are cluster operators themselves, securing and updating the cluster is a key responsibility.

In addition to keeping your cluster up to date, handling disruption, deploying node agents, and building non-root containers, this chapter takes you through the process of creating a dedicated namespace for a team of developers and how access can be granted specifically to that namespace. This is a pretty common pattern I've observed in companies where several teams share clusters.

12.1 Staying up to date

Kubernetes has a large surface area. There's the Linux kernel and the Kubernetes software running on the control plane and user nodes. Then, there are your own containers and all their dependencies, including the base image. All this means there's a lot to keep up to date and protected against vulnerabilities.

12.1.1 Cluster and node updates

One critical task for a Kubernetes operator is to ensure that your cluster and nodes are up to date. This helps mitigate known vulnerabilities in Kubernetes, and the operating system that runs on your nodes.

Unlike most of the topics discussed in this book so far, the updating of clusters and nodes is actually not part of the Kubernetes API. It sits at the platform level, so you'll need to consult the docs for your Kubernetes platform. Fortunately, if you're using a managed platform, this should be straightforward. If you're running Kubernetes the hard way via a manual installation on VMs (which I don't recommend), these updates will be a significant burden, as you are now the one offering the Kubernetes platform.

Updating Google Kubernetes Engine

In the case of GKE, staying up to date is easy. Simply enroll in one of the three release channels: Stable, Regular, or Rapid. Security patches are rolled out to all channels quickly. What differs is how soon you get other new features of both Kubernetes and the GKE platform.

When enrolled in a release channel, both the cluster version and nodes are automatically kept up to date. The older static version option is not recommended, as you need to keep on top of the updates manually.

12.1.2 Updating containers

Keeping the Kubernetes cluster up to date isn't the only updating you'll need to do. Security vulnerabilities are often found in the components of base images like Ubuntu. As your containerized application is built on these base images, it can inherit vulnerabilities that exist in them.

The solution is to rebuild and update your containers regularly, especially if any vulnerabilities are found in the base images you use. Many developers and enterprises employ vulnerability scanners (often known as *CVE scanners* after the Common Vulnerabilities and Exposures system where known vulnerabilities are documented) to look through built containers to see whether any reported vulnerabilities exist in them to prioritize rebuilds and rollouts.

When updating your containers, be sure to specify the base image that contains the latest fixes. Typically, this can be achieved by only specifying the minor version of the base image you're using rather than the specific patch version. You can use the `latest` tag to achieve this, but then you might get some unwanted feature changes.

For example, take the Python base image.[1] For any given version of Python (say, v3.10.2), you have a bunch of different options: `3.10.2-bullseye`, `3.10-bullseye`, `3-bullseye`, and `bullseye` (`bullseye` refers to the version of Debian it uses). You can also use `latest`. For images that follow semantic versioning (semver) principles, I would typically recommend going with the `major.minor` version—in this example, `3.10-bullseye`. This allows you to get patches to the v3.10 automatically while avoiding breaking changes. The downside is that you need to pay attention to when the support drops for 3.10 and migrate. Going with the major version instead (i.e., `3-bullseye` in this example) would give you longer support but with slightly more risk of breakages. In theory, with semver, you should be safe to use the major version as changes should be backward-compatible, but in practice, I find it safer to go with the minor version. Using `latest`, while great from a security perspective, is typically not recommended due to the extremely high risk of breakage from backward-incompatible changes.

Whichever way you configure your Docker file, the key principles are to rebuild often, to reference base images that are up to date, roll out updates to your workloads frequently, and employ CVE scanning to look for containers that are out of date. A further mitigation to reduce potential vulnerabilities in application containers is to build extremely lightweight containers that include only the absolute minimum needed to run your application and its dependencies. Using a typical base image like Ubuntu includes a package manager and various software packages, which make life easy but also increase the vulnerability surface area. The less code there is in your container from other sources, the less you'll need to update it due to vulnerabilities found in that code and the fewer bugs you can potentially be exposed to.

The Dockerfile in section 2.1.8 on multistage builds employed this principle by using one container to build your code and another to run the code. To reduce the potential attack surface, the key is to pick the slimmest possible runtime base image for the second stage of the container build. Google has an open source project distroless[2] to assist with providing super-lightweight runtime containers. The following

---

[1] https://hub.docker.com/_/python
[2] https://github.com/GoogleContainerTools/distroless

listing provides the distroless project's example of a building Java container, referencing the Google-provided distroless image in the second step.

Listing 12.1   https://github.com/GoogleContainerTools/distroless/tree/main/examples/java/Dockerfile

```
FROM openjdk:11-jdk-slim-bullseye AS build-env
COPY . /app/examples
WORKDIR /app
RUN javac examples/*.java
RUN jar cfe main.jar examples.HelloJava examples/*.class

FROM gcr.io/distroless/java11-debian11
COPY --from=build-env /app /app
WORKDIR /app
CMD ["main.jar"]
```

◁── The regular OpenJDK image is used to build the code.

◁── The distroless java image is used to run the code.

12.1.3 *Handling disruptions*

With all this updating, you might be wondering what happens to your running workloads. It's inevitable that as you update, Pods will be deleted and re-created. This can obviously be very disruptive to the workloads running in those Pods, but fortunately, Kubernetes has a number of ways to reduce this disruption and potentially eliminate any ill effects.

READINESS CHECKS

First, if you've not set up readiness checks (as we did in chapter 4), now is the time to go back and do that, as it's absolutely critical. Kubernetes relies on your container reporting when it's ready, and if you don't do that, it will assume it's ready the moment the process starts running, which is likely *before* your application has finished initializing and is actually ready to serve production traffic. The more your Pods are moved around, such as during updates, the more requests will error out by hitting Pods that are not ready unless you implement proper readiness checks.

SIGNAL HANDLING AND GRACEFUL TERMINATION

Just as readiness checks are used to determine when your application is ready to start, graceful termination is used by Kubernetes to know when your application is ready to stop. In the case of a Job, which may have a process that takes a while to complete, you may not want to simply terminate that process if it can be avoided. Even web applications with short-lived requests can suffer from abrupt termination that causes requests to fail.

To prevent these problems, it's important to handle SIGTERM events in your application code to start the shutdown process, and set a graceful termination window (configured with `terminationGracePeriodSeconds`) long enough to complete the termination. Web applications should handle SIGTERM to shut down the server once all current requests are completed, and batch jobs would ideally wrap up any work they are doing and not start any new tasks.

In some cases, you may have a Job performing a long-running task that, if interrupted, would lose its progress. In these cases, you might set a very long graceful termination window whereby the application accepts the SIGTERM but simply continues on as before to attempt to finish the current task. Managed platforms may have a limit on how long the graceful termination window can be for system-originated disruption.

Section 10.1.2 has examples of SIGTERM handling and `terminationGracePeriod-Seconds` configuration in the context of Jobs. The same principles apply to other workload types.

ROLLING UPDATES

When you update the containers in a Deployment or a StatefulSet (e.g., to update the base image), the rollout is governed by your rollout strategy. Rolling update, covered in chapter 4, is the recommended strategy to minimize disruption when updating workloads by updating Pods in batches while keeping the application available. For Deployments, be sure to configure the `maxSurge` parameters of the Deployment, which will do a rollout by temporarily increasing the Pod replica count, which is safer for availability than reducing it.

POD DISRUPTION BUDGETS

When nodes are updated, this process does *not* go through the same rollout process as updates to Deployments. Here's how it works. First, the node is cordoned to prevent new Pods from being deployed on it. Then the node is drained, whereby Pods are deleted from this node and re-created on another node. By default, Kubernetes will delete all Pods at once from the node and (in the case of Pods managed by a workload resource such as Deployment) schedule them to be created elsewhere. Note that it does *not* first schedule them to be created elsewhere and then delete them. If multiple replicas of a single Deployment are running on the same node, this can cause unavailability when they are evicted at the same time, as shown in figure 12.1.

To solve the problem where draining a node that contains multiple Pods from the same Deployment may reduce the availability of your Deployments (meaning too few running replicas), Kubernetes has a feature called Pod Disruption Budgets (PDBs). PDBs allow you to inform Kubernetes how many or what percentage of your Pods you are willing to have unavailable for your workload to still function as you designed it.

Listing 12.2 Chapter12/12.1_PDB/pdb.yaml

```
apiVersion: policy/v1
kind: PodDisruptionBudget
metadata:
  name: timeserver-pdb
spec:
  maxUnavailable: 1          ◁───┐  Declares the maximum
  selector:                        number of Pods that
    matchLabels:                   can be unavailable
      pod: timeserver-pod          during disruptions

                                   Selects the Pods
                                   by their labels
```

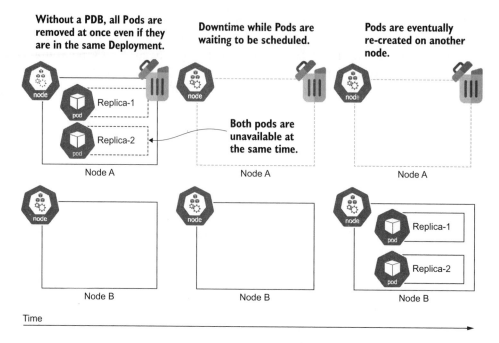

Figure 12.1   Node deletion without Pod disruption budgets. All the Pods on the node will become unavailable at once.

Deploying this PDB into your cluster will ensure that at no time during disruptions will more than one of your Pods be unavailable, as illustrated in figure 12.2. An alternative configuration uses `minAvailable` to set how many replicas you need. I prefer `maxUnavailable`, as it works better with scaling. If you use `minAvailable`, you may need to scale that value along with your replica count to retain the desired minimum availability, which is just extra work.

> **NOTE**   The PDB protects against voluntary evictions such as during node upgrades, but not every possible case of disruption, such as if a node were to fail abruptly.

The process of handling disruptions with a PDB is somewhat similar to how a rolling update avoids taking out too many Pods at the same time. To ensure your application stays available during updates that you initiate and disruptions are initiated by cluster updates, you'll need to have both the rolling update and the PDB configured.

12.2   *Deploying node agents with DaemonSet*

This book has covered a bunch of high-order workload constructs that encapsulate Pods with particular objectives, like Deployment for application deployments, StatefulSet for database deployments, and CronJob for period tasks. DaemonSet is another workload type that allows you to run a Pod on every node.

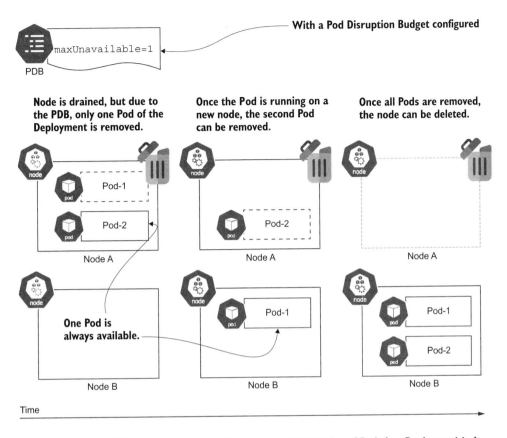

Figure 12.2   With a PDB, Kubernetes will wait for the required number of Pods in a Deployment to be available before deleting others, reducing the disruption.

When would you need that? It's almost entirely for cluster operational reasons, like logging, monitoring, and security. As an application developer, DaemonSet is generally not your go-to workload construct. Due to the ability to expose services internally on a cluster IP, any Pod in your cluster can talk to any service you create, so you don't need to run services on every node just to make them available within the cluster. And if you need to be able to connect to a service on localhost, you can do that virtually with a Service of type `NodePort`. DaemonSets are generally for when you need to perform operations at a node level, like reading load logs or observing performance, putting them squarely in the system administration domain.

DaemonSets are typically how logging, monitoring, and security vendors deploy their software. This software performs actions like reading logs off the node and uploading it to a central logging solution, querying the kubelet API for performance metrics (like how many Pods are running, their boot times, and so forth), and for security, such as monitoring container and host behaviors. These are all examples of Pods that need to be on every node to gather the data they need for the product to function.

The typical cluster will have a few DaemonSets running in `kube-system`, such as the following abridged list from a GKE cluster, which provides functionality like logging, monitoring, and cluster DNS:

```
$ kubectl get daemonset -n kube-system
NAMESPACE      NAME
kube-system    filestore-node
kube-system    fluentbit-gke
kube-system    gke-metadata-server
kube-system    gke-metrics-agent
kube-system    kube-proxy
kube-system    metadata-proxy-v0.1
kube-system    netd
kube-system    node-local-dns
kube-system    pdcsi-node
```

Typically, application developers will not be creating DaemonSets directly but rather will be using off-the-shelf ones from vendors. By way of example, though, the following listing is a simple DaemonSet that reads logs from the node into standard output (stdout).

Listing 12.3   Chapter12/12.2_DaemonSet/logreader.yaml

```
apiVersion: apps/v1
kind: DaemonSet
metadata:
  name: logreader
spec:
  selector:
    matchLabels:
      pod: logreader-pod
  template:
    metadata:
      labels:
        ds: logreaderpod
    spec:
      containers:
      - image: ubuntu
        command:
        - bash
        - "-c"
        - |
          tail -f /var/log/containers/*_kube-system_*.log
        name: logreader-container
        resources:
          requests:
            cpu: 50m
            memory: 100Mi
            ephemeral-storage: 100Mi
        volumeMounts:
        - name: logpath
          mountPath: /var/log
          readOnly: true
```

Read and output kube-system container logs from the node

DaemonSets typically use low resource requests.

Mount the volume "logpath" to /var/log.

```
        volumes:            │ Define the volume
        - hostPath:         │ "logpath" from
            path: /var/log  │ /var/log on the host.
          name: logpath     │
```

To create the DaemonSet, use

```
$ kubectl create -f Chapter12/12.2_DaemonSet/logreader.yaml
daemonset.apps/logreader created
```

Once the Pods are ready, we can stream the logs:

```
$ kubectl get pods
NAME              READY    STATUS     RESTARTS    AGE
logreader-2nbt4   1/1      Running    0           4m14s

$ kubectl logs -f logreader-2nbt4 --tail 10
==> /var/log/containers/filestore-node_kube-system_gcp-filestore-1b5.log <==
lock is held by gk3-autopilot-cluster-2sc2_e4337a2e and has not yet expired
```

In practice, you will likely encounter DaemonSets when deploying logging, monitoring, and security solutions.

12.3   Pod security context

The PodSpec has a `securityContext` property where the security attributes of the Pod and its containers are defined. If your Pod needs to perform some kind of administrative function (e.g., perhaps it's part of a DaemonSet that is doing a node-level operation), it's here where you would define the various privileges it needs. For example, the following is a Pod in a DaemonSet that requests privilege on the node:

Listing 12.4   Chapter12/12.3_PodSecurityContext/admin-ds.yaml

```
apiVersion: apps/v1
kind: DaemonSet
metadata:
  name: admin-workload
spec:
  selector:
    matchLabels:
      name: admin-app
  template:
    metadata:
      labels:
        name: admin-app
    spec:
      containers:
      - name: admin-container
        image: ubuntu
        command: ["sleep", "infinity"]
        securityContext:
          privileged: true
```

With this access, the Pod effectively has root access, and can, for example, mount the host filesystem of the node into the container, as follows:

```
$ kubectl exec -it admin-workload-px6xg -- bash
root@admin-workload-px6xg:/# df
Filesystem     1K-blocks     Used      Available   Use%   Mounted on
overlay        98831908      4652848   94162676    5%     /
tmpfs          65536         0         65536       0%     /dev
/dev/sda1      98831908      4652848   94162676    5%     /etc/hosts
shm            65536         0         65536       0%     /dev/shm
root@admin-workload-px6xg:/# mkdir /tmp/host
root@admin-workload-px6xg:/# mount /dev/sda1 /tmp/host
root@admin-workload-px6xg:/# cd /tmp/host
root@admin-workload-px6xg:/tmp/host# ls
dev_image  etc  home  lost+found  var  var_overlay  vmlinuz_hd.vblock
root@admin-workload-px6xg:/tmp/host#
```

If you attempt the same on a container without privilege, the mount will fail.

As a developer of a regular application that run on Kubernetes, you will more likely be using the `securityContext` properties to *limit* what functions your Pod can use to reduce risk. Contrasting the previous example, the following is the PodSpec for a Pod with locked-down privileges that runs as the non-root user and cannot elevate privileges.

Listing 12.5   Chapter12/12.3_PodSecurityContext/pod.yaml

```
apiVersion: v1
kind: Pod
metadata:
  name: ubuntu
  labels:
    pod: ubuntu-pod
spec:
  containers:
  - name: ubuntu-container
    image: ubuntu
    command: ["sleep", "infinity"]
    securityContext:
      runAsNonRoot: true
      runAsUser: 1001
      allowPrivilegeEscalation: false
      capabilities:
        drop:
          - ALL
```

By default, any Pod is free to request whatever capabilities it wants, even root access (unless your Kubernetes platform restricts this, as some nodeless platforms do). As the cluster operator, this may be something you want to restrict as it basically means that anyone with kubectl access to the cluster has root privileges. Furthermore, there are some other recommended principles for hardening clusters, like not running containers as the root user (which is distinct from having root on the node), something that is enforced by the `runAsNonRoot: true` configuration in the prior example.

The following sections cover these topics, starting with how to build containers so they don't need to run as the root user, and how, as a cluster administrator, you can force users of the cluster to adopt this and other desired security settings.

12.4 *Non-root containers*

One common security recommendation when deploying containers is to run them as a non-root user. The reason for this is that despite all the fancy packaging, Linux containers are basically just processes that run on the host with sandboxing technology applied (like Linux cgroups and namespaces). If your container is built to run using the root user, which is the default, it actually runs as root on the node, just sandboxed. Container sandboxing means that the process doesn't have the power of root access, but it's still running under the root user. The problem with this is that while the sandboxing prevents the process from having root access, if there is ever a "container escape" vulnerability due to bugs in the underlying Linux containerization technology, the sandboxed container process can gain the same privileges as the user it's running as. That means if the container is running as root, a container escape would give full root access on the node—not so good.

Since Docker runs all processes as root by default, this means that any container escape vulnerabilities can present a problem. While such vulnerabilities are fairly rare, they do occur, and for the security principle known as *defense in depth*, it's best to protect against it. Defense in depth means that even though container isolation offers protection of the host in the event your application is breached, ideally, you would have further layers of defense in case that protection is breached. In this case, defense in depth means running your containers as the non-root user, so in the event an attacker can breach your container and take advantage of a container escape vulnerability in Linux, they still wouldn't end up with elevated privileges on the node. They would need to string together yet another vulnerability to elevate their privileges, making for three layers of defense (your application, Linux containerization, and Linux user privileges).

> **NOTE** You may be wondering if it's the best practice not to run container processes as root, why then does Docker default to the root user when building containers? The answer is developer convenience. It's convenient to act as the root user in a container, as you can use privileged ports (those with numbers below 1024, like the default HTTP port 80), and you don't have to deal with any folder permission problems. As you'll see later in this section, building and running containers with the non-root user can introduce some errors that need to be worked through. If you adopt this principle from the start, however, you may not find it so difficult to fix these problems as they arise, and the payoff is adding one more layer of defense into your system.

Preventing containers from running as the root user is simple in Kubernetes, although the problem (as we'll see shortly) is that not all containers are designed to run this way and may fail. You can annotate your Pods in Kubernetes to prevent them from running as a root user. So, to achieve the goal of not running as root, the first step is to simply add this annotation! If you're configuring a Kubernetes cluster for a wider team or you're a member of that team using such a configured cluster, a Kubernetes admission controller can be used to automatically add this annotation to every Pod (see section 12.5.1). The end result is the same, so for this demo, we'll just add it manually. The following Deployment enforces the best practice to prevent containers from running as root.

Listing 12.6   Chapter12/12.4_NonRootContainers/1_permission_error/deploy.yaml

```yaml
apiVersion: apps/v1
kind: Deployment
metadata:
  name: timeserver
spec:
  replicas: 1
  selector:
    matchLabels:
      pod: timeserver-pod
  template:
    metadata:
      labels:
        pod: timeserver-pod
    spec:
      containers:
      - name: timeserver-container
        image: docker.io/wdenniss/timeserver:6
        securityContext:          Prevent running this
          runAsNonRoot: true      container as the root user.
```

Unfortunately, we're not done because the container itself doesn't configure a non-root user to run as. If you try to create this Deployment, Kubernetes will enforce the securityContext and won't let the container run as root. The following is the truncated output you'll see if you try and create this Deployment.

```
$ kubectl get pods
NAME                             READY  STATUS                    RESTARTS
timeserver-pod-fd574695c-5t92p   0/1    CreateContainerConfigError   0

$ kubectl describe pod timeserver-pod-fd574695c-5t92p
Name:          timeserver-pod-fd574695c-5t92p
Events:
  Type     Reason   Age                 From     Message
  ----     ------   ----                ----     -------
  Warning  Failed   10s (x3 over 23s)   kubelet  Error: container has
  runAsNonRoot and image will run as root
```

To resolve this problem, you need to configure the user that the Pod will be run under. Root is always user 0, so we just need to set any other user number; I'm going to pick user 1001. This can either be declared in the Dockerfile with USER 1001 or in the Kubernetes configuration with `runAsUser: 1001`. When both are present, the Kubernetes configuration takes priority, similar to how the `command` parameter in a Kubernetes PodSpec overrides `CMD` if present in the Dockerfile. Here's the Dockerfile option:

```
FROM python:3
COPY . /app
WORKDIR /app
RUN mkdir logs
CMD python3 server.py
USER 1001
```

Or, you can specify it in the PodSpec by adding an additional field to the security context section:

Listing 12.7   Chapter12/12.4_NonRootContainers/1_permission_error/deploy-runas.yaml

```
# ...
securityContext:
  runAsNonRoot: true
  runAsUser: 1001
```

Both approaches work, but what I recommend is to configure it on the Kubernetes side as this is better for keeping your development and production environments separate. If you specify the run-as user in the Dockerfile and want to run your container locally outside of Kubernetes and try to mount a volume, you'll hit a snag, like Docker issue #2259,[3] which prevents you from mounting a volume as a user other than root, a 7+-year-old problem. Since the original security concern is not to run containers as root is only related to production, why not relegate this whole "run as non-root" concern to production as well? Fortunately, it's easy to let your container run as root in Docker locally for maximum convenience and as non-root in production in Kubernetes for better defense in depth.

Specifying `runAsUser: 1001` is enough to run our container as non-root. Provided that the container is capable of running as non-root, your job is done. Most public, well-known containers should be designed to run as non-root, but this likely isn't the case for your own containers.

In the case of our example container, it wasn't designed to run as non-root and will need to be fixed. Two major differences when running the container as non-root are that you can't listen on privileged ports (i.e., those between 1 and 1023), and you don't have write access by default to the container's writable layer (meaning, by default, you can't write any files!). This is a problem for version 6 of the Timeserver sample app (Chapter12/timeserver6/server.py), which listens on port 80 and writes a log file to `/app/logs`.

---

[3] https://github.com/moby/moby/issues/2259

UPDATING CONTAINERS TO RUN AS NON-ROOT

If you deploy the revised Deployment from listing 12.7 with `runAsUser` specified, you will see that there is no `CreateContainerConfigError` error when deployed, but the container itself is crashing. When your container starts crashing after you change the user it runs as to non-root, it's probably a permission error related to that change. Before you start debugging the non-root user errors, be sure your container runs fine as root; otherwise, the problem could be something completely unrelated.

The steps to debug permission problems for containers running as non-root will vary, but let's walk through how to find and fix these two common errors with our example app. The following are the output and truncated logs that I see for this crashing container:

```
$ kubectl get pods
NAME                                  READY   STATUS           RESTARTS     AGE
timeserver-demo-774c7f5ff9-fq94k      0/1     CrashLoopBackOff  5 (47s ago)  4m4s

$ kubectl logs timeserver-demo-76ddf6d5c-7s9zc
Traceback (most recent call last):
  File "/app/server.py", line 23, in <module>
    startServer()
  File "/app/server.py", line 17, in startServer
    server = ThreadingHTTPServer(('',80), RequestHandler)
  File "/usr/local/lib/python3.9/socketserver.py", line 452, in __init__
    self.server_bind()
  File "/usr/local/lib/python3.9/http/server.py", line 138, in server_bind
    socketserver.TCPServer.server_bind(self)
  File "/usr/local/lib/python3.9/socketserver.py", line 466, in server_bind
    self.socket.bind(self.server_address)
PermissionError: [Errno 13] Permission denied
```

Fortunately, the port problem in Kubernetes is an easy fix without any end-user effect. We can change the port that the container uses while keeping the standard port 80 for the load balancer. First, let's update the port used by the container.

Listing 12.8   Chapter12/timeserver7/server.py

```python
//...

def startServer():
    try:
        server = ThreadingHTTPServer(('',8080), RequestHandler)
        print("Listening on " + ":".join(map(str, server.server_address)))
        server.serve_forever()
    except KeyboardInterrupt:
        server.shutdown()

if __name__ == "__main__":
    startServer()
```

If we're changing ports in the application, we'll need to update our Kubernetes Service configuration to match the new port by updating the `targetPort`. Fortunately, we don't need to change the external port of the Service, as the Service networking glue is provided by Kubernetes and doesn't run as a particular user, so it can use ports below 1024.

Listing 12.9   Chapter12/12.4_NonRootContainers/2_fixed/service.yaml

```
apiVersion: v1
kind: Service
metadata:
  name: timeserver
spec:
  selector:
    pod: timeserver-pod
  ports:
  - port: 80
    targetPort: 8080          ◁──┐  Targets the new
    protocol: TCP                 └─ container port
  type: LoadBalancer
```

Once the socket problem is fixed and we rerun the application, another error will be encountered when the app attempts to write to the log file on disk. This error didn't stop the app from starting but is encountered when a request is made. Looking at those logs, I see

```
$ kubectl logs timeserver-demo-5fd5f6c7f9-cxzrb
10.22.0.129 - - [24/Mar/2022 02:10:43] "GET / HTTP/1.1" 200 -
Exception occurred during processing of request from ('10.22.0.129', 41702)
Traceback (most recent call last):
  File  "/usr/local/lib/python3.10/socketserver.py", line 683, in
    process_request_thread
    self.finish_request(request, client_address)
  File "/usr/local/lib/python3.10/socketserver.py", line 360, in
    finish_request
    self.RequestHandlerClass(request, client_address, self)
  File "/usr/local/lib/python3.10/socketserver.py", line 747, in
    __init__
    self.handle()
  File "/usr/local/lib/python3.10/http/server.py", line 425, in
    handle
    self.handle_one_request()
  File "/usr/local/lib/python3.10/http/server.py", line 413, in
    handle_one_request
    method()
  File "/app/server.py", line 11, in do_GET
    with open("logs/log.txt", "a") as myfile:
PermissionError: [Errno 13] Permission denied: 'logs/log.txt'
```

If you see a permission denied error when running as non-root when writing a file, it's a clear sign that your folder permissions have not been set up correctly for non-root users.

The simplest way to solve this is to set the group permissions on the folder in question. I like using the group permissions, as we can use the same group (i.e., group 0)

for running locally using Docker and deploying in production to Kubernetes without environment-specific changes in the Dockerfile. Let's update the Dockerfile to give write access to group 0.

Listing 12.10   Chapter12/timeserver7/Dockerfile

```
FROM python:3.12
ENV PYTHONUNBUFFERED 1
COPY . /app
WORKDIR /app
RUN mkdir logs
RUN chgrp -R 0 logs \          Updates the permissions
    && chmod -R g+rwX logs     on the logs folder
CMD python3 server.py
```

If you want to run the container in Docker locally using a non-root user to test it before deploying to Kubernetes, you can set the user at runtime: `docker run --user 1001:0 $CONTAINER_NAME`.

So there we have it—our revised container (published as version 7) now runs happily as the non-root user. Deploy the configuration in Chapter12/12.4_NonRootContainers/2_fixed to see it running. If you want to see all the changes made to enable the container and configuration to operate as non-root, diff the before and after:

```
cd Chapter12
diff -u timeserver6 timeserver7
diff -u 12.4_NonRootContainers/1_permission_error \
      12.4_NonRootContainers/2_fixed
```

12.5   *Admission controllers*

In the previous section, we added `runAsNonRoot` to our Pod to prevent it from ever running as root, but we did it manually. If this is a setting we want for all Pods, ideally, we'd be able to configure the cluster to reject any Pod without this configuration or even just add it automatically.

This is where admission controllers come in. Admission controllers are bits of code that are executed via webhooks when you create an object, like with `kubectl create` (figure 12.3). There are two types: validating and mutating. Validating admission webhooks can accept or reject the Kubernetes object—for example, rejecting Pods without `runAsNonRoot`. Mutating admission webhooks can change the object as it comes in—for example, setting `runAsNonRoot` to `true`.

You can write your own admission controllers to implement the behavior you desire, but depending on what you're hoping to achieve, you may not need to. Kubernetes ships with an admission controller out of the box, and others may be available as commercial or open source deployments.

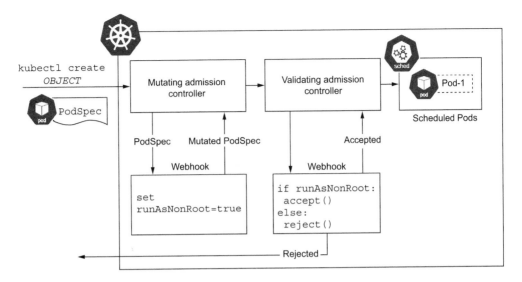

Figure 12.3 The admission process of a Pod that gets scheduled

12.5.1 *Pod Security admission*

Writing admission controllers is no walk in the park. You need to configure certificates, build an application that can be set up as webhook that conforms to the request/response API of Kubernetes and have a development process to keep it up to date as Kubernetes changes, which it does fairly frequently. The good news is that most developers don't need to write their own admission controllers. You'll typically use those from third-parties or included in Kubernetes.

Kubernetes includes admission controllers that can enforce security policies like requiring `runAsNonRoot`. Prior to Kubernetes v1.25, PodSecurityPolicy served this purpose but never left beta and was removed. Since Kubernetes v1.25, Pod Security admission is the recommended way to enforce security policies via an admission controller. You can even deploy it manually into clusters running an older version of Kubernetes or where the feature wasn't enabled by the platform operator.

POD SECURITY STANDARDS

The Pod Security Standards define[4] three security policy levels that apply at a namespace level:

- *Privileged*—Pods have unrestricted administrative access and can gain root access to nodes.
- *Baseline*—Pods cannot elevate privileges to gain administrative access.
- *Restricted*—Enforces current best practices for hardening (i.e., defense in depth), adding additional layers of protection over the baseline profile, including restricting running as the root user.

---

[4] https://kubernetes.io/docs/concepts/security/pod-security-standards/

Basically, `privileged` should only be granted for system workloads; `baseline` offers a good balance of security and compatibility; and `restricted` offers additional defense in depth at a cost of some compatibility, such as needing to ensure all containers can run as non-root, per section 12.4.

CREATING A NAMESPACE WITH POD SECURITY

In keeping with the running example of this chapter and to implement the most secure profile, let's create a namespace with the `restricted` policy. This will require Pods to run as a user other than root and will enforce several other security best practices as well.

To start, create a new namespace with the `restricted` policy. We'll call this namespace `team1`, as it can be the place for a hypothetical `team1` to deploy their code to.

> Listing 12.11   Chapter12/12.5_PodSecurityAdmission/namespace.yaml

```
apiVersion: v1
kind: Namespace
metadata:
  name: team1
  labels:
    pod-security.kubernetes.io/enforce: restricted
    pod-security.kubernetes.io/enforce-version: v1.28
```

These two labels set the policy we want to enforce and the version of the policy that will be enforced. The `enforce-version` label exists, as the definition of what the policy actually enforces may evolve as new security risks are uncovered. Instead of pinning a particular version, for example, `v1.28`, you can specify `latest` to apply the most recent policy. However, there is a high risk that policy changes between Kubernetes versions will break existing workloads, so it's advisable to always pick a specific version. Ideally, you would test the newer policy versions in a staging namespace or cluster to validate them first, before updating the `enforce-version` in your production environment.

Let's create this namespace:

```
kubectl create -f Chapter12/12.5_PodSecurityAdmission/namespace.yaml
kubectl config set-context --current --namespace=team1
```

Now, if we try to deploy a Pod from chapter 3 that doesn't set `runAsNonRoot`, the Pods will be rejected:

```
$ kubectl create -f Chapter03/3.2.4_ThePodSpec/pod.yaml
Error from server (Forbidden): error when creating
"Chapter03/3.2.4_ThePodspec/pod.yaml": admission webhook
"pod-security-webhook.kubernetes.io" denied the request: pods "timeserver"
is forbidden: violates PodSecurity "restricted:v1.28":
allowPrivilegeEscalation != false (container "timeserver-container" must set
securityContext.allowPrivilegeEscalation=false), unrestricted capabilitie
 (container "timeserver-container" must set
 securityContext.capabilities.drop=["ALL"]), runAsNonRoot != true (pod or
 container "timeserver-container" must setsecurityContext.runAsNonRoot=true)
```

If we add the appropriate `securityContext` (listing 12.12) to satisfy the Pod Security admission policy, our Pod will be admitted. It's also important to use the updated container that is designed to run as root from the previous section so that it runs correctly under these new conditions.

Listing 12.12 Chapter12/12.5_PodSecurityAdmission/nonroot_pod.yaml

```
apiVersion: v1
kind: Pod
metadata:
  name: timeserver-pod
spec:
  securityContext:
    seccompProfile:
      type: RuntimeDefault
  containers:
  - name: timeserver-container
    image: docker.io/wdenniss/timeserver:7
    securityContext:
      runAsNonRoot: true                      Security context
      allowPrivilegeEscalation: false         required by the
      runAsUser: 1001                         restricted profile
      capabilities:
        drop:
          - ALL
```

Creating this non-root Pod should now succeed:

```
$ kubectl create -f Chapter12/12.5_PodSecurityAdmission/nonroot_pod.yaml
pod/timeserver-pod created
```

Debugging Pod admission rejections for Deployments

The two examples in this section used stand-alone Pods, rather than Deployments. The reason I did that is it's easier to debug when the Pod's admission is rejected. Once you confirm it's working as expected as a standalone Pod, you can always embed the PodSpec in the Deployment of your choice.

If you create a Deployment that violates the security constraints, you won't see an error printed on the console, like in my example, when I tried to create the Pod directly. This is an unfortunate fact of Kubernetes's implementation of Deployment. Creating the Deployment object itself succeeds, so you don't see an error on the console. However, when the Deployment then goes to create its Pods, they will fail. Also, since the Deployment actually creates an object called a ReplicaSet under the hood to manage Pods of a particular version of the deployment, you won't even find this error if you describe the Deployment object but rather need to inspect its ReplicaSet.

I've not mentioned ReplicaSet yet in the book as it's essentially implementation detail. Basically, a ReplicaSet is a workload construct that manages a set of Pods. Deployment uses them by creating a new ReplicaSet for each version you deploy. So when you're doing a rolling update, the Deployment will actually have two ReplicaSets,

(continued)

one for the old version and one for the new; these are scaled gradually to achieve the rolling update. Normally, this implementation detail doesn't matter, which is why I didn't spend any time on it in the book so far, but here is one of the few times it does since the ReplicaSet is where this particular error is hidden.

It's not exactly simple, but here's how to debug this type of problem. Normally, when you create a Deployment, it will create Pods. If you run `kubectl get pods`, you should see a bunch of Pods. Now, those Pods may not always be `Ready`—there are a bunch of reasons why they might be `Pending` (and, in some cases, may get stuck in the `Pending` state forever, as covered in section 3.2.3), but these Pod objects will normally at least exist with some status. If when you call `kubectl get pods` and don't see any Pod objects at all for your Deployment, it could mean that those Pods were rejected during admission, which is why there are no Pod objects.

Since it's the ReplicaSet owned by the Deployment that actually creates the Pods, you need to describe the ReplicaSet to see the error with `kubectl describe replicaset` (`kubectl describe rs` for short). The following is an example with the output truncated to show the error message of interest:

```
$ kubectl create -f Chapter03/3.2_DeployingToKubernetes/deploy.yaml
deployment.apps/timeserver created

$ kubectl get deploy
NAME         READY   UP-TO-DATE   AVAILABLE   AGE
timeserver   0/3     0            0           12s

$ kubectl get pods
No resources found in myapp namespace.

$ kubectl get rs
NAME                  DESIRED   CURRENT   READY   AGE
timeserver-5b4fc5bb4  3         0         0       31s

$ kubectl describe rs
Events:
  Type      Reason        Age                 From                   Message
  ----      ------        ----                ----                   -------
  Warning   FailedCreate  36s                 replicaset-controller
  Error creating: admission webhook "pod-security-webhook.kubernetes.io"
  denied the request: pods "timeserver-5b4fc5bb4-hvqcm" is forbidden:
  violates PodSecurity "restricted:v1.28": allowPrivilegeEscalation != false
  (container "timeserver-container" must set
  securityContext.allowPrivilegeEscalation=false), unrestricted capabilities
  (container "timeserver-container" must set
  securityContext.capabilities.drop=["ALL"]), runAsNonRoot != true (pod or
  container "timeserver-container" must set
  securityContext.runAsNonRoot=true)
```

When you're done, you can delete this namespace and all resources as follows:

```
$ kubectl delete ns team1
namespace "team1" deleted
```

12.5.2 *Balancing security with compatibility*

In the prior section we used the example of the `restricted` Pod security profile and configured our container to be able to run as a non-root user. Hopefully, this has given you the confidence to be able to run containers in a highly secure manner. While this is the best practice and may be required in situations like regulated industries, there is a clear tradeoff with ease of development, and it may not always be practical. Ultimately, it's up to you, your security team, and maybe your regulators to determine what security profile you're happy with. I'm not necessarily recommending every single Kubernetes workload should be put into a namespace with the `restricted` profile. I do suggest that you use `baseline` for every nonadministrative workload you deploy in your cluster, as it helps protect your cluster in the event that one of your containers is compromised and shouldn't cause any incompatibility with the average app. Administrative workloads that need the `privileged` profile should be run in their own namespaces, separate from common workloads.

12.6 *Role-based access control*

Let's say that you have a requirement for Pods to run as non-root (section 12.4) and set up an admission controller to enforce this requirement using Pod Security admission (section 12.5). This sounds great, provided you trust all the users of your cluster not to mess anything up and remove those restrictions, whether accidentally or on purpose. To actually enforce the requirements of your admission controller and create a tiered user permission setup with roles like platform operator, who can configure namespaces and controller, and developer, who can deploy to namespaces, but not remove admission controllers, you can use role-based access control (RBAC).

RBAC is a way to control what access users of the cluster have. One common setup is to give developers in a team access to a particular namespace in the cluster, with all the desired Pod Security policies configured. This gives them the freedom to deploy whatever they like within the namespace, provided it conforms to the security requirements that's been set. This way it's still following DevOps principles, as developers are the ones doing the deployments, just with some guardrails in place.

RBAC is configured through two Kubernetes object types at a namespace level: Role and RoleBinding. Role is where you define a particular role for a namespace, like the developer role. RoleBinding is where you assign this role to subjects in your cluster (i.e., your developer identities). There are also cluster-level versions, ClusterRole and ClusterRoleBinding, which behave identically to their namespace-level counterparts, except that they grant access at a cluster level.

NAMESPACE ROLE

In the Role, you specify the API group(s), the resource(s) within that group, and the verb(s) that you are granting access to. Access is additive (there is no subtractive option), so everything you define grants access. Since our goal is to create a Role that gives the developer access to do pretty much everything within their namespace *except* modify the namespace itself and remove the Pod Security annotation, the following listing is a Role that can achieve that.

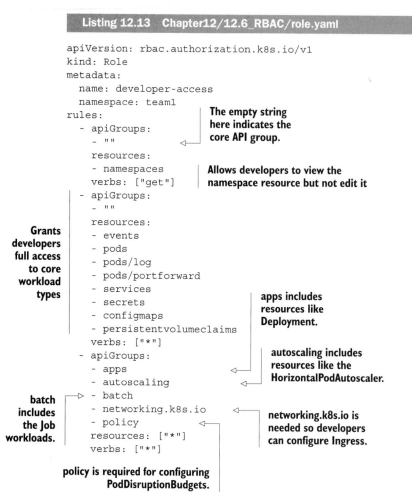

Listing 12.13   Chapter12/12.6_RBAC/role.yaml

```
apiVersion: rbac.authorization.k8s.io/v1
kind: Role
metadata:
  name: developer-access
  namespace: team1
rules:
  - apiGroups:
    - ""                      The empty string
                              here indicates the
                              core API group.
    resources:
    - namespaces              Allows developers to view the
    verbs: ["get"]            namespace resource but not edit it
  - apiGroups:
    - ""
    resources:
    - events
    - pods
    - pods/log
    - pods/portforward
    - services
    - secrets                 apps includes
    - configmaps              resources like
    - persistentvolumeclaims  Deployment.
    verbs: ["*"]
  - apiGroups:
    - apps                    autoscaling includes
    - autoscaling             resources like the
    - batch                   HorizontalPodAutoscaler.
    - networking.k8s.io
    - policy                  networking.k8s.io is
    resources: ["*"]          needed so developers
    verbs: ["*"]              can configure Ingress.
```

Grants developers full access to core workload types

batch includes the Job workloads.

policy is required for configuring PodDisruptionBudgets.

This Role grants access to the team1 namespace and allows the user to modify Pods, Services, Secrets, and ConfigMaps within the core API grouping and all resources in the apps, autoscaling, batch, networking.k8s.io, and policy groupings. This particular set of permissions will let the developer deploy nearly every YAML file in this book, including Deployment, StatefulSet, Service, Ingress, Horizontal Pod Autoscaler, and Job objects. Importantly, the namespaces resource is not listed in the core API group (which is the group listed with the empty string ""), so the user won't be able to modify the namespace.

Once the Role exists, to grant this Role to our developer, we can use a RoleBinding where the subject is our user.

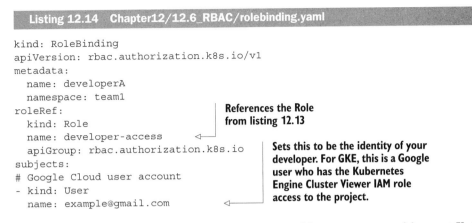

Listing 12.14 Chapter12/12.6_RBAC/rolebinding.yaml

```
kind: RoleBinding
apiVersion: rbac.authorization.k8s.io/v1
metadata:
  name: developerA
  namespace: team1
roleRef:
  kind: Role
  name: developer-access
  apiGroup: rbac.authorization.k8s.io
subjects:
# Google Cloud user account
- kind: User
  name: example@gmail.com
```

References the Role from listing 12.13

Sets this to be the identity of your developer. For GKE, this is a Google user who has the Kubernetes Engine Cluster Viewer IAM role access to the project.

Note that the acceptable values within the `User` subject are governed by your Kubernetes platform and any identity systems you have configured. With Google Cloud, the name here can be any Google user, referenced by their email address. RBAC authorizes the user to the actions specified in the Role. However, the user also needs to be able to authenticate to the cluster. In the case of Google Cloud, that is achieved by assigning a role such as Kubernetes Engine Cluster Viewer to the user. This role includes the `container.clusters.get` permission, which allows the user to authenticate to the cluster without actually being given any permissions inside the cluster (allowing you to configure fine-tuned permissions with RBAC). The exact steps here will vary depending on your platform provider.

Authentication vs. authorization

Authentication (AuthN) is the means by which the user presents their identity credentials to the system. In this case, being able to authenticate to the cluster means that the user can retrieve credentials to access the cluster via `kubectl`. Authorization (AuthZ) is the process of granting users access within the cluster. Depending on your platform's IAM system, it should be possible to allow users to authenticate to the cluster (e.g., get credentials to use `kubectl`) but not actually be able to perform any action (no authorization). You can then use RBAC to grant the precise authorization you want. In the case of GKE, granting users the Kubernetes Engine Cluster Viewer role in the IAM permissions (outside of Kubernetes) will allow them to authenticate, after which you can authorize them to access specific resources using RBAC and the examples shown here. Again, depending on your particular Kubernetes platform, it's possible, as is the case with GKE, that some IAM roles will also grant the user authorization to some resources in addition to whatever RBAC rules you have here. The project-wide Viewer role is one such example in GKE that will allow users to view most of the resources in the cluster without needing specific RBAC rules to do so.

As the cluster administrator, create the namespace and these two objects:

```
$ cd Chapter12/12.6_RBAC/
$ kubectl create ns team1
```

```
namespace/team1 created
$ kubectl create -f role.yaml
krole.rbac.authorization.k8s.io/developer-access created
$ kubectl create -f rolebinding.yaml
rolebinding.rbac.authorization.k8s.io/developerA created
```

With this role and binding deployed in the cluster, our developer user should be able to deploy most of the code in this book in the `team1` namespace but specifically not be able to change any other namespaces or edit the `team1` namespace itself. For a meaningful experiment, you'll need to set an actual user as the User subject in the RoleBinding—for example, a test developer account).

To verify the RBAC is configured correctly, switch to the test developer account by authenticating to the cluster as the user specified in the `subjects` field. Once authenticated as our developer user, try to deploy something into the default namespace, and it should fail, as no RBAC permissions were granted:

```
$ kubectl config set-context --current --namespace=default
$ kubectl create -f Chapter03/3.2_DeployingToKubernetes/deploy.yaml
Error from server (Forbidden): error when creating
"Chapter03/3.2_DeployingToKubernetes/deploy.yaml": deployments.apps is
forbidden: User "example@gmail.com" cannot create resource "deployments" in
API group "apps" in the namespace "default": requires one of
["container.deployments.create"] permission(s).
```

Switching the context to the `team1` namespace, for which we configured this test user with the previous Role, we should now be able to create the Deployment:

```
$ kubectl config set-context --current --namespace=team1
Context "gke_project-name_us-west1_cluster-name" modified.
$ kubectl create -f Chapter03/3.2_DeployingToKubernetes/deploy.yaml
deployment.apps/timeserver created
```

While this developer can now deploy things in the namespace, if they try to edit the namespace to gain the privileged Pod Security level, they will be restricted by the lack of edit permission on the namespace resource:

```
$ kubectl label --overwrite ns team1 pod-security.kubernetes.io/enforce=privileged
Error from server (Forbidden): namespaces "team1" is forbidden: User
"example@gmail.com" cannot patch resource "namespaces" in API group "" in
the namespace "team1": requires one of ["container.namespaces.update"]
permission(s).
```

CLUSTER ROLE

So far, we've set up a Role and RoleBinding to give a developer access to a particular namespace. With this Role, they can deploy most of the configuration in this book. There are, however, a couple of things they won't be able to do, and that is create a PriorityClass (chapter 6), create a StorageClass (chapter 9), or list the Persistent-Volumes in the cluster (chapter 9). Those resources are considered cluster-wide objects, so we can't amend the namespace-specific Role we created earlier to grant that permission. Instead, we'll need a separate ClusterRole and ClusterRole binding to grant this additional access.

Figuring out what permissions to grant

I've done the work here to provide a Role definition that covers all the needed permissions to deploy the code in the book, but there may be other missing permissions that you need to grant developers in the context of your own workload deployments. To figure out which groups, resources, and verbs you need to grant, you can consult the API docs. When debugging permission errors—say a developer is complaining that they don't have the access they need—you can simply inspect the error message. Consider the following example:

```
$ kubectl create -f Chapter06/6.3.2_PlaceholderPod/placeholder-priority.yaml
Error from server (Forbidden): error when creating "placeholder-priority.yaml":
priorityclasses.scheduling.k8s.io is forbidden: User "example@gmail.com"
cannot create resource "priorityclasses" in API group "scheduling.k8s.io"
at the cluster scope: RBAC: clusterrole.rbac.authorization.k8s.io
"developer-cluster-access" not found requires one of
["container.priorityClasses.create"] permission(s).
```

To add this permission to the Role, we can see that the group is `scheduling.k8s` `.io`, the resource is `priorityClasses`, the verb is `create`, and the RBAC scope is `clusterrole`. Thus, add a rule with these values to a ClusterRole definition.

The following listing shows a ClusterRole to provide the additional permissions needed to create StorageClass and PriorityClass objects.

Listing 12.15 Chapter12/12.6_RBAC/clusterrole.yaml

```
apiVersion: rbac.authorization.k8s.io/v1
kind: ClusterRole
metadata:
  name: developer-cluster-access
rules:
- apiGroups:
  - scheduling.k8s.io          Grants the developer access
  resources:                   to modify all PriorityClasses
  - priorityclasses            in the cluster
  verbs: ["*"]
- apiGroups:
  - storage.k8s.io             Grants the developer access
  resources:                   to modify all StorageClasses
  - storageclasses             in the cluster
  verbs: ["*"]
- apiGroups:
  - ""                              Grants the developer read-
  resources:                        only access to view and list
  - persistentvolumes               PersistentVolumes and
  - namespaces                      Namespaces
  verbs: ["get", "list"]
```

The next listing shows the ClusterRoleBinding to bind this to our test user, which looks very similar to the RoleBinding used earlier.

> **Listing 12.16   Chapter12/12.6_RBAC/clusterrolebinding.yaml**

```
kind: ClusterRoleBinding
apiVersion: rbac.authorization.k8s.io/v1
metadata:
  name: developerA
  namespace: team1
roleRef:
  kind: ClusterRole
  name: developer-cluster-access          References the ClusterRole
  apiGroup: rbac.authorization.k8s.io     from listing 12.15
subjects:
- kind: User                              Sets this as the identity of your developer. For GKE,
  name: example@gmail.com                 this is a Google User with Kubernetes Engine Cluster
                                          Viewer IAM role access to the project.
```

With these additional cluster roles and bindings, our developer should be able to perform every action in this book.

> ## Identity federation
>
> For RBAC to be able to reference your developer identities as Users and Groups, your cluster needs to understand how to authenticate your developer's identities. In the case of GKE, it natively understands Google users in the User field as well as Google groups when the Google Groups for RBAC feature is enabled. Depending on your platform and your corporate identity provider, you may have similar access already, or you may need to set it up. This setup is outside the scope of this book, but you may consider configuring the OpenID Connect (OIDC) integration so that RBAC can reference identities provided by your identity system.
>
> Furthermore, when using an identity system plugin that offers Groups support, instead of needing to list every User as a subject of our role bindings, you can specify a single Group instead.

APPLYING THE POD SECURITY PROFILE

The namespace in this section was created without using Pod Security. If we go back and configure the namespace with the Pod Security labels from section 12.5, it would lock down this namespace to the Restricted Pod Security profile, and thanks to RBAC, our developer would not be able to modify that restriction. Mission accomplished.

RBAC FOR SERVICEACCOUNTS

In the examples in this section, we used RBAC with the User subject because our developers are actual human users of our cluster. Another common use case for RBAC is to grant access to services—that is, code running in the cluster.

Let's say you have a Pod that belongs to a Deployment in the cluster that needs to access the Kubernetes API—say, it's monitoring the Pod status of another Deployment.

To give this machine user access, you can create a Kubernetes ServiceAccount and then reference that in the subject of your RBAC binding instead of a user.

You may see some documentation that sets up ServiceAccounts for human users, where the user then downloads the certs of the service account to interact with Kubernetes. While this is one way to configure your developers and bypasses the need to set up identity federation, it is not recommended as it sits outside of your identity system. For example, if the developer quit and their account was suspended in the identity system, the tokens they downloaded for the ServiceAccount would continue to be valid. It's better to properly configure identity federation and only use User subjects for human users so that if the user is suspended from the identity system, their Kubernetes access will also be revoked. Once again, managed platforms like Google Cloud make this integration easy; for other platforms, you may need to do a bit of setup to get it working.

Kubernetes ServiceAccounts are intended for when you have, for example, a Pod inside the cluster that needs its own access to the Kubernetes API. Say you want to create a Pod to monitor another Deployment. You can create a ServiceAccount to use as the subject of the RoleBinding and assign that service account to the Pod. The Pod can then utilize that credential when making API calls, including with kubectl.

12.7   Next steps

Pod Security admission can be used to control what permissions the Pod has on the Node, and RBAC governs what resources users can manage in the cluster. This is a good start; however, if you need further isolation at a network and container level there is more you can do.

12.7.1   Network policies

By default, every Pod can talk to every other Pod in the cluster. This is useful, as it allows teams operating in different namespaces to share services, but it means that Pods, including a potentially compromised Pod, can access other internal services. To control traffic to and from the network and other Pods, including the ability to restrict Pods in a namespace from accessing Pods in other namespaces, you can configure network policies.[5]

The way network policies work is that if no NetworkPolicy applies to a Pod (by selecting it), then all traffic is allowed (and there are no network policies by default, thus all traffic is allowed). However, once a NetworkPolicy selects the Pod for either ingress or egress traffic, then all traffic in the chosen direction is denied other than what you explicitly allow. This means to deny egress traffic to a particular destination, you need to build an exhaustive list of what is allowed by understanding the requirements of your Pods.

---

[5] https://kubernetes.io/docs/concepts/services-networking/network-policies/

For example, to restrict traffic to Pods in other namespaces you might create a rule to allow traffic within the namespace and to the public internet. Since such a ruleset omits Pods in other namespaces, that traffic will be denied, thus achieving the objective.

This nature of network policies to deny all traffic other than what you explicitly allow means you need to carefully study what access is required (including potentially some specific requirements of your platform), and it might take some trial and error to get right. I've published a series of posts on this topic at https://wdenniss.com/networkpolicy, which can help get you started.

12.7.2 *Container isolation*

Containerization offers some isolation of the process from the node, and Pod Security admission allows you to limit the access that containers have, but from time to time there are so-called container escape vulnerabilities that can result in the process gaining node-level access. It is possible to add an additional isolation layer between the container and the host for an added layer of defense in depth, beyond what is afforded by containerization alone. This isolation typically comes with a performance penalty, which is why you don't usually see it configured by default. If you are running untrusted code in the cluster, for example, for a multi-tenant system where users are providing their own containers, then you almost certainly want an additional layer of isolation.

You can configure your Pods for additional isolation by defining a secure runtime with RuntimeClass.[6] A popular choice, developed and open sourced by Google, is gVisor[7], which implements the Linux kernel API and intercepts system calls between the container and the system kernel to provide an isolated sandbox.

12.7.3 *Cluster hardening*

I hope this chapter has provided some practical security considerations as you develop and deploy your applications to Kubernetes, and potentially find yourself operating in clusters with RBAC permissions and restricted admission rules such as running non-root containers. For cluster operators, the broader topic of hardening your cluster and its operating environment (such as the network, nodes, and cloud resources) is a lengthy one, and many of the considerations are specific to the precise platform that you choose.

I recommend reading up-to-date hardening information with a search for "Kubernetes Hardening Guide." Since so much depends on your specific operating environment, a good starting point is to read the hardening guide for your specific platform, such as *Harden your cluster's security*[8] from GKE. The security space is constantly evolving, so be sure to stay up to date with the latest best practices from authoritative sources.

---

[6] https://kubernetes.io/docs/concepts/containers/runtime-class/
[7] https://gvisor.dev/
[8] https://cloud.google.com/kubernetes-engine/docs/how-to/hardening-your-cluster

Summary

- It's important to keep your cluster and its nodes up to date to mitigate against security vulnerabilities.
- Docker base images also introduce their own attack surface area, requiring monitoring and updating of deployed containers, which a CI/CD system can help with.
- Using the smallest possible base image can help to reduce this surface area, decreasing the frequency of application updates to mitigate security vulnerabilities.
- DaemonSets can be used to run a Pod on every node and are commonly used to configure logging, monitoring, and security software in the cluster.
- The Pod security context is how Pods are configured to have elevated or restricted permissions.
- Admission controllers can be used to make changes to Kubernetes objects as they are created and enforce requirements, including around the Pod security context.
- Kubernetes ships with an admission controller named Pod Security admission to enable you to enforce security profiles, like Baseline, for mitigating most known attacks, and Restricted, for enforcing security best practices on Pods.
- RBAC is a role-based permission system that allows users with the cluster administrator role to grant fine-grained access to developers in the system, like restricting a team to a particular namespace.
- By default, Pods can communicate with all Pods in the cluster. Network Policies can be used to control network access to Pods.
- To offer another layer of isolation, especially if you are running untrusted code in the cluster, apply a RuntimeClass like gVisor.
- Review your platform's Kubernetes hardening guide for comprehensive and platform-specific security considerations.

index